T0184613

Lecture Notes in Computer Science 12621

More information about this subseries at http://www.springer.com/series/7409

Robert Krimmer · Andriana Prentza ·
Szymon Mamrot (Eds.)

The Once-Only Principle

The TOOP Project

 Springer

Editors
Robert Krimmer ⓘ
TalTech Tallinn University of
Technology/University of Tartu
Tallinn/Tartu, Estonia

Andriana Prentza ⓘ
University of Piraeus
Piraeus, Greece

Szymon Mamrot ⓘ
Łukasiewicz Research Network – Institute of
Logistics and Warehousing
Poznan, Poland

ISSN 0302-9743   ISSN 1611-3349   (electronic)
Lecture Notes in Computer Science
ISBN 978-3-030-79850-5   ISBN 978-3-030-79851-2   (eBook)
https://doi.org/10.1007/978-3-030-79851-2

LNCS Sublibrary: SL3 – Information Systems and Applications, incl. Internet/Web, and HCI

This Springer imprint is published by the registered company Springer Nature Switzerland AG
The registered company address is: Gewerbestrasse 11, 6330 Cham, Switzerland

Preface

The Once-Only Principle (OOP) is part of the seven underlying principles of the eGovernment Action Plan 2016–2020. Its importance is highlighted by the Tallinn Declaration on eGovernment, signed on October 6, 2017, and the Berlin Declaration on Digital Society and Value-Based Digital Government, signed on December 8, 2020. OOP aims to make the government more effective and more superficial and to reduce administrative burdens by asking citizens and companies to provide certain (standard) information to the public authorities only once.

Thus, the goal of this TOOP book is to describe and document the developments and results of the Once-Only Principle Project (TOOP). TOOP was not a typical example of the type of large-scale pilot usually funded by the EU Framework Programme for Research and Innovation. It was a horizontal project that was policy-driven, with the aim of showing that the implementation of OOP in a cross-border and cross-sector setting is feasible. More than 50 partners from more than 20 Member States and associated countries of the EU participated in the TOOP project. Several things happened during the project, such as the outbreak of the COVID-19 pandemic, but the most essential "game-changing" event was the establishment of the Single Digital Gateway Regulation (SDGR). With the TOOP book, we wanted to summarize the results of the TOOP project from different points of view, from policy, organizational, architectural, and, last but not least, technical perspectives.

We would like to express our gratitude to the European Commission, DGs CONNECT, GROW, and DIGIT, as well as REA, for the support and good collaboration. Moreover, we want to thank the external reviewers of the project for their valuable input. Special thanks go to the national governments of the beneficiaries and the other organizations that have participated in the project for their active contribution. Moreover, the project would not have been possible without the enduring, productive, cheerful crowd working on the TOOP. Thank you all for making our project a reality!

Finally, we are also thankful for the financial support received through the European Union's Horizon 2020 research and innovation program under grant agreement no. 737460.

June 2021

Robert Krimmer
Andriana Prentza
Szymon Mamrot

Introduction
The Once-Only Principle (TOOP)

Jean-François Junger

European Commission, Place Rogier 16/Rogierplein 16,
1210 Bruxelles/Brussel, Belgium
jean-francois.junger@ec.europa.eu

Over the past two decades, digital tools and the internet have been at the heart of the transformation of our industries but more widely of our society. Behavior of citizens and consumers has significantly changed. Things that have long been thought too complex to implement are possible today. Information is at the end of our fingertips. Expectations from citizens have, however, also changed. When Amazon brought the concept of 'one click' to order goods on the internet, people wanted to see the same ease of service delivery from any service provider, including from the public sector.

The public sector, the heavily paper-based administration, has been shaken. The pressure on administrations to evolve has grown to the brink of risking them becoming obsolete. Many in the younger generation in particular see them as just a burden, slow and inefficient.

In Europe, public sector organizations and procedures are not the responsibility of the European Union. Still, the European Commission and the Member States have been working together to jointly prepare the public sector for its digital transformation since as early as 2001, which was was indeed the year when setting up cross-border digital public services, allowing citizens and businesses from a Member State to interact with a public service in another Member State electronically, was first declared a priority for Europe (European Commission 2003).

As a first step, through work in the eGovernment group, Member States and the Commission identified a few key domains where common solutions had to be developed at a European level. In 2005, three topics were identified: eID, eProcurement, and eHealth. With the financial support of the Information and Communication Technologies Policy Support Programme (ICT-PSP)[1], the Commission launched the STORK, PEPPOL, and EPSOS projects. Quickly, the idea of launching projects together gained momentum with the eventual launch of the eSENS project. This family of projects[2] led to a paradigm shift. To deliver user-friendly, burden-free digital public services, a change of practice was needed between the different corners of the administration. Administrations needed to reuse, as far as possible, common services, common building blocks.

Thus, the holy grail in public service delivery is the application of the 'Once-Only Principle', eliminating the need for citizens and businesses to provide over and over

---

[1] https://ec.europa.eu/cip/ict-psp/index_en.htm.

[2] STORK, PEPPOL, EPSOS, SPOCS, eCODEX, eSENS.

again the same information for receiving a public service. Some Member States have demonstrated the operational feasibility of the principle. Still, for many it was considered too complex, either for legal reasons or for legacy system problems. So, applying the principle at European level was considered non-achievable for the coming decades. Implementing the Once-Only Principle will bring time-savings, lower administrative burdens, reduce costs, and accelerate the fulfillment of legal obligations through reduced information requirements, less frequent reporting from businesses, and, eventually, even pre-filled forms. Administrations will benefit through improved service quality and administrative efficiency. The shared data between public administrations remain under the control and the consent of the businesses or citizens involved; personal data is now in the hands of the citizen, who is in control of whom to share that data with.

Nonetheless, with the help of these preparatory activities and the political commitment of the Commission and in particular of Vice President Andrus Ansip, the Commission adopted in 2015 in the "eGovernment Action Plan 2016–2020[3]" the Once-Only Principle, and in regulation (EU) 2018/1724[4] established a single digital gateway in respect of the General Data Protection Regulation (GDPR), with the objective of seeing it implemented within a few years. This achievement was possible thanks to the commitment of Member States, of key, highly passionate people. The outcome will European demonstrate how the Union can reduce borders and the burden for businesses and citizens.

---

[3] https://ec.europa.eu/digital-single-market/en/european-egovernment-action-plan-2016–2020.

[4] https://eur-lex.europa.eu/legal-content/EN/TXT/?uri=uriserv:OJ.L_.2018.295.01.0001.01. ENG&toc=OJ:L:2018:295:TOC.

Contents

The Once-Only Principle: A Matter of Trust

Robert Krimmer[1,2] 🆔, Andriana Prentza[3(✉)] 🆔, Szymon Mamrot[4(✉)] 🆔,
and Carsten Schmidt[1,2(✉)] 🆔

[1] Ragnar Nurkse Department of Innovation and Governance, Tallinn University of Technology
(TalTech), Akadeemia tee 3, 12618 Tallinn, Estonia
{robert.krimmer,carsten.schmidt}@taltech.ee

[2] Johan Skytte Institute for Political Studies, Center for IT Impact Studies, University of Tartu,
Lossi 36, 51003 Tartu, Estonia
{robert.krimmer,carsten.schmidt}@ut.ee

[3] Department of Digital Systems, University of Piraeus Research Center, 18532 Piraeus, Greece
aaprentza@unipi.gr

[4] Łukasiewicz Research Network – Institute of Logistics and Warehousing, ul. Estkowskiego 6,
61-755 Poznań, Poland
szymon.mamrot@ilim.lukasiewicz.gov.pl

Abstract. The Single Market is one of the cornerstones of the European Union. The idea to transform it into a Digital Single Market (DSM) was outlined several years ago. The EU has started different initiatives to support this transformation process. One of them is the program Horizon 2020 to support the process from a technical point of view. In parallel to this, initiatives were started to set up a sound legal framework for the DSM. The Single Digital Gateway Regulation (SDGR) is an outcome of these initiatives. The key aspect of the SDGR is the underlying Once-Only Principle (OOP), outlining that businesses and citizens in contact with public administrations have to provide data only once. "The Once-Only Principle Project (TOOP)" is the EU-funded project initiated for research, testing, and implementation of the OOP in Europe. The authors give an overview of the research questions of the different parts of TOOP. Besides that, they introduce the other chapters of this book and what the reader can expect as the content of them.

Keywords: Once-only Principle · Single digital gateway · SDGR · Digital single market · TOOP · Building blocks · e-Delivery

1 Introduction

The TOOP Book aims to describe and document the developments and results of the Once-Only Principle Project (TOOP). The once-only principle (OOP) is a concept in the broader context of e-government that aims to ensure that business, citizens, and other organisations have to provide specific information to administrations and governmental authorities only once. The principle was defined as one of the key enablers for e-Government in Europe by the Tallinn Declaration on e-Government at the ministerial meeting during the Estonian Presidency of the Council of the EU on 6 October 2017.

R. Krimmer et al. (Eds.): The Once-Only Principle, LNCS 12621, pp. 1–8, 2021.
https://doi.org/10.1007/978-3-030-79851-2_1

However, these exchanges require public administrations to have a certain degree of trust in each other, which is built on a shared legal basis. Together with the organisational and technical concepts of the OOP, the first time in the history of the EU, a specific horizontal, non-sector legal framework for the direct exchange of digital evidence between public administrations in different Member States and associated countries was created. This legal basis for the EU is the Single Digital Gateway Regulation.

TOOP was launched by the European Commission in January 2017 within Horizon 2020 research and innovation programme. The approach of the EC, Member States and associated countries was to introduce TOOP as the large-scale project for research, testing and implementation of the OOP in Europe.

The main objective of TOOP was to explore and demonstrate the OOP across borders, focusing on data from businesses. The OOP is one of the underlying principles stated in the European Union's eGovernment Action Plan 2016–2020, as well as the Single Digital Gateway Regulation. The application of the OOP is the prerequisite for building modern and user-friendly digital services. An important concept to realize the OOP is from a technical point of view the interconnection of base registries. Such registries are defined as being the consolidated source of information for specific domains, such as business, properties, persons, etc. The concept of OOP then means using base registries as information sources that always keep the latest version, and that can provide information on request or subscription. To explore and demonstrate the functionality of OOP, multiple pilots have been selected, and a set of guiding concepts as well as appropriate methodologies are developed. The TOOP project ran pilots in three different domains, General Business Mobility (GBM), Maritime, and eProcurement, in fifteen Member States:

In the GBM pilot, it is considered that a Legal or Natural Person requires data about their company to use in a service, e.g., to issue a certificate for their company

In the Maritime pilot, it is considered that a Legal or Natural Person requires a certificate for their or their company's ship and crew

In the eProcurement pilot, the objective is to get qualification evidence from a data provider for economic operators that are submitting a tender

To support the active or interested partners in piloting, a generic reference architecture for TOOP (TOOPRA) was developed. A reference architecture is a set of standardized enterprise Architectures that provides a frame of reference for a particular domain, sector, or field of interest [1]. The TOOPRA is offered to be used by architects responsible for the design of cross-border solution architectures.

During the lifetime of the project more than 50 organisations from more than 20 EU Member States and associated countries were part of the TOOP consortium, including a number of academic and research institutions.[1]

Caused by the number of partners in the project, a specific structure was developed to ensure on the one side the participation and involvement and on the other side to keep the administration simple and manageable. The partners of the TOOP consortium participated in the project as so-called national consortia via a lead beneficiary. The

---

[1] The number of participating countries and partners has changed over the duration of the project.

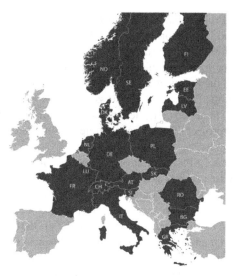

Fig. 1. Map of Countries Participating in TOOP (at the end of the project)

ultimate decision-making body of the project was the General Assembly. Each consortium/beneficiary had one vote in the assembly. The decisions were prepared inside the national consortia based on the rules given to them. The outcomes of this process set the guidelines for the Management Board responsible for the execution of the decision and the maintenance of the daily business of the project. The Management Board consisted of the leaders of the different work packages and the Project Director, as representative of the Project Coordinator.

The participation of different European countries has enabled the exchange of national experiences, and best practices followed intensive discussions on the interoperability issues. The testing activities demonstrated the feasibility of cross-border application and revealed room for further research. Taking into consideration the experience gathered in the field of OOP, the TOOP partners developed several scientific papers covering various aspects of the project. The articles discuss findings from over 4 years of research in the OOP area and are based on the lessons learned in the project.

2   Overview of Large-Scale Piloting in Europe

TOOP has not started from scratch. As already stated in the preface of the book, the TOOP project was another project in the long row of so-called "Large-Scale Pilot Projects" (LSPs) initiated by the European Commission with the support of the Member States and associated countries. The large-scale piloting and the preparation of the corresponding setting were initiated at the beginning of the 21st century. A dialog was commenced on the European level between the European Commission (EC) and the Member States. As the outcome of this fruitful collaboration, the preparations for the LSPs took place in 2005. During these groundworks, the main areas were identified as worthwhile for further investigation; eID, eProcurement, and eHealth. They got financial contributions based on the ICT Policy Support Programme (ICT PSP), one of the three specific programmes of The Competitiveness and Innovation Framework Programme (CIP) of the EU. Inspired by the success of these initial LSPs, further projects were initiated. As the first step, some additional vertical (sector-specific) projects were kicked off. The focus of these projects was set on the support of the Points of Single Contact in the EU and the area of e-Justice. As a second step within the EU horizontal (cross-sector) projects were introduced, one of the projects (e-SENS) focussed on the technical aspects of a generic cross-border data exchange, and the other project (TOOP) concentrated additionally on the policy aspects of the data exchange.

Some of the previous LSPs had a strong influence on the TOOP project. TOOP used the outcomes of these projects as a foundation for its own work and developments. Especially the following existing LSPs supported by the European Commission produced – mainly technical results – that were re-used for the purpose of the TOOP project. These solutions were developed for different domains, STORK/STORK2.0 for the eID domain; PEPPOL for the eProcurement domain; SPOCS for the Business start-up domain; epSOS for the eHealth domain; and e-CODEX for the e-Justice domain, as well as by the e-SENS project, which aimed to consolidate and align results of the five LSPs.

- The STORK and STORK 2.0 have developed and piloted an interoperability infrastructure for electronic identities.
- The PEPPOL Project would facilitate EU-wide interoperable public eProcurement.
- The overarching goal of the SPOCS Project was to establish a next-generation Point of Single Contact (PSC).
- The epSOS Project was an Open eHealth initiative for piloting patient summary and electronic prescription services
- The e-CODEX Project aimed to provide cross-border interoperable e-Justice infrastructure for the Member States.
- The e-SENS Projects objective was to strengthen the Single Market by facilitating and promoting interoperable public services across borders based on the existing and previous Large-Scale Projects results. This objective comprised planning and design of sustainability and long-term governance of the LSP building blocks, such as e-ID, e-Signatures, e-Documents, and e-Delivery.

3 Overview of the TOOP Book

During the lifetime of the TOOP project it become clear that there is not much literature about the OOP aside of the papers that are produced by the members of the project [2–8].

Therefore, it was the main motivation for this book to provide information from the context of the TOOP project to enable or deepen the discourse amongst policymakers, researchers, administrators, and vendors so that understanding, cooperation, future research, and development can emerge. As such, this book consists of 12 chapters that cover the following topics:

3.1 Implementation of the 'Once-Only' Principle in Europe

The implementation of OOP on the national level is one of the corner stones of the initiatives around OOP and the SDGR. This article presents the OOP definition and discusses the most important EU initiatives to make it a reality in Europe. Furthermore, the chapter of *Szymon Mamrot* and *Katarzyna Rzyszczak* provides an overview of national OOP implementations of EU Member States and European Economic Area countries and the related aspects. The analysis focuses on the different stages and different kinds of implementation of the OOP in Europe. It will highlight the states of play in different countries and the (first) outcomes of implementing the OOP.

3.2 Drivers, Barriers, and Opportunities

Drivers and barriers are playing an essential role for the implementation of the OOP in Europe. To support the ongoing transition of the SDGR into reality in the different countries, an analysis within several Member States and associated countries based on the experiences and findings within the TOOP project was initiated. This chapter focuses on the identification of influencing factors that are more prevalent in one area than another. The authors *Nele Leosk, Irma Põder, Carsten Schmidt, Tarmo Kalvet,* and *Robert Krimmer* furthermore investigated the institutional factors to be the most influential on the OOP implementation. In general, the most important drivers, barriers, and also opportunities that are identified discovered in the TOOP project are summarized here.

3.3 Good Practices of OOP Across Europe

Besides the more theoretical approaches of other chapters, it is also essential to give practical information and to highlight good practices related to the OOP in Europe. *Maria Wimmer* sums up the findings from the OOP good practice analysis, good practice cases, and enablers in different countries. Besides that, an examination of the strategic policies in Europe, the OOP visions, top-down implementation of digitalization, and the bottom-up engagement of stakeholders will be given. On top, there is a look into further projects that are dealing with the OOP, like the DE4A project and the SCOOP4C project.

3.4 Impact of the Once Only Principle for Businesses Across Borders

An essential part of the analysis around the once-only principle is especially its impact during and after the implementation. As the OOP is relatively new, the information about the impact of the OOP on businesses, and in particular on its cross-border impact is limited. In this chapter, *Tjerk Timan, Anne Fleur van Veenstra* and *Kristina Karanikolova* explore an impact assessment framework for measuring the impact of the OOP on cross-border services for businesses. The outcomes of the measurement for business but also other related actors, e.g., governments will be displayed. Besides that, the validation of this framework with members from the TOOP project will be described. The authors also provide an insight into the preparation and execution of the validation process.

3.5 The Single Digital Gateway Regulation and Other Legal Aspects

As the OOP is strongly related to its legal bases, it is crucial to look at the legal framework for the OOP on a national and supranational level. *Hans Graux* provides a specific chapter with an insight into the Single Digital Gateway Regulation as the common legal basis for the EU, its Member States, and the EFTA countries. As part of the description, the requirements for public administrations are highlighted and how especially which role the trust in each other for the success of the OOP plays.

To complement the picture drawn from the European level, a specific focus on the national legal framework is set by *Francesco Gorgerino*. This study presents how the OOP is related to the constitutional and institutional principles concerning the good performance and impartiality of public authorities and the protection of citizens' rights against the action of public administration, with special regard to the Italian regulatory framework and an additional look into the legal impact of the OOP for development of the European digital single market and in public procurement.

3.6 Architecture

A stabile technical architecture is a core pillar for the success of developing and piloting the technical solutions of each project. As TOOP has not started from scratch and is re-using the outcomes of previous LSPs and technical building blocks provided by the EC it is even more critical and difficult to provide an architecture that covers the need of all interested parties. Part of the activities was to assist the members of TOOP and further partners that are concerned in the cross-border implementation of the OOP. The chapter of *Jaak Tepandi, Carmen Rotuna, Giovanni Paolo Sellitto, Sander Fieten,* and *Andriana Prentza* outlines the TOOP Reference Architecture (TOOPRA) users, principles, and requirements presents an overview of the architecture development, describes the main views of TOOPRA, discusses architecture profiling, and analyses the TOOPRA sustainability issues.

All kinds of information need to be secured. The level of security needed is directly related to the sensitivity of the data exchanged. As for the OOP, the very sensitive data from base registries are provided, the success of the project is directly bound to the trust in the data. As follow-up, in the chapter of *Jaak Tepandi, Luca Boldrin,* and *Giovanni Paolo Sellitto*, the TOOP trust architecture is presented, starting from a simple abstract model of interaction between two agents down to the detailed end-to-end trust establishment architecture, modeled onto the TOOP Reference Architecture.

3.7 Testing Methodology for the TOOP Pilots

Testing is vital for the development of a sound technical basis for the OOP. Therefore, already in an early stage, the members of the TOOP project have agreed on the approach for the piloting of the OOP and the area where the piloting is taking place. The goal is to uncover errors and gaps in program function, behaviour, and performance. *Andriana Prentza, Marie-Laure Watrinet,* and *Lefteris Leontaridis* describing how the testing methodology was developed and implemented. Besides that, an overview of the set of testing tools created to facilitate testing between the different parties in the three different piloting domains is given.

Furthermore, the generic definition and adaption of the testing methodology for each of the pilot is described. This includes the whole process, how it is started from a low level, and how it finishes at a higher level by a particular approach by testing the connections between the different partners within the same piloting domain.

3.8 Pilot Experiences: Challenges and Achievements in Implementing Once-Only

Piloting is the proof of the pudding for each project. On the other side,, piloting is a complex endeavor where a number of actors and related stakeholders cooperate and interrelate to implement technical solutions that facilitate business processes in new ways. TOOP, as an LSP, required a set of work processes to be defined and a number of procedures and tools to be used by the participating entities to implement the planned activities in ways that achieve results of maximum value that fulfill the objectives of the project. In order to explore and demonstrate the functionality of OOP, multiple pilots have been selected, and a set of guiding concepts as well as appropriate methodologies were developed. *Andriana Prentza, David Mitzman, Madis Ehastu,* and *Lefteris Leontaridis* present in the chapter the three different pilot workgroups, General Business Mobility, e-Procurement, and Maritime, that are selected for the demonstration. The advances that are attained are highlighted and also details about the lessons learned are provided.

3.9 Future of the Once-Only Principle in Europe

The sustainability of the results of a project like TOOP is of utmost importance. Therefore, after a decent and detailed overview of the developments in and along the lines of the TOOP project is given, to complete the picture, an outlook into the future of the OOP is provided by *Robert Krimmer, Andriana Prentza, Szymon Mamrot, Aleksandrs Cepilovs,* and *Carsten Schmidt.* Part of the outlook is a summary of the conclusions of the main parts of this book. It includes an overview of the results of TOOP as a project and the different chapters, e.g., drivers and barriers, impacts, legal and technical aspects, piloting methods and outcomes, and the gaps that are discovered by the project members. This compendium is the basis for the outlook into the future of the OOP and the suggestions for the next steps on the EU- and national level.

4 The Once-Only Principle and the Further Development of the Single Digital Gateway

This book with its multidisciplinary chapters published by summer 2021 at the end of TOOP is ideally suited to provide foundation for the further developing of Europe's Single Digital Gateway as outlined before. With the Implementing Act just to be published for the technical system in line with Article 14 SDGR, it sets the scene for an incredible next step in the digital transformation of Europe: Providing seamless cross-border digital public services in just some 2,5 years. May these following chapters provide you with the insights needed for the intense work to come!

References

1. Proper, H.A., Lankhorst, M.M.: Enterprise architecture.- towards essential sensemaking. Enterp. Model. Inf. Syst. Architect. \textbf{9}(1), 5–21 (2014)
2. Wimmer, M.A., Neuroni, A.C., Frecè, J.T.: Approaches to good data governance in support of public sector transformation through once-only. In: Viale Pereira, G., et al. (eds.) EGOV 2020. LNCS, vol. 12219, pp. 210–222. Springer, Cham (2020). https://doi.org/10.1007/978-3-030-57599-1_16
3. Krimmer, R., Kalvet, T., Toots, M.: Contributing to a digital single market for Europe Barriers and Drivers of an EU-wide Once-Only Principle. dg.o '18: dg.o 2018: Proceedings ofthe 19th Annual International Conference on Digital Government Research, May 30-June 1, 2018, pp. 1–8, (2018). https://doi.org/10.1145/3209281.3209344.
4. Cirnu, C.-E., Rotuna, C.-I.: Cross-border eServices for public administration driven by Once-Only Principle. Revista Română de Informatică şi Automatică **30**(4), 99–110 (2020). https://doi.org/10.33436/v30i4y202008S1-12M4-Citavi
5. Siapera, M., Douloudis, K., Dimitriou, G., Prentza, A.: Employing the once-only principle in the domain of the electronic public procurement, pp. 236–246 (2020)
6. Krimmer, R., Kalvet, T., Toots, M., Cepilovs, A., Tambouris, E.: Exploring and demonstrating the once-only principle. In: 18th Annual International Conference on Digital Government, pp. 546–551 (2017) https://doi.org/10.1145/3085228.3085235.
7. Krimmer, R., Kalvet, T., Toots, M.: The Once-Only Principle Project Drivers and Barriers for OOP (2017)
8. Tepandi, J., et al.: Towards a cross-border reference architecture for the once-only principle in Europe: an enterprise modelling approach, pp. 103–117 (2019)

Implementation of the 'Once-Only' Principle in Europe – National Approach

Szymon Mamrot[✉] and Katarzyna Rzyszczak

Łukasiewicz Research Network – Institute of Logistics and Warehousing, ul. Estkowskiego 6, 61-755 Poznań, Poland
{szymon.mamrot,katarzyna.rzyszczak}@ilim.lukasiewicz.gov.pl

Abstract. The 'once-only' principle (OOP) in the context of the public sector means that citizens and businesses supply data only once to a public administration. The role of public administrations is to internally share these data also across borders so that no additional burden falls on citizens and businesses. This paper presents what steps are taken to implement the OOP both on the European and national level. The national approach in European countries towards implementing the OOP is analysed and compared in terms of legislation, strategies and infrastructure. The most important benefits of the OOP are described as well. One of the most important initiatives in Europe to explore and demonstrate the OOP in practice is the TOOP project. The paper presents how TOOP technical solution is practically implemented within three pilot areas: general business mobility, e-procurement, maritime domain.

Keywords: The once-only principle · Public administration · e-government · Digital public services · Digital government

1 Introduction

The 'once-only' principle (OOP) is a crucial element in the delivery of the user-friendly digital public services and modernisation of public administration. Providing the same data over and over again is troublesome and time-consuming both for citizens and businesses. It is also not reasonable since most of the data is already stored in authoritative sources. The key is to enable public administration to retrieve it in an efficient and safe way.

EU-wide implementation of the OOP is one of the priorities of the European Commission, which is reflected in the strategic documents. The principle appeared for the first time in 2009, when the Member States committed themselves to, among others, jointly investigate how public administrations can reduce the frequency with which citizens and businesses have to resubmit information, by signing the Malmö Ministerial Declaration on eGovernment [38]. Reduction of administrative burdens by applying the principle of "once-only" registration of data for citizens was one of the actions of the eGovernment Action Plan 2011 – 2015 [25]. Furthermore, the principle has been highlighted in the European Council Conclusions in October 2013 [29] by stating that "efforts should

R. Krimmer et al. (Eds.): The Once-Only Principle, LNCS 12621, pp. 9–37, 2021.
https://doi.org/10.1007/978-3-030-79851-2_2

be made to apply the principle that information is collected from citizens only once, in due respect of data protection rules". Another the OOP milestone was signing the 'eGovernement Declaration' in Tallinn on 6 October 2017 [28], in which 32 countries of the European Union and the European Free Trade Area made a political commitment to implement the principle for key public services. Furthermore, in the EU eGovernment Action Plan 2016–2020 [26] the OOP is listed among other principles for effective eGovernment such as digital by default, inclusiveness and accessibility, openness and transparency, cross-border by default, interoperability by default, trustworthiness and security. According to the Plan, "public administrations should ensure that citizens and businesses supply the same information only once to a public administration. Public administration offices take action if permitted to internally re-use this data, in due respect of data protection rules, so that no additional burden falls on citizens and businesses". Additionally, a recommendation to "as far as possible under the legislation in force, ask users of European public services once-only and relevant-only information" is provided in the new European Interoperability Framework [27] within the user-centricity principle for establishing interoperable European public services. Finally, the Single Digital Gateway Regulation [30] provided legal basis for the cross-border application of the OOP, that should result in citizens and businesses not having to supply the same data to public authorities more than once, the possibility to use those data at the request of the user to complete cross-border online procedures involving cross-border users. According to the Regulation, by December 2022 a dedicated technical system will connect the 21 online procedures, key for citizens and businesses, established in each Member State with the data sources across Europe.

Even there is no one concrete definition of the OOP, based on the EU level documents mentioned above, the following elements of the OOP can be identified:

1. collecting only necessary information,
2. exchanging data so the citizen or entrepreneur is never asked again,
3. respecting data protection rules when re-using data.

2 National Approaches Towards Implementing the OOP

Although the OOP is relatively new in the actions of the European Commission, it seems that the Member States realized its benefits a long time ago. In many countries, this has been a natural reaction on isolation of databases. The existence of numerous registries not linked with each other caused low quality of the data, redundancy of data collected, work duplication of administrative workers, and dissatisfaction of the citizens and businesses due to the growing red tape. Although most countries face similar challenges, understanding and the way of application of the OOP may vary. National differences such as different administrative structures, IT systems, database models affect the deployment of the EU-wide OOP.

The table presented in Appendix provides an overview of national OOP implementations of EU Member States and European Economic Area countries (Norway, Island, Lichtenstein). The table was developed based on the available online sources (Digital Government Factsheets of 2019 published by the European Commission's National Interoperability Framework Observatory, collection of Joinup cases, national sources) as well as information gathered from the TOOP partners and representatives of Member States. The table includes information on the legal basis of the OOP, national programs/actions supporting the OOP and the solutions enabling realization of the principle. The information in the table, especially related to the solutions enabling the OOP, refers to the business data exchange (among other data). Therefore, the OOP applications in sectors such as health, justice, social security etc., which are often supported by a dedicated infrastructure are intentionally not presented (Fig. 1).

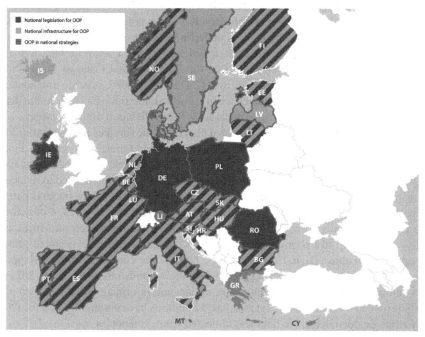

Fig. 1. Legislation, strategies and infrastructure for OOP in the EU Member States and EEA countries

Legislation can be an important driver for the application of the principle. Most of the countries (22 out of 30) have national legislation for OOP in place. Not all regulations directly prohibit requesting data more than once. Legislation obliging authorities to obtain and reuse data stored in public administration databases as well as introduction of meta/base registries are also treated as OOP enabling regulation (e.g. case of Slovakia, Norway, Finland, Croatia, Czech Republic). Base registries provide authentic sources of data for public administrations, and therefore, are the key to making the OOP a reality [23]. In some EU countries, law does not only prevent the collection of data more than once but also ensures that data are stored only in one place. For example, the Estonian law prohibits the creation of separate databases for the collection of the same data [46]. Public institutions exchange information between each via a system called X-Road. Information, stored in decentralized registers can be securely accessed through a data exchange layer. Additionally, in the case of Estonia, the legislation is used to force the use of the X-road solution, which is a recommended good practice [23], facilitating the broad uptake. In the Netherlands, the common rules for the base registries [22] do not permit to collect data that is already stored in any of the registers. Sharing and exchange of data are enabled by four system services Digikoppeling, Digilevering, Digimelding and the Stelselcatalogus [18]. Duplication of data held in the central business registries (the Business Registry and the Private Entrepreneur Registry) is also not allowed in Hungary. Public administration bodies are obliged to retrieve data from the registries via secure data exchange. The legal obligation for OOP does not exist in Denmark, Greece, Iceland and Sweden. Lack of the OOP legal basis in Sweden may be justified by the "Swedish tradition" that common infrastructure is governed through guidelines and recommendations. Therefore, the OOP is underlined in the national digitization plans but not dedicated legislation. No data was found for Cyprus, Latvia, Lichtenstein and Malta. It must be however remembered that the Single Digital Gateway Regulation, which mandates the use of the principle from 12 December 2023, became immediately enforceable as law in all Member States when it entered into force in 2018. In this way, each EU country has legal basis to enable at least key OOP based digital services.

The OOP is often seen as a part of a global plan of public services modernization and cutting red-tape and therefore is part of national programs and strategies related to digital government. 18 (out of 30 countries have highlighted the principle in the documents such as digitalisation strategies, interoperability strategies, or programs dedicated to reducing administrative burden. For example, The Dites-le-nous une fois (Tell us once) is part of a global plan to modernise public services in France and is one of a range of actions being taken to digitalise processes and improve collaboration between ministries and public services [35]. In Luxembourg, the OOP is one of the five eGovernment principles, approved within "Digital Luxembourg". OOP is the core goal of the "Mapping Tomorrow", which is a strategic plan for the public administration for 2019–2021 in Malta, aiming at internal sharing and re-use of data and information that has been previously provided by a citizen or organisation. 5 countries have not highlighted the OOP in any strategic documents. No data was collected from 7 countries.

The infrastructure enabling the OOP is in place in 22 (out of 30) countries. The solutions are at various maturity levels and cover different scope of information.

The MAGDA platform (Maximum Data Sharing between Agencies) of Belgium is connected with base registries at the federal level through the relevant service integrators. In France, where the OOP principle was implemented along with a wide range of base registry initiatives, public administrations can access this information through APIs (Apientreprisesl) that provide information from different base registries. In Hungary, the Central Governmental Service Bus, the technical interoperability platform, which is online since 1 January 2018, enables automatic information exchange from 27 base registers indicated in the e-Administration Act. Others can also connect to provide their services over the central data exchange platform voluntarily. Furthermore, the Public Connectivity System [51], one of the Italian OOP solutions, is a network that connects Italy's government agencies, allowing them to share and exchange data from six base registries based on Domain Gateways (Data Providers and Consumers). Another OOP solution in Italy is the National Digital Data Platform (PDND). The X-Road system, which is the backbone of the OOP in Estonia, enables multiple databases to communicate. Apart from Estonia, the solution is already implemented in Finland and Iceland. Not all Member States realize the OOP by the deployment of the data exchange infrastructure. In Denmark for example, Data Distribution Platform, an authoritative data source infrastructure makes basic data from several authorities accessible in the same place. In this way, the Platform ensures that authorities are provided with easy and safe access to basic data in one collective system.

The OOP solutions are often interconnected with the Points of Single Contacts (PSC) for businesses operated in each Member States, following the implementation of the Directive 2006/123/EC on services in the internal market [49]. The business portals facilitate access to information and the completion of administrative procedures online. Luxembourg has implemented the OOP by making it a component of the Guichet.lu whilst in Norway, the exchange of information from business registries at the Altinn system (PSC) is possible thanks to the Central Coordinating Register for Legal Entities. In Sweden, the Composite Service of Basic Information on Companies, which supports the exchange of business-related data, collects and forwards replies from the PSC - verksamt.se portal, (as well as municipalities, government authorities) to data sources (Swedish Tax Agency, Statistics Sweden, Swedish Companies Registration Office). In Estonia the X-Road system is the basis for the core-functionality of eesti.ee among other portals.

No central infrastructure supporting the OOP is currently available in Germany, Greece, Poland and Romania, although for selected services the automatic data exchange is gradually being enabled (e.g. business registration service in Poland). No information was found for 3 countries.

Looking from the European perspective of the once-only, different maturity levels as well as fragmentation of the OOP applications significantly hamper extending the principle to the cross-border level. Still, in some Member States, the OOP is not applied horizontally but has a limited – service-oriented character. Exchange of data in selected processes or a single database is an indisputable added value for a business but does not realize the OOP in general. This quite low level in the OOP advancement is reported in countries such as Poland and Greece, although a more holistic approach is envisaged in national plans and strategies.

3   Benefits of the OOP

The once-only principle puts the public services user in the centre. Public administration eliminates burdens in access to public services by reorganizing internal processes and enabling cooperation between public bodies. Implementation of the OOP is not only about exploiting the advantages of new technologies but overcoming organizational as well as legal challenges. Thanks to this effort, handling administrative matters becomes more efficient and friendly. The principle refers both to retrieving documents required as attachments to the form as well as filling the form with necessary information. The time required to prepare a form to be submitted to the public office is limited to the minimum as only data and documents that the administration is unable to obtain on its own are requested. Keeping data up-to-date, which is citizens and business responsibility imposed by law, also becomes less cumbersome. In the case of dispersed and not interconnected registries, there is a risk that citizens or businesses might lose control over data submitted in various databases. The interconnection of databases enables swift notification of respective sources in case of change submitted to the one place. Furthermore, the OOP has a great potential of minimizing administrative burden for businesses in meeting the reporting obligations. The businesses during its operation need to submit numerous reports related to taxes, employment, working conditions, fixed assets, financial information and many others. The research conducted in 2019 Poland reviled [32] that an average Polish entrepreneur in a medium-size company needs to submit 208 reports. The authors of the report say the data submitted to the different bodies (up to 14) are often duplicated or unnecessary. This area has been the case of OOP application in some countries. The Register of the Reporting Obligations of Enterprises in Norway is responsible for a constant overview of the reporting obligations of enterprises to central authorities and finding ways to coordinate and simplify these obligations. In the Netherlands, Standard Business Reporting was introduced. It provides governments and businesses with a secure method for the exchange of business information between organisations in a reporting chain [18].

The OOP is expected to bring savings to businesses in terms of time devoted to multiple submissions of the same data and in turn complying with administrative requirements. According to an OECD Survey [35], 3 companies out of 4 consider that reducing repeat requests for information should be a government priority. As an example, it is estimated that data related to revenues and the workforce is, on average, requested from companies by public services between 10 and 15 times, which generates the cost between 3% and 5% of GDP a year.

A breach in the OOP has an impact on creating an administrative burden for citizens but public administrations are negatively affected as well. It fosters building administrative silos and lowers the efficiency of public processes. Ineffective processes related to data management generates extra workload. Additionally, duplication of the same actions by different bodies is costly for governments as extra effort needs to be put on ensuring data quality and reliability.

Investing in solutions related to enabling the OOP pays off. One of the examples is the Basic Data Programme in Denmark which introduced the OOP for many data collected in 10 electronic registries. According to estimations, it is expected to have annual revenues of around € 100 million, since the number of transactions between citizens/businesses is limited and the burden of reporting information is reduced [31]. Another example is the estimation on the application of the OOP, which has been carried out based on the Register of non-residents (RNI) in the Netherlands. RNI allows for data sharing among Ministries and National Agencies, which generates time savings related to the reduced number of transactions related to collecting and managing data. In line with the OOP principle, users registered in the RNI have to communicate their data only once to public authorities. As a result, a 50% decrease in potential transactions between users and public authorities was reported. According to estimation, the RNI generated benefits of €112 million [31].

Bringing the principle to the European level is expected to bring further benefits. For many years, the European Commission is devoted to making the citizens and business life easier by enabling seamless digital public services. Application of the OOP further improves their quality and contributes to the creation of the real Digital Single Market. Furthermore, it is expected that extending the OOP to the EU level could result in significant savings, estimated for as much as €5 billion per year [24]. However, the final benefits, as well as savings, will depend on the scale of the OOP application – the more data from various registries is exchanged the higher savings can be expected. Currently, information about citizens and businesses is reused only in 48% of cases.

4   Implementing the OOP in the TOOP Project

On 1 January 2017, the Once-Only Principle Project (TOOP) was launched with the aim to investigate and demonstrate the practical operation of the "once-only principle" in the field of cross-border public services to businesses in the EU Member States.

The substance of the OOP across borders is shown in the diagram below. It shows the case where a user from country B intends to execute a public e-service in country A. To do so, he starts the service in the service portal of country A (Data Consumer). The one-off principle is fulfilled in such a way that the service portal in country A retrieves the data of the user from country B directly from the system in country B (Data Provider). The aim of the TOOP project was to create an architecture that would enable data exchange as shown in the figure. The architecture developed in the project is federative as it is dispersed and does not create a single central system but enables data exchange between existing public administration systems in different EU Member States and associated countries (Fig. 2).

The technical solution developed in the TOOP project has been tested in three pilot areas: general business mobility, e-procurement and maritime pilot.

4.1   General Business Mobility

The TOOP architecture is used to facilitate the provision of cross-border services related to obtaining licences and permits for companies planning to do business in a Member State associated country other than their home country. The developed IT architecture enables business data to be automatically transferred from one system of a country to another, without the need for the entrepreneur to submit it again. This not only saves costs and time, but also improves data quality and consistency.

An exemplary cross-border implementation of e-services looks based on the TOOP project architecture is following:

1. an entrepreneur from Poland visits the eGovernment portal in Germany in order to obtain the permission necessary to provide the service in Germany;
2. the eGovernment portal in Germany authenticates the Polish entrepreneur through the eIDAS solution[1];

---

[1] The eIDAS solution allows citizens from Member States to prove and verify their identification when accessing on-line services in other Member States. It allows citizens to authenticate themselves by using their eIDs and connecting with their Identity Provider (IdP) from their country.

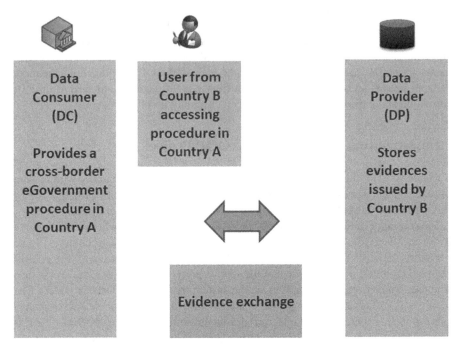

Fig. 2. The TOOP architecture concept

3. the Polish entrepreneur begins the process to obtain a permit in Germany. The eGovernment Portal in Germany verifies through the TOOP architecture what data is already stored in the Polish register. In case the data is available, it notifies the Polish entrepreneur and asks him/her for consent to download the data directly from the Polish register;

4. if the consent is given, the data is retrieved directly from the Polish register and the Polish entrepreneur completes only data, which are not available but necessary to obtain permission in Germany.

4.2 E-procurement

In the area of public procurement, TOOP solutions will facilitate the implementation of procedures related to the contractors' compliance with the requirements for participation in the tender procedure. The technical solution created in the project enables automatic completion of the European Single Procurement Document (ESPD)[2], which is one of the documents required to be presented by the contractor participating in the tender procedure. Thanks to this, the process of verification of documents submitted by contractors participating in public procurement procedures is faster and easier. The TOOP solution can also support further stages of the procurement process. In the award

---

[2] European Single Procurement Document is a self-declaration of the business used as a preliminary evidence of fulfilment of the conditions required in public procurement procedures across the EU, created under the EU's 2014 Directive on Procurement.

phase, the contracting authority will retrieve the evidences, which have been declared in the ESPD by the winner of a tender procedure, directly from the competent authority of the country in which the tenderer is registered. To make this automatic data exchange possible the contractor needs to give an appropriate consent so the data can be accessed by the contracting party. The process can be repeated multiple times after awarding a contract.

4.3 Maritime Pilot

The application of the OOP in maritime transport is aimed at eliminating the need to provide ship and crew certificates, which are currently issued and kept in paper form by national maritime authorities. Ship and crew certificates are issued by various organisations such as the Maritime Administration and the Recognised Organisation. According to International Maritime Organisation (IMO) Conventions, these certificates should be "available in its original form on board the ship on which the holder is serving". The shipowner and, in practice, the ship master acts as an intermediary between the issuer of the certificates and the entity that requires them to be presented, i.e. the Port State Control Officers (PSCOs). Thus, an entrepreneur - the shipowner in this case, is burdened with providing information which is already in the possession of the public administration. The purpose of implementing the OOP is to enable PSCOs to access directly the databases of certificate issuers. This would result in automating a largely manual and paper-based procedure, which is used now.

5 Summary

The article presents the definition of the OOP and discusses the most important EU initiatives to make it a reality in Europe. The analysis carried out indicates that in most EU countries, the principle is both embedded in national legislation and indicated in national eGovernment strategies. However, having legislation is not equivalent to the practical functioning of the OOP. Some countries still have only solutions limited to selected group of services or registers and the priority is given to the national level applications. Such an approach already brings tangible benefits of reducing bureaucracy, but much higher savings can be generated at cross-border level and broad application of the OOP. This is the aim of the TOOP project, which has created a generic IT architecture, tested by a number of eGovernment systems in 19 European countries. The solutions developed in the TOOP project will be used in the implementation of the Single Digital Gateway. Its launch in 2023 will be a significant landmark for the OOP in the EU and the EEA countries and the next milestone in the development of seamless cross-border digital services.

Appendix

Country	Oop – legal basis	Program/strategy	National infrastructure supporting the OOP for business
Austria	The Austrian eGovernment Act (§ 17 (2)) stipulates that whenever technically possible, citizens shall not be asked to present proof of data that already exists in an electronic register in the public sector. Instead, public sector organisations need to make requests of data directly to the relevant databases [6]. The legal framework for the system for electronic data exchange between public registers, the Austrian Information Hub, is currently being created and will be embedded in the Austrian Business Service Portal Act	The OOP has been a pivotal part of Austria's digital government efforts in recent years, with a strong focus within the current Austrian government program, as well as the Austrian Digitisation Strategy [6]	The Business Service Portal (Unternehmensserviceportal, USP) is a one-stop-shop for businesses which offers information and transaction services that help businesses fulfil their legal obligations. In combination with the infrastructure of two national once-only core components, the Information Obligation Database ("DLK") and the Information Hub ("RSV"), data exchange with different registers is achieved

(*continued*)

(*continued*)

Country	Oop – legal basis	Program/strategy	National infrastructure supporting the OOP for business
Belgium	The Belgian law requires the federal government's public administrations to retrieve all available data from official registers with a unique identification feature instead of asking citizens and companies to make this data available more than once The Flemish Public Governance decree introduced the Once Only obligation to use base registries in Flemish administrative processes, with the obligation to notify back any errors found in these base registries [7]	No data	The MAGDA platform (Maximum Data Sharing between Agencies) is the once-only principle implementation supporting electronic delivery of public services, at the federal, regional, and local levels of the government. The platform enables the reuse and sharing of citizens' and companies' data between the Flemish government authorities (190 agencies and 13 departments) MAGDA is connected with base registries at federal level through the relevant service integrators. When consuming the data in various formats, it transforms the data to a single format
Bulgaria	According to the eGovernment Act, entered into force on 13 June 2008, administrative bodies, persons charged with public functions and organisations providing public services cannot require citizens and organisations to produce or to prove data which has already been collected or created [8]	One of the priorities of the Governance Programme of the Bulgarian Government is connection of key registers and provision of interoperability for switching to automated/semi-automated exchange of data and electronic documents	The Registry Information Exchange System (RegiX) is an environment for automated interconnections between registries. With RegiX it is possible for the authorised users of information to automatically retrieve data from basic registers such as the National Population Database, BULSTAT Register, Property Register, Commercial Register and other (62 registries in total) [8]

(*continued*)

(*continued*)

Country	Oop – legal basis	Program/strategy	National infrastructure supporting the OOP for business
Denmark	There is no legislation for OOP	The Digital Strategy puts forward the ambition that, as far as possible, citizens and businesses should not have to spend time submitting the same information to several public authorities or providing documentation for information that is already in public registries [1]	There is currently no government-wide data exchange infrastructure in Denmark however Data Distribution Platform offers an authoritative data source infrastructure. The Data Distribution Platform is the distribution channel that makes basic data from several authorities accessible in the same place. The Data Distribution Platform replaces a series of public distribution solutions and ensures that authorities and companies are provided with easy and safe access to basic data in one collective system, rather than having many different systems and interfaces
Czech Republic	The Act amending certain acts in connection with adoption of the Act on Base Registries (Act No 227/2009 Coll.) defined the rights and duties related to information editing, publishing and receiving data through the System of Base Registries. Act No. 111/2009 Coll. introduced base Registries into operation in other agendas of public services and created a cooperative network of various agendas around base registries including rules for information interoperability [10]	The Digital Czechia Programme covers the use and upgrade of base registries and their inter-connection [10]	The Registry of Economic Entities is one of 4 Base Registries. The interoperability between these base registries is ensured through the Information System of Base Registries [23]. National public administrations not only have access to the reference data in base registries, of which accuracy and validity is guaranteed by the state, but also to other attributes and data from other public administration information systems, in compliance with national legislation [10]

(continued)

Country	Oop – legal basis	Program/strategy	National infrastructure supporting the OOP for business
Cyprus	No data	No data	No data
Croatia	On 15 July 2014, the Croatian Parliament adopted the Law on the State Information Infrastructure, which introduced a meta-register thus ensuring preconditions for the 'Paperless government' and realisation of the "once-only" principle [9]	No data	The Metaregistry is a public register used to control the system of all public registers. It contains detailed information on public registers, the data they hold, as well as how to connect with other systems. The Metaregistry is still not yet fully operational [9]
Estonia	Since 2007, the Public Information Act prohibits the establishment of separate databases for the collection of the same data (§ 43). Also, the General Part of the Economic Activities Code Act (2011), establishing the general conditions and procedures for exercising the freedom of economic activity, states that economic administrative authorities are prohibited to require companies to provide information that is already entered in a public database. The prohibition also applies to information which can be obtained from the relevant register of another Contracting State (§ 13)	No data	X-tee (X-Road) is based on an interoperable ecosystem and a technical ability to exchange data. To exchange data, one member of X-tee describes the shared data and other members are able to use this data based on an agreement

(continued)

(continued)

Country	Oop – legal basis	Program/strategy	National infrastructure supporting the OOP for business
Finland	The Act on Public Administration Information Management requires government agencies to utilise datasets of other government agencies whenever possible, if they by law have access to such data via electronic interfaces. Regular exchange of data between agencies has to be organised via electronic interfaces. The Act also prescribes to the Ministry of Finance a general coordination task of interoperability of public sector data sets. The act entered into force on 1 January 2020 [11]	No data	Data Exchange Layer Palveluväylä is the Data Exchange Layer, which was based on Estonian X-Road technology. It is connected to Suomi.fi, which provides e-services to citizens, businesses and government organisations [11]

(continued)

(continued)

Country	Oop – legal basis	Program/strategy	National infrastructure supporting the OOP for business
France	Code des relations entre le public et l'administration which came into force on 1 January 2016 contains, among others, the exchange of information between administration (once-only) rules. Book III of the code deals with the access to administrative documents and re-use of public information [12] Additionally, following the law of 10 August 2018 for a State in the Service of a Company of Trust, a decree published in the Official Journal of 20 January 2019 supplements the principle of "Tell us once", where a user of the administration (individual or company) carrying out an action will no longer be obliged to provide certain information or supporting documents as soon as these elements are already held by the administration's services [12]	The Dites-le-nous une fois (Tell us once) is part of a global plan to modernise public services and is one of a range of actions being taken in France to digitalise such processes and improve collaboration between ministries and public services [35]	The OOP principle was implemented along with a wide range of base registry initiatives introduced through a number of strategies and respective initiatives. The digital tool enabled the pre-filling and digitisation of administrative forms that businesses were required to complete, in particular, to consent the exchange of information between the different departments and agencies. Public administrations can access this information through APIs (Apientreprisesl) that provide information from different base registries. The base registries available through APIs are: INSEE (Administrative information / contact details and identity); Infogreffe (Legal information / legal status); DGFiP (fiscal information / taxation / turnover); ACOSS (social situation / social security contributions); Caisses retraites (pension funds) [12]

(continued)

(continued)

Country	Oop – legal basis	Program/strategy	National infrastructure supporting the OOP for business
Germany	The possibility for Once-Only has been created in the eGovernment Act of the Federal Government and those of some countries (§5 (2) EGovG) which states that the competent authority can electronically obtain necessary evidence originating from a German public body directly from the issuing public body with the consent of the party to the procedure. For this purpose, the requesting authority and the issuing public authority may collect, process and use the necessary personal data	No strategy highlighting the OOP	At the moment there is no infrastructure supporting the OOP. In the future, an online gateway portal network will connect the administrative portals of the countries and enable their exchange of information. Using basic components, the decentralised data sets are exchanged and updated via all portals, so that all service descriptions can be found and online services can be called up via each portal With this decentralized approach, the project Online Gateway Portal Network will address the different development stages, technology approaches and IT strategies of the federal countries. The participation possibilities in the portal network are manifold and will be solved easily and cost-efficiently via standard interfaces[a]
Greece	At the moment the OOP is not regulated[a]	The OOP is not highlighted in any national strategy. At the moment the Ministry of Digital Governance is working on the design and implementation of the government's digital transformation policy	There is no infrastructure supporting the OOP

(continued)

(*continued*)

Country	Oop – legal basis	Program/strategy	National infrastructure supporting the OOP for business
Hungary	According to law, a person cannot be obliged to provide any data which is publically known or being stored in any authoritative data sources. At the same time it is not allowed to duplicate the data of base registries by other public administration bodies, they have to retrieve data from the given registries via secure data exchange[b]	The National Infocommunication Strategy 2014–2020 contains the necessity of simplifying administrative processes, reducing the administrative and bureaucratic burdens, and the establishment of interoperability among the major base registries until 2020	The technical infrastructure to support the OOP in Hungary is the Central Governmental Service Bus, the technical interoperability platform which is online since 1 January 2018. It enables automatic information exchange from 27 base registers indicated in the e-Administration Act. Others can also connect to provide their services over the central data exchange platform on a voluntary basis
Iceland	There is no legislation, however it is being analysed what needs to be changed in Icelandic laws to ensure the legitimacy of digital services and data sharing between parties	A new digital strategy is underway for Iceland. In the green book, which is the foundation for the new strategy, it is recommended that the OOP will be a part of it	The infrastructure enabling the OOP is already in place as a working X-Road implementation called Straumurinn,. Icelandic government is working on connecting all governmental organisations to this solution

(*continued*)

(*continued*)

Country	Oop – legal basis	Program/strategy	National infrastructure supporting the OOP for business
Italy	The Italian law (Legislative Decree no. 82 of 2005, the Digital Administration Code (CAD) Articles 50 and 58) states that public administrations should cooperate to obtain information and not as to provide information more than once [14]. Additionally, it establishes that public administrations shall exchange data between each other by default. Article 60 defines the Business Register as one of the Base Registries in Italy of national interest. Additionally, OOP is also explicitly mentioned and supported in the Public Contracts Code (Legislative Decree no. 50 of 2016) [5]	The OOP is one of the principles in the national strategy for digitization and in the three years Plan for digitization of public administrations 2019–2021 [3]	The infrastructure to enable OOP is the so called the Public Connectivity System (SPC) [51], which is a network that connects Italy's government agencies, allowing them to share and exchange data and information resource. The System is an eGovernment Digital service Infrastructure based on Domain Gateways (Data Providers and Consumers), a common format for the Data Request/Response (the so called eGov XML envelope) and Registers to publish the agreements (TOOP register) [48]
Ireland	Data Sharing and Governance Act 2019 provides a generalised legal basis for the sharing of data between public bodies for making public services more seamless by reducing the burden of providing the same information to different public bodies [13]	The Public Service Data Strategy for the period 2019–2023 aims to put in place a series of measures to improve how data is governed, managed and re-used in a secure, efficient and transparent manner, for the benefit of citizens, businesses and policy makers	No data

(*continued*)

(*continued*)

Country	Oop – legal basis	Program/strategy	National infrastructure supporting the OOP for business
Latvia	No data	The OOP is highlighted in the Information Society Development Guidelines 2014–2020 within Action Direction "Advanced and Effective Public administration" (Single Public administration Data Space) [33]	The IVIS is tasked with the unification and central management of the integration of platform-independent standardised data exchange between national registries and information systems. It provides a platform for sharing resources and for the public administration in using electronic services in the creation and delivery. Together with the state portal latvija.lv, it creates a single national electronic service delivery platform. One of the IVIS components is the public administration documents management system integration environment (DIV), which provides safe and secure environment between different record keeping systems of public administration [15] State information system register (SISR) was set up for the registration of State Information Systems (SIS), in which data on the national information systems - their use, technical resources and administrators - is stored. It supplies information to natural and legal entities on the data contained in the registers, as well as to system developers and organisations that integrate SIS. There are 173 registered SIS in the SISR [15]
Lichtenstein	No data	No data	No data

(*continued*)

(continued)

Country	Oop – legal basis	Program/strategy	National infrastructure supporting the OOP for business
Lithuania	Article 36 of the Law on Public Administration states that an economic entity shall enjoy the right not to submit documents to a supervising entity, if it has already submitted the same documents to at least one supervising entity. However, when refusing to submit documents, the economic entity must indicate in writing the supervising entity to which it has submitted the said documents [47]	No data	The State Information Resources Interoperability Platform (SIRIP) is the public interoperability platform, which consists of two main parts: Data exchange platform and Central electronic services portal eGovernment gateway [16]

(continued)

(*continued*)

Country	Oop – legal basis	Program/strategy	National infrastructure supporting the OOP for business
Luxembourg	The Law of 25 June 2013 concerning the digital identification of physical persons forms is the main basis for the OOP by prescribing that authentic data, already contained in the National Register of Natural Persons, have to be reused by public administrations. These administrations are not allowed to ask once more for these data and citizens do not need to provide evidence that the data in the register is correct. Nevertheless the OOP is also applied for other registers or databases not covered by the Law of 25 June 2013 but containing other authentic data: Cadastre, Cars register, Driving licence, VAT balance sheet [36]	The OOP is highlighted in the Digital Luxembourg initiative [50]	Luxembourg has implemented the OOP as efficiently as possible by making it a component of the Guichet.lu One Stop Shop [36]. It is possible to integrate authentic sources within the Guichet.lu back-office to retrieve and/or verify authentic data. The OOP is implemented in three distinct ways: data is reused automatically in the context of procedures at back office level without any explicit intervention of the user; for some cases citizens' or businesses' explicit consent is necessary in order for the administration to retrieve the necessary data from the central registers and databases; the citizen or the business decides to reuse information that he inserted himself in his personal space and that therefore is not information coming from an authentic source, i.e. from a central authoritative register or database
Malta	No data	Mapping Tomorrow is a strategic plan for the public administration for 2019–2021. Once-only is the core goal, aiming at internal sharing and re-use of data and information that has been previously provided by a citizen or organisation	No information about the implementation status. The Maltese Government Common Database (CdB) was enhanced with some minor amendments. An ongoing effort is being done for the simplification of processes by internally sharing data and re-use previously gathered information, in line with the OOP [17]

(*continued*)

(*continued*)

Country	Oop – legal basis	Program/strategy	National infrastructure supporting the OOP for business
The Netherlands	All base registries are anchored in legislation according to 12 agreed common principles [22]. One of them is that the use of basic registries is mandatory for all bodies that perform public tasks. It is not permitted to collect data that is already present within a basic register and citizens and businesses have to provide data once	No data	The System of Base Registries was created to share authentic data provided by citizens and businesses. It is composed of 10 base registries. In order to enable sharing and exchange of data, four system services were developed: Digikoppeling, Digilevering, Digimelding and the Stelselcatalogus [18]

(*continued*)

(*continued*)

Country	Oop – legal basis	Program/strategy	National infrastructure supporting the OOP for business
Norway	The Act relating to the Central Coordinating Register for Legal Entities LOV-1994–06-03–15 and the regulation regarding the registration of legal entities in the Central Coordinating Register for Legal Entities mandates public authorities to re-use information from the Central Register. Moreover, the Act regarding the Register of the Reporting Obligations of Enterprises (LOV-1997–06-06–35) obliges public authorities to coordinate reporting obligations in order to reduce multiple reporting[a]	OOP is supported in the Norwegian Digital strategy for the public sector 2019–2025	'Altinn' is the governmental system for digital communication between state, businesses and citizens. The exchange of information from business registries at the Altinn system is possible thanks to the Central Coordinating Register for Legal Entities, which identifies legal entities. The Register of the Reporting Obligations of Enterprises takes care of the re-use of data, enables the extracting of data from administrative systems and supplies metadata for electronic reporting solutions. CCR serves as a link between the entities and registries, making key data accessible. Associated registers shall use information registered in the CCR, and submit information they receive to the CCR. This is important in order to pre-fill forms and confirm whether a person is authorized to act on behalf of an entity
Portugal	The Decree-Law no. 135 of 1999, reviewed by the Decree-Law no. 73 of 2014, approved in May 2014, established important administrative modernisation measures, including the OOP, according to which the citizen must not be obliged to give the public administration the same document twice [19]	According to the Portuguese Government's interoperability strategy, public services should be allowed to exchange data in real time, facilitating the OOP, whereby citizens don't have to provide information to a public administration that is already in a public administration database [37]	The administration interoperability platform (iAP) connects various services between public entities and digital platforms that accumulate public information. The technology platform is based on a SOA and open standards, providing real time access to authentic sources of information and an Identity Federation mechanism [37]

(*continued*)

(continued)

Country	Oop – legal basis	Program/strategy	National infrastructure supporting the OOP for business
Poland	The Polish law (The Code of Administrative Procedure [34]) forbids public bodies to request information that is already stored by any other public body	The OOP is part of the action for the citizens and businesses oriented services in the national Integrated Program for Digitalization [44]	There is no general infrastructure to enable secure exchange of data between public registries. This kind of exchange is enable only for selected services
Romania	The 41/2016 Ordinance, issued in June 2016, introduced the obligation for public authorities, on request from citizens, to accept documents in electronic format and reuse any personal data previously delivered to the public administration. The ordinance stipulated new rules concerning source code for ICT systems developed under an eProcurement contract. The ordinance also established a national CIO in partnership with the Ministry of Communication and Information Society and the rest of government	The OOP is part of the Strategy for enhancing the Public Administration 2014–2020 (with the purpose of establishing the general framework for public administration reform), MDRAP [39]; the Action Plan - Strategy for enhancing the Public Administration 2014–2020 [40]; the Integrated plan for simplifying administrative procedures applicable to citizens, CNCISCAP, 2016 [41]; the Romania's development strategy for the next 20 years, Romanian Academy, 2017 [2]	There is no a national infrastructure enabling the OOP in relation to business data

(continued)

(continued)

Country	Oop – legal basis	Program/strategy	National infrastructure supporting the OOP for business
Spain	Law 39/2015 of 1 October 2015, on Common Administrative Procedure of Public Administrations, art. 28 and law 40/2015 art. 155 facilitate the OOP. Public administration cannot require data and documents that have been previously delivered. Each administration must facilitate access to data in its possession [4]	The Action Plan for Digital Transformation in the Ministry of Finance includes Initiatives that are proposed for compliance with article 28 of Law 39/2015, related to the 'once-only' principle [21]	The Data Intermediation Platform (PID) is a horizontal service that simplifies administrative procedures, so that citizens or businesses do not have to deliver data or documents already held by public authorities [21]. Using the PID with the SCSP protocol, public bodies in charge of administrative procedures can automatically check the required information. The SCSP protocol is aimed to substitute paper certificates by electronic data exchanges and it defines a common structure for the messages and a governance model that considers four roles as result of two dimensions: data consumer/provider and business/technical actor [21]
Sweden	There is no legal obligation for the OOP	OOP is underlined in the national digitization plans	The Composite Service of Basic Information on Companies - CSBIC supports exchange of business related data in line with the OOP. The CSBIC works as an intermediary and forwards basic data requests from consumers (municipalities, government authorities, verksamt.se business portal) to data sources (Swedish Tax Agency, Statistics Sweden, Swedish Companies Registration Office) and then collects and forwards the replies from the producers to the consumers. The service is based on xml/soap

(continued)

(*continued*)

Country	Oop – legal basis	Program/strategy	National infrastructure supporting the OOP for business
Slovenia	According to art. 139 of General Administrative Procedure Act [52], the official who conducts the proceeding shall obtain the data on the facts of which the agency competent for deciding, any other State agency, local community agency or statutory authority keeps official records	At the moment only guidelines for information solution development [45] cover the OOP. The new Public Administration Development Strategy, which is under preparation, will highlight the OOP	The TRAY is a central system for electronic data enquires, which enables efficient, reliable and secure collection of data for different clients, from numerous and heterogeneous data sources, by handling electronic data enquiries and electronic answers. It also enables the handling of data sources in a customised and parameterised way. In 2019 an AI based algorithm for data traffic optimization was added to the system, minimizing congestion risks with data collection
Slovakia	Act no. 177/2018, on measures to reduce administrative burden by using public administration information systems and on amendments and supplements to certain acts (Act Against Bureaucracy), came into force on 1 September 2018. According to the provisions of § 1 par. 1 of the Act, in their official activities public authorities were obliged and authorised to obtain and use data recorded in public administration information systems, to make extracts from them, and to provide such data and extracts when necessary [20]	National strategy for public governance informatization (document National Concept of Public Administration Informatization of the Slovak Republic [42]) contains also several OOP mentioning in context of public services improvements. The European scope of OOP is mentioned in document 2030 Digital Transformation Strategy for Slovakia [43]	The digital service OVER SI started in September 2018. Based on the Central Data Integrated Platform, was set up in response to the Government´s Stop to Bureaucracy initiative. In due course, more than 16000 public administration clerks performing duties at different domains were registered in order to provide themselves with the requested evidence (in the first phase evidence came from business registers of companies and self-employed, from cadastre and from criminal register). By the end of 2019, another batch of 11 sources of evidence was expected to be made available via the OVER SI. The portal allows the verification and exchange of four documents between government authorities [20]

[a]Questionnaire with a TOOP partner.
[b]Information obtained from the Ministry of Interior, Hungary.

References

1. A stronger and more secure digital Denmar Digital Stratey 2016–220. https://en.digst.dk/media/14143/ds_singlepage_uk_web.pdf. Accessed 06 Mar 2020
2. ACADEMIA ROMÂNĂ website. https://acad.ro/bdar/strategiaAR/doc14/Strategia-SumarExecutiv.pdf. Accessed 20 Mar 2021
3. Agenzia per l'Italia digitale. https://docs.italia.it/italia/piano-triennale-ict/pianotriennale-ict-doc/it/2019-2021/01_piano-triennale-per-informatica-nella-pa.html#strategia-per-la-trasfo rmazione-digitale. Accessed 05 Mar 2020
4. Amutio, A.M.: https://www.slideshare.net/MiguelAmutio/onceonly-as-a-means-of-admini strative-simplification-in-spain. Accessed 24 Feb 2020
5. CodiceAppalti.it website. https://www.codiceappalti.it/glossario_appalti/PRINCIPIO_DI_UNICITA'_DELL'INVIO_(DLGS_50_2016)/9361. Accessed 05 Mar 2020
6. Digital Government Factsheet 2019 – Austria. https://joinup.ec.europa.eu/sites/default/files/inline-files/Digital_Government_Factsheets_Austria_2019_3.pdf. Accessed 24 Apr 2020
7. Digital Government Factsheet 2019 – Belgium. https://joinup.ec.europa.eu/sites/default/files/inline-files/Digital_Government_Factsheets_Belgium_2019_1.pdf. Accessed 24 Apr 2020
8. Digital Government Factsheet 2019 – Bulgaria. https://joinup.ec.europa.eu/sites/default/files/inline-files/Digital_Government_Factsheets_Bulgaria_2019_1.pdf. Accessed 24 Feb 2020
9. Digital Government Factsheet 2019 – Croatia. https://joinup.ec.europa.eu/sites/default/files/inline-files/Digital_Government_Factsheets_Croatia_2019.pdf. Accessed 24 Feb 2020
10. Digital Government Factsheet – Czech Republic. https://joinup.ec.europa.eu/sites/default/files/inline-files/Digital_Government_Factsheets_Czech%20Republic_2019.pdf. Accessed 06 Mar 2020
11. Digital Government Factsheet 2019 – Finland. https://joinup.ec.europa.eu/sites/default/files/inline-files/Digital_Government_Factsheets_Finland_2019.pdf. Accessed 24 Feb 2020
12. Digital Government Factsheet 2019 – France. https://joinup.ec.europa.eu/sites/default/files/inline-files/Digital_Government_Factsheets_France_2019.pdf. Accessed 24 Feb 2020
13. Digital Government Factsheet 2019 – Ireland. https://joinup.ec.europa.eu/sites/default/files/inline-files/Digital_Government_Factsheets_Ireland_2019.pdf. Accessed 27 Feb 2020
14. Digital Government Factsheet 2019 – Italy. https://joinup.ec.europa.eu/sites/default/files/inline-files/Digital_Government_Factsheets_Italy_2019_0.pdf. Accessed 05 Mar 2020
15. Digital Government Factsheet 2019 – Latvia. https://joinup.ec.europa.eu/sites/default/files/inline-files/Digital_Government_Factsheets_Latvia_2019.pdf. Accessed 24 Feb 2020
16. Digital Government Factsheet 2019 – Lithuania. https://joinup.ec.europa.eu/sites/default/files/inline-files/Digital_Government_Factsheets_Lithuania_2019_0.pdf, last accessed 2020–02–24
17. Digital Government Factsheet 2019 – Malta. https://joinup.ec.europa.eu/sites/default/files/inline-files/Digital_Government_Factsheets_Malta_2019.pdf. Accessed 24 Feb 2020
18. Digital Government Factsheet 2019 – The Netherlands. https://joinup.ec.europa.eu/sites/default/files/inline-files/Digital_Government_Factsheets_Netherlands_2019_0.pdf. Accessed 24 Feb 2020
19. Digital Government Factsheet 2019 – Portugal. https://joinup.ec.europa.eu/sites/default/files/inline-files/Digital_Government_Factsheets_Portugal_2019_vFINAL.pdf. R Accessed 24 Feb 2020
20. Digital Government Factsheet 2019 – Slovakia. https://joinup.ec.europa.eu/sites/default/files/inline-files/Digital_Government_Factsheets_Slovakia_2019.pdf. Accessed 24 Feb 2020
21. Digital Government Factsheet 2019 – Spain. https://joinup.ec.europa.eu/sites/default/files/inline-files/Digital_Government_Factsheets_Spain_2019_1.pdf. Accessed 24 Feb 2020

22. Digitale Overheid website. https://www.digitaleoverheid.nl/overzicht-van-alle-onderw erpen/gegevens/naar-een-gegevenslandschap/themas/twaalf-eisen-stelsel-van-basisregistr aties/. Accessed 24 Apr 2020
23. European Commission: Access to base registries (2016)
24. European Commission: Communication From the Commission to the European Parliament, The Council, The European Economic and Social Committee and The Committee of the Regions a Digital Single Market Strategy for Europe (2015)
25. European Commission: eGovernment Action Plan 2011–2015 (2010)
26. European Commission: EU eGovernment Action Plan 2016–2020 – Accelerating the digital transformation of government (2015)
27. European Commission. New European Interoperability Framework (2017)
28. European Commission (2017). "Tallinn Declaration on eGovernment"
29. European Council: European Council conclusions 169/13 (2013)
30. European Union: Regulation (EU) 2018/1724 of the European Parliament and of the Council of 2 October 2018 establishing a single digital gateway to provide access to information, to procedures and to assistance and problem-solving services and amending Regulation (EU) No 1024/2012 (Single Digital Gateway Regulation) (2018)
31. Gallo, C., Giove, M., Millard, J., Thaarup, R., Valvik, K.: Study on eGovernment and the Reduction of Administrative Burden: final report (2014)
32. Grant Thornton (2020). "Sprawozdawczość firm2019"
33. Information Society Development Guidelines 2014–2020. https://www.varam.gov.lv/en/pol icy-planning-documents. Accessed 27 Feb 2020
34. ISAP – Internetowy System Aktów Prawnych. http://prawo.sejm.gov.pl/isap.nsf/download. xsp/WDU19600300168/U/D19600168Lj.pdf. Accessed 24 Feb 2020
35. Joinup website. https://joinup.ec.europa.eu/collection/open-government/document/dites-le-nous-une-fois-programme. Accessed 28 Feb 2020
36. Joinup website. https://joinup.ec.europa.eu/collection/nifo-national-interoperability-framew ork-observatory/document/oop-luxembourg. Accessed 27 Feb 2020
37. Joinup website https://joinup.ec.europa.eu/collection/egovernment/document/iap-common-language-ensure-real-interoperability-public-administration. Accessed 24 Feb 2020
38. Ministerial Declaration on eGovernment. https://ec.europa.eu/digital-single-market/sites/dig ital-agenda/files/ministerial-declaration-on-egovernment-malmo.pdf. Accessed 05 Mar 2020
39. Ministry of Development, Public Works and Administration website. http://www.dpfbl. mdrap.ro/documents/strategia_administratiei_publice/Strategia_pentru_consolidarea_adm inistratiei_publice_2014-2020.pdf. Accessed 20 Mar 2021
40. Ministry of Development, Public Works and Administration website. http://www.dpfbl. mdrap.ro/documents/strategia_administratiei_publice/Strategia_pentru_consolidarea_adm inistratiei_publice_2014-2020.pdf. Accessed 20 Mar 2021
41. Ministry of Development, Public Works and Administration website. https://www.mlpda.ro/ uploads/articole/attachments/5daea2f3b042e096613155.pdf. Accessed 20 Mar 2021
42. Ministry of Investments, Regional Development and Informatization of the Slovak Republic website. https://www.vicepremier.gov.sk/wp-content/uploads/2018/10/NKIVS-SR_2016-1.pdf. Accessed 26 May 2020
43. Ministry of Investments, Regional Development and Informatization of the Slovak Republic website. https://www.vicepremier.gov.sk/wp-content/uploads/2019/10/SDT-English-Ver sion-FINAL.pdf. Accessed 26 May 2020
44. National Integrated Program for Digitalization. https://www.gov.pl/web/cyfryzacja/program-zintegrowanej-informatyzacji-panstwa. Accessed 2020–02–24
45. NIO - National Interoperability Framework of Slovenia website. https://nio.gov.si/nio/asset/ smernice+mju+za+razvoj+informacijskih+resitev-768?lang=en. Accessed 20 Mar 2021

46. Public Information Act – Riigi Teataja. www.riigiteataja.ee. Accessed 26 Feb 2020
47. Republic of Lithuania Law on Public Administration. https://e-seimas.lrs.lt/portal/legalAct/lt/TAD/09ebba107b9311e49386e711974443ff?jfwid=rivwzvpvg. Accessed 24 Feb 2020
48. Sistema pubblico di cooperazione: QUADRO TECNICO D'INSIEME, DigitPA, 2011
49. The European Parliament and the Council of the European Union: Directive 2006/123/EC of the European Parliament and of the Council of 12 December 2006 on services in the internal market (2006)
50. The Luxembourg Government website. https://gouvernement.lu/en/actualites/toutes_actualites.gouvernement%2Bfr%2Bactualites%2Btoutes_actualites%2Bcommuniques%2B2015%2B07-juillet%2B24-conseil-gouvernement.html. Accessed 27 Feb 2020
51. Wikipedia.   https://it.wikipedia.org/wiki/Sistema_pubblico_di_connettivit%C3%A0. Accessed 28 Feb 2020
52. Zakonodaja website. https://zakonodaja.com/zakon/zup/139-clen. Accessed 26 May 2020

Drivers for and Barriers to the Cross-border Implementation of the Once-Only Principle

Nele Leosk[1], Irma Põder[1(✉)], Carsten Schmidt[1,2(✉)] (iD), Tarmo Kalvet[1(✉)] (iD), and Robert Krimmer[1,2(✉)] (iD)

[1] Tallinn University of Technology, Ehitajate tee 5, 12616 Tallinn, Estonia
{nele.leosk,irma.poder,carsten.schmidt,tarmo.kalvet,
robert.krimmer}@taltech.ee
[2] Center for IT Impact Studies, Johan Skytte Institute for Political Studies, University of Tartu,
Lossi 36, 51003 Tartu, Estonia
{carsten.schmidt,robert.krimmer}@ut.ee

Abstract. The once-only principle (OOP) aims to reduce interactions between citizens and governments, but many factors challenge its cross-border implementation. Building on the results of the "The Once-Only Principle Project" (TOOP, 2017–2021), an analysis was undertaken of the factors that either support or hinder implementation of the cross-border OOP. Five domains of factors were examined - technological, organizational, institutional aspects, actors and miscellaneous. This research highlights the importance of awareness of the OOP, and its inherent benefits, as a key driver. Also, the activities of supranational entities are of key significance, as it is establishing a critical legal framework. Co-ordination between different levels of government and different countries remains an important barrier. One specific issue discovered and addressed during the project but uncovered here, relates to identity matching, and this requires EU level intervention to reach an effective and efficient solution.

Keywords: The once-only principle · Drivers · Barriers · Cross-border public services · Interoperability · The once-only principle project

1 Introduction

The once-only principle (OOP) aims to reduce interactions between citizens and governments. It is driven by the goal of designing user-centric public services and reducing administrative burdens for citizens and businesses when fulfilling government-imposed administrative requirements and consuming public services (Gallo et al. 2014). In order to reduce administrative burdens, public administrations seek to minimize instances in which citizens and businesses must provide data to the government. To this end, public administrations seek to replace requesting data from citizens with machine-to-machine data exchange; and reuse of data already stored digitally in public sector databases, hence allowing citizens to provide data to the government "only once" (Meyerhoff Nielsen and Krimmer 2015, Krimmer et al. 2017, Kalvet et al. 2018a, Kalvet et al. 2018b, Olesk 2020).

© The Author(s) 2021
R. Krimmer et al. (Eds.): The Once-Only Principle, LNCS 12621, pp. 38–60, 2021.
https://doi.org/10.1007/978-3-030-79851-2_3

Although the OOP is not yet a widespread practice across European countries (Cave et al. 2017; Gallo et al. 2014), the European Commission recently took major policy steps to promote and adopt the OOP on a Europe-wide level, with the aim of developing cross-border e-government services for European citizens and businesses. The European Commission and 21 European countries launched a large-scale European interoperability initiative as a significant milestone – The Once-Only Principle Project (TOOP) – in 2017. TOOP is seeking to facilitate a Europe-wide OOP by developing a federated technical architecture, capable of interconnecting databases and data exchange layers in different countries (see Krimmer et al. 2017 for more details). Since cross-border OOP is an emerging concept, not yet practiced widely or discussed in literature, TOOP provided us valuable empirical information on drivers, barriers and obstacles for the OOP in Europe.

This section of the TOOP Book is structured as follows. After this introductory section, the second section identifies and categorizes, using state of the art for different determinants of the success of OOP initiatives (i.e., aspects identified as drivers or barriers in existing literature). After that, the third section briefly presents the method used to assess the importance of those factors. The following section of the chapter presents the results of data analysis. Finally, a discussion of the main findings, implications and some recommendations to address some aspects we identified, which hinder concretization and success of future OOP initiatives, is presented in section four. The section ends with our conclusions.

2 The Factors Impacting OOP Initiatives in a Cross-border Context

2.1 Factors Generally Impacting OOP Initiatives in a Cross-border Context

The aim of this chapter is to explore the barriers and drivers of cross-border OOP. Despite being fairly common concepts in e-governance literature, we nevertheless find it important, first of all, to clarify the use of the two terms. Said simply, drivers and barriers relate to the respective positive or negative impacts that a certain factor (or variable) presumably has on implementation and execution of OOP initiatives (or any type of undertaking for that matter). Therefore, the same factor, depending on its value, and sometimes even the context (e.g., country, domain), may either be a driver or a barrier for an initiative involving the OOP. Additionally, the effect, and even direction of certain factors could presumably also vary, depending on the stage of implementation of an OOP initiative we have determined.

Research on implementation of the OOP is still scarce – only a few studies on the implementation of the OOP exist, with the most notable studies on the topic being by Gallo et al. (2014) and Cave et al. (2017). However, existing literature on e-government, interoperability, public sector innovation, as well as acceptance of technology, can help us identify the key factors perceived to affect public administrations´ readiness, and ability to adopt the OOP for both national and cross-border transactions. This literature consistently suggests that factors impacting the provision of cross-border digital are plentiful and not related exclusively to technological dimensions (e.g., Gil-Garcia and Pardo 2005; Savoldelli et al. 2014; Cave et al. 2017). Furthermore, it has been postulated that there is no one single factor influencing digitalization, but rather a combination of several determinants instead (Gil-Garcia 2012).

There are several typologies used to classify, and group together different factors affecting digital provision of public services. One early attempt to categorize these factors was made by Gil-Garcia and Pardo (2005). According to the authors, factors affecting ICT projects in the public sector can be grouped into five categories: 1) information and data; 2) information technology; 3) organizational and managerial; 4) legal; and 5) institutional and environmental (Gil-Garcia and Pardo 2005). While the first two concern the availability and quality of data and technology, respectively, the remaining three extend beyond the technological domain, relating to the existence of an organizational, legal and institutional environment that stimulates, or hinders, the provision of digital services. Some examples of these factors are: the size of a project or organizations´ staff, the project alignment with existing goals, the presence of a regulatory framework or incentives; and, finally, pressures from political actors, businesses, or civil society.

Subsequent works followed a similar approach to classify factors affecting e-government and adoption of ICTs. Regarding the development of e-government in the European Union (EU), Germanakos et al. (2007) also identified factors from several categories such as technical, legal, as well as social and institutional environments too. Similarly, Savoldelli et al. (2014) stressed, in addition to technological/operational aspects, the significance that managerial-organizational and political-institutional factors have for the adoption of e-government. Looking at determinants of e-procurement, in two European regions, Gascó et al. (2018) also take the source of the barriers into account, making a distinction between "outer context" and "inner" factors. While the former refers to wider environmental factors, such as economic, social and political factors, as well as the inter-institutional environment and dynamics, inner factors are the ones intrinsically related to the organizations (i.e., organizational, individual and technical). Even though the authors find political aspects to be significant, internal factors seem to be the most weighty determinants. Overall, whether examining the provision of e-services, the adoption of ICTs, or e-government maturity levels, the frameworks, or typologies, developed to identify determinants for these outcomes have remained relatively constant.

Olesk (2020) also found that collaborative digital government initiatives are subject to influences of a number of factors in their context. These factors relate to technology and innovation, stakeholders (characteristics, beliefs and the behavior of public officials and citizens), organizational and institutional contexts, public sector quirks and particularities, and developments in the broader environment. While some of the factors (e.g., championing innovations, political will or favorable regulatory environments) serve as drivers and enablers of innovation, many others (e.g., stakeholders' beliefs, organizational resistance to change, resource limitations) tend to pose constraints and barriers to adoption and institutionalization of innovative public governance practices (Table 1).

The research which exists on the OOP produced similar results. According to (Cave et al. 2017), regarding the European context, the key barriers for implementation of the OOP can be grouped into five distinct categories. Those categories are 1) legal; 2) organizational; 3) semantic; 4) technical; and 5) other. The last, less well-defined, category covers aspects such as political will, users' awareness or the existence of bi(multi)lateral

Table 1. Key categories and examples of context factors of collaborative digital public sector innovation

Technology	Innovation characteristics	Public officials	Citizens
Availability of hardware and software Features of specific technologies (e.g. security) Interoperability	Ease of use Cost Compatibility Trustworthiness Relative advantage	Characteristics of individual innovators Attitudes, beliefs Knowledge and competences Trust in citizens Leadership Human error in innovation management	Motivation to engage with government Interests Knowledge and competences Trust in government Time constraints Perceptions (e.g. usefulness of the innovation)
Organizations	Institutions	Public sector context	Broader environment
Capabilities Incentives Financial resources Human resources Organizational structures Organizational cultures Resistance to change Top management support Participation in networks	Regulations and legal constraints Informal norms Institutional histories Legal and administrative culture Coordination and governance mechanisms Existing power relations	Influence of politics and political will Stakeholder complexity, different agendas Multi-rationality Bureaucratic and democratic principles Organizational competition for power and legitimacy Expanding domain of public intervention	Public attention Media attention Mimetic pressures Technological development

Source: Olesk (2020)

agreements. Two points should be emphasized from this exhaustive examination focusing on the OOP. The first is that perspectives of individuals/businesses and public officials diverge in terms of perceived barriers to the OOP. The second stresses the importance of semantic aspects, particularly the need for certified translations and deviation in the content of documents and data (Cave et al. 2017). In this sense, this study places importance on the interoperability dimension and cross-country dynamics, which are, to a great extent, distinctive and crucial aspects of the OOP.

A similar and also enhanced taxonomy has been proposed, based on previous results of the TOOP project (Table 2).

Summing up, literature used fairly consistent models, or similar sets of independent variables, to study modernization of the public sector and adoption of e-government. However, with a few exceptions (e.g., Leosk 2019), the aspect of time has been overlooked in written works examining determinants of e-government. The importance of

Table 2. Barriers to cross-border OOP

Stakeholders	Organizational, institutional	Legal	Technology, interoperability
Lack of awareness of the OOP Unclear perceived benefits of the OOP Unclear motivation to adopt the OOP Hesitancy adopting cross-border data sharing	Organizational silos Complexity of organizational change Resource limitations Cultural resistance Lack of political priority	Legal restrictions on data sharing Data protection and confidentiality requirements Absence of legal basis for cross-border OOP Lack of legal validity of evidence exchanged	Heterogeneous ICT systems Heterogeneous data handling approaches Legacy systems Data fragmentation Differences in data quality Limited availability of digital data

Source: Olesk (2020), based on (Kalvet et al. 2018a)

barriers and drivers of OOP, particularly when discussing perceptions of the main intervening actors, should vary not only between contexts (e.g. countries, area of implementation) but also between different stages of implementation. This problem is addressed in this study, by considering two distinct phases of implementation of OOP projects. This approach allows us, among other things, to explore whether the significance of certain factors, perceived to be important, persists over time.

Overall, the same lenses that were used to focus on our study of determinants for electronic provision of public services, or e-government in general, also prove useful for exploring key barriers and drivers, in the case of the OOP. Nonetheless, we can also identify factors, or variables, that are particularly important in the case of OOP initiatives. The improved framework of technical enactment (Fountain 2001; 2008) is valuable for structuring the array of factors, which we have grouped for this study into 5 dimensions: 1) technological; 2) organizational; 3) institutional; 4) actors; and 5) others (or miscellaneous), largely context specific factors. Each dimension, and respective factor, is detailed in the paragraphs below.

2.2 Technological Factors

Technological factors are particularly relevant in the case of OOP due to its reliance on heterogeneous information and process models. In fact, technical issues, particularly those relating to interoperability, are perceived as the most challenging aspects of modern cross-organizational information systems (Mocan et al. 2011). Interoperability, a key element of the OOP, can be defined as the exchange of data between different organizations and respective ICT systems. It therefore requires organizations have the capacity to interact with each other to achieve mutually beneficial and common goals (Cave et al. 2017). This becomes more important, particularly on a semantic level, in the case of cooperation between different countries. Besides the interoperability aspect, in the case of the cross-border context of the OOP, other relevant factors concern data quality, the particularities of various databases or information systems and, finally, countries' overall e-government architecture/infrastructures (Cave et al. 2017).

The European Commission also acknowledges that, in order to put the OOP into practice, various organizations must collaborate to develop technical and semantic interoperability (European Commission 2017). Ensuring technical interoperability requires adopting common technical specifications and building infrastructures that enable linking systems, in order to secure data exchange between information systems. Ensuring semantic interoperability requires agreement to common data formats and developing vocabularies to allow communicating systems to understand the meaning of the data in the same way. The EC's concept of interoperability extends beyond technical factors, also covering the importance of organizational and legal interoperability; as described in the following sections.

2.3 Organizational Factors

The organizational dimension consists of all factors intrinsically related to organizations. This accounts for the significant changes imposed by the OOP in organizational structures and workflows. The required level of collaboration and coordination between different organizations, one core aspect of the OOP (e.g., Wimmer et al. 2020), is bound to face a number of organizational and administrative barriers affecting organizations' will and capacity to implement OOP. The most common barriers faced during implementation of OOP at a national level have been found to include governmental silos and lack of communication between government departments, the complexity of changes in organizational structures, working practices and cultures, and concerns about high implementation costs (Gallo et al. 2014). A set of constraints that are also very frequently present at a cross-border level (Cave et al. 2017).

The literature confirms the importance of organizations' capacity to adapt, transform and innovate, which in turn depends, to a great extent, on aspects such as organizational structure and culture, the existing networks and the existence/ development of cross-organizational and cross-border knowledge transfer networks (de Vries et al. 2016; Albury 2005; Ferguson et al. 2013). Finally, one cannot overlook the importance that organizations' financial and human resources may naturally convey for the adoption and successful implementation of electronic services or use of ICTs (Drew 2011; Bekkers et al. 2013). The lack of financial, technical and personnel (staffing) capacities in an organization are major obstacles to development of e-government (Moon 2002).

2.4 Institutional Factors

The third dimension of factors affecting the OOP deals with the institutional aspect and concerns the sets of rules, laws and principles that may influence the development of digital governance (Bellamy and Taylor 1996; Fountain 2008; Heeks and Bailur 2007; Luna-Reyes and Gil-García 2011). It is common knowledge that public sector organizations are also heavily affected by variables beyond the power of individual organizations, such as the legal culture and administrative traditions of a state (Bekkers et al. 2013). Even though these factors are exogenous to the organizations, and usually more stable, or slower to change, regulations can be determinants for change, and promote innovation by imposing, for example, legal obligations on administrations to implement innovative solutions (de Vries et al. 2016). The political environment is also another critical aspect, with factors such as political stability having a positive effect on the development of e-government (Rodriguez et al. 2011).

Particularly in the case of the OOP, institutional and legal rules are critical for setting limits on data sharing and personal data protection systems. According to Gallo et al. (2014), resolving any legal obstacles and establishing a sound legal basis is one of the most important strategic issues for implementation of OOP. The role of intergovernmental and supranational institutions is fundamental for the case of the OOP. Although some directives and regulations have been adopted to support interoperability at the EU level (e.g., Single Digital Gateway Regulation – SDGR, regulation on electronic identification and trust services for electronic transactions – eIDAS, Services Directive and the General Data Protection Regulation – GDPR), there is still a need to establish a common legal basis at the EU level to fully support an EU-wide OOP (Cave et al. 2017).

2.5 Actors

The fourth important dimension of factors considered in this study are the actors. This dimension results from a revision of the technology enactment framework and the acknowledgment that technology, organizations and institutions cannot account alone for e-government and public sector's modernization (Dawes 1996; Gil-Garcia 2006; Dunleavy et al. 2006). As they are accountable to a number of public and private stakeholders, public sector organizations are highly dependent on political goals and tensions (Rashman et al. 2009). However, the modernization of services may be highly dependent not only on political will, but also on public and business demands (Heeks 2005; Panopoulou et al. 2010; De Vries et al. 2016).

The public is a pivotal element of e-government and "governments must be careful, in their zeal to modernize, not to unwittingly betray the public interest" (Fountain 2001:203). Here, aspects such as citizens´ level of education, one important predictor of internet usage according to Chinn and Fairlie (2007), may influence individuals' demand for digital solutions. In the case of OOP, the support of political actors, business and civil society, both at national and supranational level, is perceived as a crucial aspect (Cave et al. 2017). This support, however, seems to depend on previous experience with OOP and on its benefits having been clearly demonstrated to individuals, businesses and public administrations (Cave et al. 2017).

Overall, different types of actors are important for the adoption of OOP. Previous experience with this principle is likely to bolster different actors' support and the will for it. However, if certain groups also benefit from the inefficiency or complexity of a service, the organizations and political actors might encounter some resistance for the implementation of OOP. Moreover, as Akkaya and Krcmar (2018) highlight, some concerns regarding privacy and data-protection may also ease the demand, or support, for the OOP.

This takes us to the expected or anticipated benefits of OOP which different actors have attached to the OOP, and which serve as one of the main drivers of the OOP. The most essential ones are brought to the fore here. The main benefit associated with OOP relates to the increased efficiency of government apparatus and, generally, to better governance (Cave et al. 2017; van Veestra et al. 2017; Wimmer and Marinov 2017; Wimmer et al. 2020). Scholars agree that sharing data across organizations, as well as across national boundaries, reduces administrative burdens and simplifies administrative processes which, in turn, leads to a reduction in time and financial resources required to support those administrative processes. In the same way, the OOP is seen as a contributor to increased user-friendliness and efficiency of digital service provision, but is also expected to leverage service quality across organizations or countries involved in providing these services (Bekkers et al. 2013; van Veenstra et al. 2013). There is an extended analysis of perceived benefits of the OOP in the chapter "Measuring the Impact of the Once Only Principle for Businesses Across Borders" in this book.

2.6 Other Factors

There are also other factors, which do not fit, or are transverse to the dimensions previously discussed. Factors which may, nevertheless, have an important impact on implementation and success of OOP initiatives. Variables such as gender, age, level of education, experience with a specific or related technology, and degree of voluntary use are considered to influence the adoption process (Carrizales 2008; Morris and Venkatesh 2000). The issue of ICT skills and the digital divide in society was also emphasized by Cave et al. (2017). In their review of literature, Van Veenstra et al. (2011) similarly conclude that a deficiency in or lack of IT skills presents hurdles for adoption of new technologies by public administrations. Furthermore, this category also accounts for unexpected, or extraordinary, factors that could account for the implementation, or smooth and efficient functioning of a particular OOP project (for example, the continued existence of supranational projects of a similar nature). It is crucial that these factors, which are difficult to specify a priori, are also taken into consideration in any study of OOP.

3 Methodology

This study builds on a multi-method approach, including several qualitative research methods such as semi-structured interviews, focus groups and surveys. The most informative collection of empirical data was completed via qualitative methods. A qualitative approach is broadly considered suitable for tackling research problems that are not clear-cut and require investigative processes and interactions in their natural, 'messy' context (Yin 2003).

By and large, the empirical data was collected in two waves. The first wave of data collection took place at the beginning of the TOOP Project in 2017, when project pilot activities had not yet commenced. This means the data collected then largely reflects TOOP Project participants' perceptions and expectations of the OOP cross-border determinants. The second wave of data collection took place towards the end of TOOP Project, in 2019 and in 2020, i.e., after implementation of TOOP pilot projects. These data reflect TOOP Project participants' real-life experiences when planning and testing the cross-border OOP. This allowed us to understand whether the perceptions of the OOP determinants, both drivers and barriers that were identified at the beginning of the Project played a role in TOOP pilot projects' progress and in implementation of the OOP.

To begin with, a thorough review of existing literature was completed; first, to understand the expected benefits of the OOP and; secondly, to understand the determinants, either supportive or otherwise, for implementation of the OOP. As a result of the review of the literature, the benefits associated with the OOP, but also with the OOP drivers and barriers, were identified and used as an input for developing the first survey questionnaire.

Based on the results of the first survey (but also the first focus groups), the inventory of perceived factors was updated and served as an input for refining the codebook. The final codebook used to analyze the data collected at the end of TOOP project includes 5 main dimensions: technology, institutions, organizations, actors, and other factors - overall comprising an exhaustive list which was further whittled down. More detailed information on the collection of empirical data is provided in a sequential order below.

First of all, at the outset of TOOP Project, a survey was conducted amongst TOOP Project participants in May to July 2017 in order to fathom and understand TOOP participants' perceptions of barriers and drivers for the OOP. The survey was sent out via e-mail to a total of 18 countries, and 15 country responses were returned.

As a second step, we organized focus groups. The first focus group was held on April 19, 2017 in The Hague, Netherlands over three sessions, one for each pilot area, each with 3–5 participants. The second focus group was held on May 23–24, 2017 in Rome, in Italy over two different sessions and included all pilot area participants. During these two focus group meetings, the expected OOP determinants of TOOP Project participants were identified, as described above. For a more detailed analysis of their results, see the publications by Kalvet and colleagues (Kalvet et al. 2018a and 2018b).

The second wave of data collection started in 2019 with the organization of focus groups, which were then held in Ljubljana, Slovenia on April 10, 2019 and in Tallinn, Estonia on June 3–4, 2019. In Ljubljana, two sessions were held with a total of 30 participants, whereas in Tallinn, three sessions were held, one for each pilot area. As already stated above, during the second wave of data collection, the OOP drivers and barriers were collected and analyzed based on the participants' real-life/actual experience in planning and testing cross-border OOP, that they had acquired through progression of TOOP pilot areas. The focus group sessions were organized in cooperation with TOOP Project impact assessment team, thus, the aim was to analyze both determinants and impacts of the OOP. The results of the impact assessment are discussed in detail in the chapter "Measuring the Impact of the Once Only Principle for Businesses Across Borders" of this book.

As part of the second wave of data collection, we also carried out semi structured interviews with TOOP participants from June-September 2020, totaling 11 people from 6 countries, representing all three pilot areas. Lastly, the second survey questionnaire was sent to 15 countries involved in TOOP pilot areas and a total of 16 responses were received from 13 countries.

This study presents a few limitations. The main one relates to comparability of the OOP determinants listed at the beginning and those that were identified towards the end of the TOOP project. As we already mentioned, in 2017, only the participants' perceptions of the OOP were identified whereas in 2019 and in 2020, participants reflected their real-time experiences with the cross-border OOP, acquired during the progress of the three pilot areas. TOOP Project members' experience with the OOP, however, may extend beyond the Project so one could presume that there is a heterogeneity of experiences with OOP among TOOP members. In brief, the OOP level may vary between TOOP members at different points in time, to the extent that some members of TOOP could have reflected their real-time experience with the OOP in 2017 too, and some could still be reflecting theses perceptions in 2019 or 2020. Estonia and Finland, for example, had started preparations for cross-border data exchange between the two countries within the Nordic Institute for Interoperability Solutions (NIIS), to ensure development and strategic management of bilateral data exchange, before the start of TOOP Project which materialized in 2018 and focusing on multilateral data exchange.

4   Results

4.1   Technological Factors

An analysis of implementation of TOOP pilots suggests that implementation of the OOP is largely determined by technological readiness at a country-wide (nationwide) level – higher levels of digitalization are connected to faster progress also in implementation of cross-border OOP. Previous experience at national level with the OOP and with current technological solution for OOP help with the implementation of OOP cross-border. Examples included Estonia, Finland, but also Slovenia, that had launched the national level OOP solution before the TOOP Project, with swift progress in TOOP Pilot areas.

Despite the fact that the level of technological readiness and prior experience with implementation of the OOP at national level serves as an essential precondition for the OOP, the results of both waves of data collection revealed an interesting fact, which to some extent contradicts our initial expectations and the previous result. More concretely, the organizations' and countries´ high levels of digital technology, in certain contexts, could also hinder the progress of cross-border OOP initiatives. This fact results, for example, from concerns for sharing information with organizations and countries with lower levels of technological modernization and advancement, also connected to lower levels of security. As a representative commented during pilot phases "Data protection has a different meaning in different countries. For us it must be very secure, how data exchange proceeds and how people are identified, how do we know that we have not accidentally shared someone else's information or data or even how to gain access to the data".

Besides that, countries with long-term historical national OOP solutions, that are functioning well and widely used, may be less willing to adapt to alternative interoperability solutions used in other countries or/and on an EU/wide level, partly because of technological path dependency but also because of the additional human resources and financial means using that alternative systems may require, especially if the expected benefits are not entirely clear.

While the technical and semantic problems relating to operability initially entailed a crucial barrier to implementation of the OOP, they were also frequently mentioned as factors which TOOP pilots were able to overcome. Concerns for security and connectivity had also been reduced by the end of the pilots. Still, in a few cases, some technological issues relating to semantic interoperability, such as heterogeneity of concepts and meanings of data but also language differences continued to be troublesome issues throughout TOOP pilot projects. A large part of the semantic interoperability cross-border concerns, also identified by interviewees, concerned the matter of data harmonization and the question of documents vs. data. A number of IT solutions have been developed over the years, in attempts to solve the data harmonization process. However, as already identified by the HUMBOLDT project in 2011 (Fichtinger et al. 2011), where the semantics of concepts are too heterogeneous or diverse, such solutions are not sufficient not advanced enough to understand language as well as people do. Therefore, more work between the domain experts themselves is needed to solve for the semantic issues. This was confirmed in many interviews, where the interviewees mentioned the limited work on semantics and lack of collaboration between the domain experts as a barrier to both the project and future implementation of the OOP - the project was directed more towards finding a technical architecture solution. In this case, semantic interoperability means not only that shared data is understood to be shared cross-border, and that language has been correctly translated and interpreted, but that that an understanding of the documents exists, which can be used to authenticate or authorize these same processes. For the sake of successful implementation of the OOP, continuing along the lines of using technological solutions which already exist and are in use in European Union Member States, we would need to solve the semantic questions rather than overwhelm public sector administrations across Europe with every type of document available, especially at a time where more and more Member States are moving away from documents and towards data.

Similarly, requirements and credentials may vary from Member State to Member State, which means that in the case of cross-border data exchange there could be difficulties in proving certain credentials. Digital authentication and signatures continued to be a problem until the end of the pilots and in this regard, the need to harmonize implementation levels of eIDAS across EU Member States remained an issue, slowing progress of the OOP.

4.2 Organizational Factors

Regarding the organizational dimension, the significance seems to have decreased slightly over time. Concerns regarding financial means and human capital, as well as organizations' capacity to implement the necessary technological changes remained of note; nevertheless, these were more salient at the start of the TOOP pilot than at the end. Moreover, factors such as inter-organizational communication and cultural differences, in line with organizations' willingness to share data, were very seldom perceived as important factors. With regard to the results from two waves of questionnaires, more concretely, our study suggests that concerns relating to financial and human resources, or alignment of processes between organizations' structures and processes, remained significant (Figs. 1 and 2).

A reason why these concerns could have been minimized was the legal push from the Single Digital Gateway Regulation (SDGR) that encouraged public administrations to take action to solve the problems regarding their bureaucratic proceedings. Pilot phase participants also identified SDGR as a solution to pushing OOP higher up the list of national political interests, in addition to solving some regulatory gaps in this field.

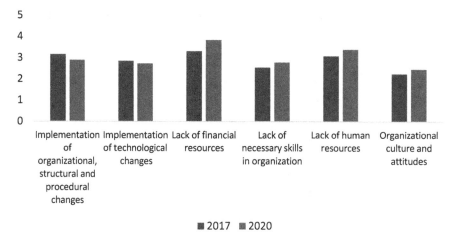

Fig. 1. Factors negatively impacting OOP implementation (scores are the mean value of all answers using a 5 point scale from 1 = very unlikely to 5 = very likely). Source: The Authors, based on survey responses.

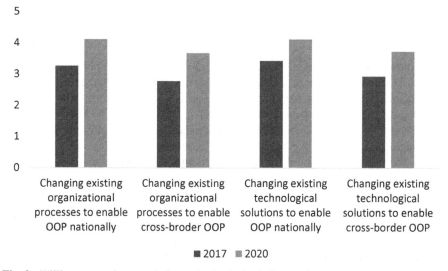

Fig. 2. Willingness to change existing technological solutions and organizational structures (5 = very open, 1 = very cautious) Source: The Authors, based on survey responses.

Even though there is a lower level of willingness to share personal information between countries, the implementing bodies' willingness to share this data with other organizations in the same country is not considerably lower. Furthermore, the results of the interviews and surveys show high levels of willingness to pursue organizational changes, in terms of processes, procedures, structures, as well as to adopt technological solutions, in order to enable OOP, both nationally and cross-border. The results indicate that the benefits of the OOP became evident to most of the participants in TOOP pilots (Fig. 3).

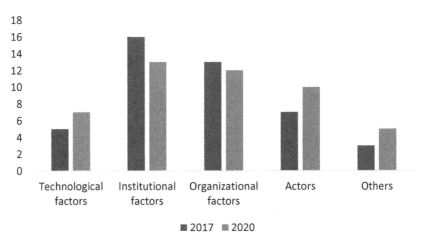

Fig. 3. Comparison of the most named barriers from the two surveys. Source: The Authors, based on survey responses (The number of respondents indicating as a barrier, multiple answers were possible).

One interesting finding uncovered here concerns the organization of IT developments in a given TOOP project partner or country, a factor not identified at the beginning of the Project. Namely, it turned out that TOOP Project partners and/or countries with in-house IT development units progressed faster with implementation of the OOP, compared to those outsourcing their IT developments to the private sector. Still, this organizational aspect might be specific to the TOOP Project as several country level TOOP developments had not been budgeted for, and those with local IT units and capacity, had the option to add TOOP Project related developments to their list of IT developments, whereas those relying on outsourcing were compelled to follow their budget cycle to allocate the financial resources required.

This last finding is in line with research on public procurement of innovation. Research shows that in cases where there are limited administrative capacities to procure innovative solutions, and if the solutions are purchased off-the-shelf (which OOP-related software elements are), there are barriers that slow down such developments and/or increase the risks (see Lember et al. 2014; Kalvet and Lember 2010).

4.3   Institutional Factors

Differently to technology and organizational dimensions, the institutional factors did not lose their importance throughout implementation of TOOP pilots. Our results suggest that two of the most important determinants for implementation of the OOP are both a sound legal basis and a clear political will and vision. In this sense, implementation of the OOP seems to rely heavily on the regulations put in place, but also on the key actors' will and conviction to pursue or demand that regulation and, at the same time, the ability to also integrate the OOP with rules and institutions already existing and in place. Legal obligation was previously categorized as more of a barrier during the ex-ante assessment due to limited legislation around implementation of the principle. The SDGR in some way filled that gap and was identified by many as the most influential driver for implementing OOP. As we can see, the prioritization to implement OOP on a cross-border scale increased at the central and regional government levels (Fig. 4).

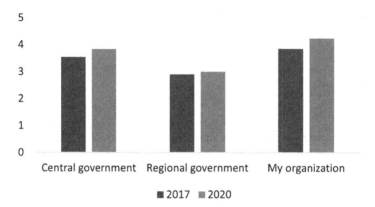

Fig. 4. Prioritization of OOP at different levels of implementation (5 = high priority, 1 = not a priority) Source: The Authors, based on survey responses.

While the SDG was regarded by most of the Member States in the project as a driver making the technological experiment that was TOOP a more purposeful and necessary endeavor, the Maritime pilot study had less impact due to the global nature of the sector. For the OOP to solve problems of efficiency in the maritime sector, it would need to be implemented on a much larger scale than just EU-wide; and the SDGR cannot solve for this.

More so than with the General Business Mobility pilot, the GDPR was mentioned as a factor contributing to the implementation of the OOP within the Maritime pilot. One of the reasons for this is the fact that crew certificates contain more personal information in them than certificates and licenses relating to businesses, which are often public information. The GDPR sets certain requirements for handling personal information, which could be a driver for favoring the TOOP solution for digital checks for crew certificates instead of the centralized system that is currently used by European Maritime Safety Agency (EMSA) to check ships' certificates. Maritime administrations already have the legal authority to store personal information while a centralized database would place the responsibility to securely store this data squarely on the shoulders of EMSA.

When piloting partners were asked to judge the willingness of their organizations towards different aspects of data sharing, the results were on average the same as for the original questionnaire completed in 2017. The only aspect towards which Member States actually became more cautious, if at all, was the sharing of personal data. One reason for this could be that the GDPR did not apply until 2018, which meant that, at the start of the project, no wide-spread practice was in existence yet. At the end of the project, when considerable time in the project was dedicated to discussions on the impact of the GDPR to cross-border OOP, this resulted in higher openness of organizations to change (Fig. 5).

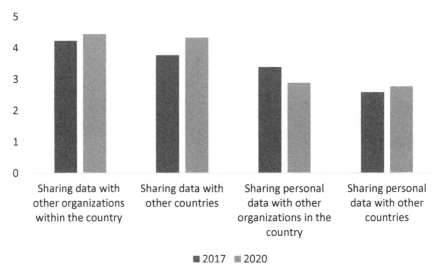

Fig. 5. Openness to sharing data (5 = very open, 1 = very cautious) Source: The Authors, based on survey responses

4.4 Actors

Government officials are critical for implementation of the OOP. Not only are their motivation and skills important, but a positive relationship also seems to exist between previous experience with the EU project, especially with the large-scale pilot project and willingness to drive the push forward and implement the OOP at a country level. TOOP pilot project participants also valued the contribution from their peers highly, in particular from more digitally advanced countries, for planning and implementation of national as well as cross-border OOP. There seems also to be a correlation between a partner implementing TOOP and/or a national coordinator with prior experience of EU Project management and/or involvement and national progress of the OOP, and personnel and staff with greater levels of EU project management experience, constituting more rapid progress of the OOP.

One aspect that was mentioned as a barrier on multiple occasions by interviewees across the pilot areas was the involvement or lack thereof of international regulatory organizations. In the Maritime pilot, this specifically includes regulatory bodies that have a wider scope than just EU such as the International Maritime Organization (IMO) and the Paris Memorandum of Understanding. Similarly, to issues with the SDGR, unless the once-only principle is taken on board by regulatory bodies with a wider scope than just the EC, implementation cannot achieve its full potential.

The importance of both institutional factors and actors is also evident in the barriers and obstacles pilot studies were unable to overcome. The low priority given to OOP, legal harmonization, low appeal to businesses (and therefore also to political agendas) and the existence of a national legal basis were all mentioned by respondents as barriers that persisted over time. Our results support the idea that the most important barriers to cross-border OOP come from external variables, rather that aspects intrinsic to the organization.

4.5 Other Factors

When it comes to implementing parties' perceptions after the end of pilot projects, there were primarily two perceived drivers of the OOP. On the one hand, most implementing bodies mentioned the importance of a legal basis existing, either on a national or supranational level. From the start, until the end of pilots, the institutional dimension continued to be perceived as a key, or perhaps even 'the key', driver for cross border implementation of OOP initiatives.

On the other hand, many participants also perceive the expected outcomes from the OOP as important drivers for implementation (e.g., simplification for citizens, businesses and public officials; reduced administrative barriers and burdens; and increased efficiencies of time and costs). This is an important aspect that implies that implementation and success of OOP projects relies on cost/benefit calculations carried out by their implementing parties. In this way, our results suggest that organizational and technological factors only indirectly drive implementation of the OOP, by affecting implementation costs and making the benefits of implementation easier to achieve. Previous experiences with national OOP implementations facilitate assessing the benefits and costs of cross-border OOP. This complements the findings on technical and operational level as mentioned in Sects. 4.1 and 4.2 (Fig. 6).

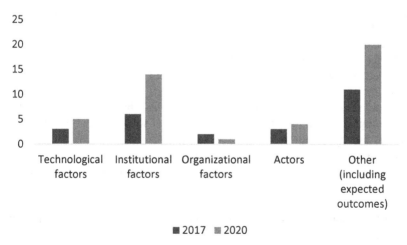

Fig. 6. Comparison of the most named drivers from the two survey results. Source: The Authors, based on survey responses (The number of respondents indicating as a driver, multiple answers were possible).

5 Discussion

The results of the research are clustered into (five) different areas.

Next to the influence of the law to the design of the technology, as laid out in the conceptual framework, it was identified that the **technological factors** further refined the legal framework as well as the organizational set up. The topology for solutions used across Europe is quite heterogeneous and technological path dependencies have emerged. Driven mainly by organizations or countries, different approaches were not, however aligned with one another (interoperability). Furthermore, in the past there was no coherent approach for interconnecting different actors (data providers and data consumers) relating to the OOP. In several cases, interconnections between actors were established just on a point to point / bilateral basis, and this led to optimization between a limited number of systems and caused a lack of interoperability. This situation gave rise to the need for some changes in technical and architectural approaches to create opportunities to exchange information between a wider range of parties. With the decision to create a technical layer permitting a multi connector exchange, a decision for a sound technical basis had been made.

On the part of **organizational factors**, the lack of a strong legal basis slowed down the whole process, when - based on the creation of SDGR - opportunities become necessities. These limiting factors are mainly determined by the capacity of the organizations involved. And these limitations are set into different dimensions, e.g. financial, organizational and capacity-wise.

Two different options are quoted to overcome these hurdles. These options were, on the one hand, to increase the resources required internally by organizations (insourcing) and, on the other hand, to buy in resources e.g,. via contracts with other entities (outsourcing).

- Two different options are quoted to overcome these hurdles. These options were, on the one hand, to increase the resources required internally by organizations (insourcing) and, on the other hand, to buy in resources e.g., via contracts with other entities (outsourcing).
- Insourcing on the plus side, ensures flexibility, and human resources in particular can be handled in a dynamic manner, in general reducing the related costs in comparison to costs for outsourcing. Furthermore, on the minus side, the risk for developing a proprietary solution is higher. This often includes the subject of interoperability.
- Outsourcing, on the plus side, reduces the internal workload and ensures that the necessary human and technical resources are available. Besides that, the opportunity to create a fully interoperable solution, complying with all respective standards is higher than with an in-house approach. One disadvantage is that this may lead to higher costs and limit flexibility.

An **institutional factor** was the lack of responsibility and coordination between different actors. Interconnections between different parties, especially in cross-border cases were made more based on needs than based on a structured and coherent approach. In an early stage of setup of the SDGR, the European Commission identified that European businesses criticized the lack of coordination and interoperability in ca. 80% of cross-border cases as a major hurdle for administrative procedures Bieńkowska (2018). This caused additional costs and workloads for administrative procedures.

The different **actors** involved impacted the development of the SDGR in several ways: This first and foremost is the European Commission as a co-legislator of the SDGR that acts on the supra-national level., and then second the Member States, as aside of the EU Parliament, the other co-legislator and associated countries that bring in the national level perspective. With the initiative to set up the SDGR, the European Commission took on the responsibility for the first outline of the new regulation. The EC detected the wishes and needs on the one hand and the criticism that were addressed by businesses and citizens in Europe on the other hand. The main findings of this evaluation of the EC were, that the EU's national level services for information and assistance, and online procedures available now, are highly fragmented, with varying levels of cover and different levels of quality. They are also not user-centric, and are difficult to find and to use, especially for foreign users (European Parliament 2017). Thus, it is difficult for EU citizens and businesses to exercise their Single Market rights. As a co-legislator, the EC has initiated a process to create a regulation harmonizing the legal basis within Member States and associated countries. Those parties involved are at an early stage via representatives of the Points of Single Contact, chambers of commerce and several national and international authorities. Not only were they involved in the process to create the SDGR, but - to ensure the balance between the supra-national level of the EC and the national point of view - are still involved via the so-called SDG Coordination Group in the transition of the SDGR; and with setting up the subsidiary implementing act(s) and the associated technical specifications. It shows that the EC and the countries has chosen a collaborative and iterative approach to set up the legal framework for implementation and transition of the OOP in Europe.

Last but not least, **other factors** must also be taken into account. These are for example other players/stakeholders, e.g. supra national standardization bodies, such as ETSI and OASIS, but also GLEIF carrying its influence on the continued debate on updating the eIDAS regulation. Setting up the eIDAS regulation was a big step forward on the road to creating a common legal basis for the EU. Since the regulation assumed full legal effect in September 2018, implementation of a digital identity even within the eIDAS framework is recognized as being fragmented and not harmonized across Member States. This caused two main issues for interoperability.

Identity Matching Issue

Databases used by different administrations in the Member States are mostly designed for specific cases or services. The underlying structure of registers are often set up before generic rules for exchanging eIDs, such as in the eIDAS regulation have been established. The data schemes are strongly related to the services provided. This causes a gap for attributes permitting automated exchange of information and mapping of identities. Different information is collected about citizens and businesses and may identify people and organizations differently. To make things even more troublesome, some Member States (e.g., Germany) do not have persistent identifiers or only provide such persistent identifiers as optional attributes. This causes a range of problems for matching the identity of a legal or natural entity even at a national but especially at a supranational level.

Record Matching Issue
Identification in Europe occurs via eIDs notified under eIDAS. In this case, there is a record matching issue depending on MS infrastructure. While using notified eIDs under the eIDAS Regulation, for the most part, allows data providers to match an identity with a record (evidence requested), using the attributes of the natural person provided by the eIDAS minimum data set, in some cases additional attributes are required to ensure a match. This is based on a lack of interoperability and the credentials defined in the eID schemes of the Member State.

Finally, for the OOP initiatives to succeed and in order to on-board the key stakeholders, the benefits of cross-border (such as administrative burden reduction, reduced time and costs for administrative processes, better quality data, improved reliability and validity) require further examination, and results of these studies must also be communicated.

6   Conclusions

This chapter offers an original empirical analysis of different factors affecting the adoption and functioning of cross-border initiatives of the Once Only Principle (OOP). We do so using a deductive approach and an exhaustive listing, based on relevant literature, for the different aspects have already been identified as potential barriers (or drivers) for the OOP. Those different factors were tested through interviews, surveys and focus group data.

Even though the readiness for implementation of the OOP varies considerably between countries, and financial/human resources are certainly an important factor for that, there are three aspects that consistently crop up as significant drivers/barriers for implementation of the OOP. The first one concerns the awareness of the OOP and its inherent benefits. The second one is enticements from external/supranational entities to make the cross-border OOP a national political priority. The third relates to establishing a critical legal framework, both at the EU and on a national level. In this sense, the political/decision-makers' will and institutional aspects are perceived as the most important drivers for the start and success of the OOP initiatives. When it comes to perceptions of the participants surveyed regarding implementation of the OOP, the "when" is far more relevant than the "how" can we do it. In this sense, to different degrees, all the countries studied demonstrated having the required technical and organizational conditions to implement the OOP.

When it comes to the OOP barriers, a major concern for the implementing parties is still the dimension of coordination required for implementation of a cross-border OOP project. This involves not only coordination between countries and organizations, but rather coordination at the EU level, including with other EU level projects. According to respondents, this barrier arises from different levels of readiness in countries/organizations, differences in the business models used by them, and also from concerns relating to the circulation of data and personal information. Even though the importance of this barrier decreased slightly during implementation of the project (i.e. there was an improvement in cooperation by the end of the pilot phases implemented), this is still a key factor to address/overcome in future cross-border OOP initiatives. Other barriers frequently mentioned dealt with semantic concerns, namely some level of distrust for translated documents and the differences of national standards on, where these exist.

When looking at key barriers towards implementation of pilot projects analyzed in this study, one could say that there has been some mystification regarding the EU countries' readiness to implement cross-border OOP. Not only are the existing perceived barriers relatively easy to overcome nowadays, but they also seem to have eroded considerably throughout the implementation process of TOOP pilot studies. This study suggests that, in very general terms, there are few factors, other than key actors´ will, hindering implementation of the OOP. However, we have also found some differences between the pilot study phases, regarding their barriers and drivers mentioned. When it comes to the different challenges faced by the TOOP pilot studies analyzed, there is some clear exceptionality in the case of piloting Online Ship and Crew Certificates. The barriers faced in that pilot were very specific to the global scale of that area (meaning that collaboration efforts, to have an impact, cannot be coordinated simply at an EU level. In addition to that, the fact that maritime certificates are produced in paper-based formats proves to be a great challenge to online data exchange. Concerns regarding security and privacy were also more relevant in this pilot).

To solve the issues relating to the problems described of identity matching mostly on the data provider side and record matching mainly on the data consumer side, a further alignment of the schemes and attributes in use is required. It is important to find solutions that cover the needs on national and international levels at the same time. Therefore, a European initiative is the most valuable approach. The recommendation would be to record the outcomes of the ongoing discussions on implementation of the SDGR in Members States, associated countries and on a European level and input them into updates of the eIDAS regulation. Preparation of the amendment of the eIDAS regulation is a great opportunity from a legal and technical point of view, to fix the existing problems.

Acknowledgments. Authors are grateful to the project partners that contributed with data on pilots and with overall comments and edits. This research was funded by the European Commission grant number 737460 - The Once Only Principle Project (TOOP). The work by Tarmo Kalvet was in addition financed in parts by grant 952410 - Industrial Strategy and Competitiveness Studies at TalTech (TalTech Industrial).

References

Akkaya, C., Krcmar, H.: Towards the implementation of the EU-wide "once-only principle": perceptions of citizens in the DACH-region. In: International Conference on Electronic Government, pp. 155–166. Springer, Cham, September 2018

Albury, D.: Fostering innovation in public services. Public Money Manage. **25**, 51–56 (2005)

Bekkers, V.J.J.M., Tummers, L.G., Voorberg, W.H.: From Public Innovation to Social INNOVATION in the Public Sector: A Literature Review of Relevant Drivers and Barriers. Erasmus University Rotterdam, Rotterdam (2013)

Bellamy, C., Taylor, J.: New information and communications technologies and institutional change: the case of the UK criminal justice system. Int. J. Public Sect. Manag. **9**(4), 51–69 (1996)

Bieńkowska, E.: European Commissioner for Internal Market, Industry, Entrepreneurship and SMEs, plenary debate European Parliament, 12.08.2018

Carrizales, T.: Functions of e-government: a study of municipal practices. State Local Govern. Rev. **40**(1), 12–26 (2008)

Cave, J., Botterman, M., Cavallini, S., Volpe, M.: EU-wide digital Once-Only Principle for citizens and businesses. Policy options and their impacts. European Commission, DG CONNECT (2017). https://ec.europa.eu/digital-single-market/en/news/eu-wide-digital-once-only-principle-citizens-and-businesses-policy-options-and-their-impacts

Chinn, M.D., Fairlie, R.W.: The determinants of the global digital divide: a cross-country analysis of computer and internet penetration. Oxf. Econ. Pap. **59**(1), 16–44 (2007)

Dawes, S.: Interagency information sharing: expected benefits, manageable risks. J. Policy Anal. Manage. **15**(3), 377–394 (1996)

De. Vries, H., Bekkers, V., Tummers, L.: Innovation in the Public Sector: A Systematic Review and Future Research Agenda. Public Administration **94**(1), 146–166 (2016)

Drew, M.A.S.J.: E-government principles: implementation, advantages and challenges. Int. J. Electron. Bus. **9**, 255–270 (2011)

Dunleavy, P., Margetts, H., Bastow, S., Tinkler, J.: New public management is dead—long live digital-era governance. J. Public Adm. Res. Theory **16**(3), 467–494 (2006)

European Commission: New European Interoperability Framework - Promoting seamless services and data flows for European public administrations (2017). https://doi.org/10.2799/78681

European Parliament: Impact Assessment Accompanying the document Proposal for a regulation of the European parliament and of the Council on establishing a single digital gateway to provide information, procedures, assistance and problem solving services and amending Regulation (EU) No 1024/2012; SWD/2017/0213 final - 2017/086 (COD) (2017). https://eur-lex.europa.eu/legal-content/EN/TXT/?uri=SWD:2017:0213:FIN

Ferguson, S., Burford, S., Kennedy, M.: Divergent approaches to knowledge and innovation in the public sector. Int. J. Public Adm. **36**(3), 168–178 (2013)

Fichtinger, A., Rix, J., Schäffler, U., Michi, I., Gone, M., Reitz, T.: Data harmonisation put into practice by the HUMBOLDT project. Int. J. Spatial Data Infrastruct. Res. **6**, 234–260 (2011)

Fountain, J.E.: Building the virtual state: Information technology and institutional change. Brookings Institution Press (2004)

Fountain, J.E.: Bureaucratic reform and e-government in the United States: An institutional perspective. The handbook of Internet politics, pp. 99–113 (2008)

Gallo, G., Giove, M., Millard, J., Thaarup, R.: Study on eGovernment and the Reduction of Administrative Burden (2014). http://ec.europa.eu/newsroom/dae/document.cfm?doc_id=5155

Gascó, M., Cucciniello, M., Nasi, G., Yuan, Q.: Determinants and barriers of e-procurement: a European comparison of public sector experiences. In: Proceedings of the 51st Hawaii International Conference on System Sciences, January 2018

Germanakos, P., Christodoulou, E., Samaras, G.: A European perspective of E-Government presence – where do we stand? the EU-10 Case. In: Wimmer, M.A., Scholl, J., Gronlund, A. (eds.) Lecture Notes in Computer Science. Presented at the Electronic Government: Proceedings of the 6th [IFIP WG 8.5] International Conference, EGOV 2007, pp. 436–447 (2007). https://doi.org/10.1007/978-3-540-74444-3

Gil-Garcia, J.R., Pardo, T.A.: E-government success factors: mapping practical tools to theoretical foundations. Gov. Inf. Q. **22**, 187–216 (2005)

Gil-Garcia, R.J.: Enacting Electronic Government Success. An Integrative Study of Government-wide Websites, Organisational Capabilities, and Institutions. Springer, New York (2012)

Heeks, R.: e-Government as a carrier of context. J. Publ. Policy **25**(1), 51–74 (2005)

Heeks, R., Bailur, S.: Analyzing e-government research: perspectives, philosophies, theories, methods, and practice. Gov. Inf. Q. **24**(2), 243–265 (2007)

Kalvet, T.; Lember, V.: Risk management in public procurement for innovation: the case of nordic-baltic sea cities. Innov. Eur. J. Soc. Sci. Res. **23**(3), 241–262 (2010). https://doi.org/10.1080/13511610.2011.553509

Kalvet, T., Toots, M., Krimmer, R.: Contributing to a digital single market for europe: barriers and drivers of an EU-wide once-only principle. In: Zuiderwijk, A., Hinnant, C.C. (eds.) Proceedings of the 19th Annual International Conference on Digital Government Research: Governance in the Data Age (dg.o '18) (Article 45, pp. 1–8). Association for Computing Machinery (2018a)

Kalvet, T., Toots, M., Van Veenstra, A.F., Krimmer, R.: Cross-border e-Government services in europe: expected benefits, barriers and drivers of the once-only principle. In: Ojo, A., Kankanhalli, A., Soares, D. (eds.) Proceedings of the 11th International Conference on Theory and Practice of Electronic Governance (ICEGOV' 18), pp. 69–72. Association for Computing Machinery (2018b)

Krimmer, R., Kalvet, T., Toots, M., Cepilovs, A., Tambouris, E.: Exploring and demonstrating the once-only principle: a european perspective, dg.o, 546–551 (2017)

Lember, V., Kattel, R., Kalvet, T. (eds.): Public Procurement, Innovation and Policy: International Perspectives. Springer, Heidelberg (2014). https://doi.org/10.1007/978-3-642-40258-6_2

Leosk, N.: Understanding the development of digital governance: a study of the relations between institutions, organisations, and actors in the member states of the OECD and EU (Doctoral dissertation, European University Institute) (2019)

Luna-Reyes, L.F., Gil-García, J.R.: Using institutional theory and dynamic simulation to understand complex e-Government phenomena. Gov. Inf. Q. **28**(3), 329–345 (2011)

Meyerhoff Nielsen, M., Krimmer, R.: Reuse of Data for Personal and Proactive Service: An Opportunity Not Yet Utilised. CeDEM15 Conference for E-Democracy and Open Government, 273–282 (2015)

Mocan, A., Facca, F.M., Loutas, N., Peristeras, V., Goudos, S.K., Tarabanis, K.: Solving semantic interoperability conflicts in cross-border e-government services. In: Semantic Services, Interoperability and Web Applications: Emerging Concepts, pp. 1–47. IGI Global (2011)

Moon, M.J.: The evolution of e-government among municipalities: rhetoric or reality? Public Adm. Rev. **62**(4), 424–433 (2002)

Morris, M.G., Venkatesh, V.: Age differences in technology adoption decisions: Implications for a changing work force. Pers. Psychol. **53**(2), 375–403 (2000)

Olesk, M.: Challenges of Collaborative Digital Government: e-Participation, Open Government Data and Cross-Border Interoperability. Doctoral Thesis. Tallinn: TalTech Press (2020)

Panopoulou, E., Tambouris, E., Tarabanis K.: "eParticipation initiatives in Europe: learning from practitioners. In: Electronic Participation, eds. E. Tambouris, A. Macintosh, O. Glassey, Lecture Notes in Computer Science, 6229, Springer, 54–65 (2010)

Rashman, L., Withers, E., Hartley, J.: Organizational learning and knowledge in public service organizations: a systematic review of the literature. Int. J. Manag. Rev. **11**(4), 463–494 (2009)

Rodríguez, L., Sánchez, I.M., Alvarez, I.: Determining factors of e-government development: a worldwide national approach. Int. Public Manag. J. **14**(2), 218–248 (2011)

Savoldelli, A., Codagnone, C., Misuraca, G.: Understanding the e-government paradox: learning from literature and practice on barriers to adoption. Gov. Inf. Q. **31**(S1), S63–S71 (2014)

Van Veenstra, A.F., Klievink, B., Janssen, M.: Barriers and impediments to transformational government: insights from literature and practice. Electron. Gov. Int. J. **8**(2/3), 226–241 (2011)

Van Veenstra, A.F., et al.: Ubiquitous Developments of the Digital Single Market. European Parliament's Committee on Internal Market and Consumer Protection, Brussels. Ubiquitous Developments of the Digital Single Market (europa.eu). (2013). https://www.europarl.europa.eu/RegData/etudes/etudes/join/2013/507481/IPOL-IMCO_ET(2013)507481_EN.pdf

Yin, R.K.: Case Study Research: Design and Methods. Sage, Thousand Oaks (2003)

Wimmer, M.A., Marinov, B.: SCOOP4C: reducing administrative burden for citizens through once-only-vision & challenges. Jusletter IT **2020**, 2–5 (2017)

Wimmer, M.A., Neuroni, A.C., Frecè, J.T.: Approaches to good data governance in support of public sector transformation through once-only. In: International Conference on Electronic Government, pp. 210–222. Springer, Cham, August 2020

Once-Only Principle Good Practices in Europe

Maria A. Wimmer[(⊠)] [iD]

University of Koblenz-Landau, Universitätsstr. 1, 56070 Koblenz, Germany
wimmer@uni-koblenz.de

Abstract. Digital transformation has become a recent keyword in the evolution of public sector modernization through the once-only principle (OOP). The once-only principle is among the seven driving principles in the eGovernment Action Plan 2016–2020 of the European Commission (EC). It requires that citizens and businesses need not to provide the same data to governments if that data is already in their hands. The ultimate goal of the principle is to reduce administrative burden and to simplify public service provisioning therewith also reducing costs and improving public service. To boost developments towards administrative burden reduction and simplification in public service provisioning, the SCOOP4C project has investigated good practice solutions across Europe. In this contribution, we provide an overview of good practice OOP cases and OOP enablers studied in the project, followed by a synthesis of the benefits and key enablers to boost the OOP implementation across Europe.

Keywords: Once-only principle · OOP · Good practices · OOP cases · OOP enablers

1 Introduction

The eGovernment Action Plan 2016–2020 of the European Union (EU) commits Member States to modernize public services along seven principles of public sector transformation in order to contribute to economic growth, jobs as well as sustainable and resilient societies [16]. The vision of the EU Member States set in this strategic document is that *"by 2020, public administrations and public institutions in the European Union (EU) should be open, efficient and inclusive, providing borderless, personalized, user-friendly, end-to-end digital public services to all citizens and businesses in the EU"* [16]. The Action Plan requires new and innovative concepts to design and deliver improved public services that better meet the needs of citizens and businesses.

The Once Only Principle (OOP) is among the seven underlying principles of this action plan to make government more effective and simpler and to reduce administrative burdens by asking citizens and companies to provide certain (standard) information to the public authorities only once. Public authorities are required to *"take action if permitted to internally re-use this data, in due respect of data protection rules, so that no additional burden falls on citizens and businesses"* [16]. The sharing and re-use of sensitive and non-sensitive data of citizens and businesses demands for broad acceptance of this revolutionary concept by all stakeholders.

© The Author(s) 2021
R. Krimmer et al. (Eds.): The Once-Only Principle, LNCS 12621, pp. 61–82, 2021.
https://doi.org/10.1007/978-3-030-79851-2_4

To implement the once-only principle and to spur innovation, the European Commission has funded the SCOOP4C project (the sister project of TOOP) in the Horizon 2020 program [18], which focused OOP public services for citizens. The aims of SCOOP4C were a) to build up a stakeholder community for the once-only principle for citizens and b) to investigate, discuss and disseminate how the once-only principle can be implemented in contexts of co-creation and co-production of public services for citizens in order to contribute to significant administrative burden reduction [50, 58]. Along with the second aim, the project partners have systematically analyzed a number of OOP good practices. This contribution aims to summarize the findings from the good practice study of the SCOOP4C project. The main research questions are:

– What OOP good practice solutions exist in the Member States and across borders in the European Union?
– What enablers do exist in Member States, and what enablers need to be in place to enable OOP implementations at large?

In order to investigate these two research questions, structured qualitative case analysis and scenario technique were used. The remainder of the paper is as follows: The next section summarizes the theoretical and political foundations for the research, i.e. digitalization in the public sector and digital transformation with the OOP as a revolutionary concept. Subsequently, the methodical foundations outline the research design for the case study (Sect. 3). In Sect. 4, an overview of OOP good practice examples is provided and individual examples are briefly outlined. Based on the insights from the good practices, Sect. 5 discusses insights on the benefits for stakeholders as well as necessary enablers to widely implement the OOP across Europe. The conclusions sum up the findings and reflect further research needs.

2   Theoretical and Political Foundations of the OOP

Public sector digitalization is on the agenda of research for several decades. Its focus evolved and changed along the social, economic, political, technical and other challenges the public sector is exposed to over time. Likewise, the readiness of public institutions to transform themselves impacted its characteristics and success [41]. Subsequently, we therefore briefly summarize the evolution of digitalization and of digital transformation in the public sector.

The use of innovative information and communication technologies (ICTs) is an integral part of modernization strategies of governments [30]. Nowadays, digital transformation characterizes this attempt of modernizing government and public service provisioning. Over two decades ago, this concept was coined as electronic government or digital government (both concepts evolved and are used synonymously). Many scholars expect that the use of ICTs in electronic or digital government (i.e. in the modernization of public service provisioning) helps realizing added value such as increased efficiency, effectiveness, openness, transparency and improved quality of service for citizens and businesses [3, 4, 7, 22, 27, 30, 35, 37, 39]. Public value, increased government responsiveness and openness are further value expectations [35].

A customer-centric approach conveys the proposition of creating value for society and economy. As the once-only principle demands that citizens and businesses will only have to provide certain standard information to the public agencies once, public authorities are in need to share and re-use sensitive and personal data to reduce administrative burden for citizens and businesses [16, 33, 34, 58, 59]. However, sharing and re-use of such data must be done with due respect of data protection regulations [19], as otherwise trustworthiness of public service provisioning would be hampered tremendously. Hence, trust is an essential ingredient in implementing the once-only principle. Furthermore, digital transformation is not a smooth process, and digital tools do not per se contribute to before mentioned success factors. Since the digital transformation in government is considered to be a quite complex endeavour, coordination and engagement concepts as well as overarching architectures to enable secure and trustworthy access to data and information in inter-agency information sharing are further success criteria [25, 27, 59].

As argued in the introduction, the implementation of the once-only principle in the European Union is a policy goal settled in the eGovernment Action Plan 2016–2020 [16] and one of the pillars of the Digital Single Market Strategy [17]. It has been reinforced in the "Tallinn Declaration" signed by the European Digital Ministers [20] in 2017. The Single Digital Gateway (SDG) Regulation [21] requires European Member States to build up and connect to a single European portal and infrastructure, through which citizens, businesses and public administrations can execute public services across borders with the OOP as underlying principle. To realize the SDG, a successful implementation of the once-only principle requires transfer and re-use of sensitive or personal data between government agencies across borders involving actors on different levels of a political system. To develop the necessary trustworthy cross-border architecture and organizational frameworks for the SDG, significant effort is put by the European Commission and by the Member States (e.g. the European-wide projects TOOP [53] and DE4ALL [8]). TOOP developed a trust architecture [28, 44].

To implement interoperable data and information sharing, the European Interoperability Framework (EIF) provides a conceptual model for public services and considers data-related services as a basic component for service provision [14]. The SCOOP4C and TOOP projects rely on this EIF to structure their investigations of barriers, enablers and architecture for a comprehensive OOP implementation.

As outlined along the review of academic and policy literature on the OOP implementation, the realization of the once-only principle turns out to be a complex endeavour, where a number of factors need to be aligned and coordinated. To gather insights from existing OOP implementations, the SCOOP4C project investigated good practice cases and enablers of the once-only principle. Before presenting insights into the good practice analysis, the next section outlines the methodical foundations for the analysis.

3   Methodical Foundations

The research design for investigating OOP good practice solutions in the Member States and across borders in the European Union, for eliciting barriers and enablers along such initiatives, and for extracting recommendations to successfully implement the OOP consisted of three steps:

a) Analysis of relevant literature and policy documents as summarized in Sect. 2;
b) Analysis of OOP good practices across Europe (see Sect. 4), separated into OOP cases, and OOP enablers and building blocks;
c) Elicitation of gaps and lessons from the good practice analysis, and formulation of policy recommendations for successful OOP implementation (see Sect. 5).

The review of academic literature depicted the evolution of public sector modernization through ICT towards digital transformation and its added value. Furthermore, policy documents were studied to gather the political dimension of the OOP. A descriptive analysis [40, 43] approach was applied in step 1. The study of strategic documents and studies encompassed the EU eGovernment Action Plan 2016–2020 [16], theEU Digital Single Market strategy [17], the European Interoperability Framework [14], the EU General Data Protection Regulation [19], the study on "eGovernment and the Reduction of Administrative Burden" [24], and the study on "EU-wide digital Once-Only Principle for citizens and businesses" [6].

The OOP good practice analysis in step 2 embarked on case study methodology [23, 61]. Based on initial literature and policy document analysis in step 1, the team developed in an iterative step a template for collecting information on the cases to be studied. Along this step, a distinction between OOP cases and OOP enablers was necessary, which resulted in the definitions as follows:

OOP cases refer to the provision of public services, where the once-only principle is implemented. Processing, sharing and re-using of citizen related data is enabled within a network of services used by public administrations to access the relevant data stored in different registers and applications. Consequently, citizens do not need to repeatedly provide the same data to the authorities. Furthermore, OOP cases can be grouped along particular policy domains such as education, healthcare, moving, social protection, taxation, etc.

The implementation of the OOP in public services (c.f. OOP cases) is supported by a set of enabling components. Therefore, *OOP enablers* are defined as crucial building blocks that support the implementation of OOP cases in different policy domains through e.g. central infrastructure components for sharing and re-using sensitive data, semantic and technical architecture and solutions building blocks, as well as organizational, legal and political enablers. The enablers reach a wider scope than cases as one enabler may support the implementation of many different OOP cases in different policy domains.

Based on this distinction of OOP cases and OOP enablers, two correlating templates evolved in the preparation of the case study analysis to describe each case and enabler in the same way to ensure comparability. Besides demographic data, the template collected information such as a short summary about the project, what the legal and political enablers are/were for the OOP project, what architecture the OOP case or OOP enabler is built upon, which actors are involved and in which role (data owner, data provider, data consumer), what data exchange logics is applied, and what type of data sharing is embodied, what socio-cultural factors and other soft factors might be relevant, and what are the lessons from the project [50]?

The identification of cases and enablers was an iterative process involving the community network of the experts in the project. For example, steering board members were asked to inform the project team about relevant OOP solutions, project members investigated their communities to identify OOP cases or OOP enablers. The next task in this step was to collect the relevant case study descriptions along the developed template. This was done on the one hand by conducting desk research and studying relevant information on the public websites of the projects or institutions. On the other hand, relevant contact persons were identified and these experts were asked to either fill in the data along the provided template themselves (this was provided as an online form over the project's stakeholder community site) or to perform an online interview with project staff that recorded the answers. In a next task, the data was quality-assured by persons of the project team other than those that recorded the data, and reviewed and updated the collected data if necessary. The review and quality-assurance of the data of OOP cases and enablers was in some cases iterated several times between the contact point of the case study and the project team. Finally, the quality-assured project descriptions were published on the project's knowledge base [50].

In a final task of step 2, the OOP cases were analyzed in regards to success factors and OOP enablers involved in the OOP cases. Furthermore, barriers to implement OOP solutions were studied and extracted from the cases. This task applied a systematic analysis of the OOP cases and enablers for which the data was collected. For the analysis of the cases and enablers, the European Interoperability Framework (EIF) [14] and the European Interoperability Reference Architecture [13] represented major sources to group barriers and enablers along the interoperability levels and along crucial factors fostering interoperability in public service provisioning. In particular, the conceptual model of public service provisioning in the EIF guided in determining different types of enablers. From the literature analysis and from initial case studies, crucial soft "enabling factors" for successful OOP implementation were added, such as motivators, benefits, public value, data protection and privacy, trust and transparency, socio-cultural influence factors, citizen-centered design or data quality [37, 58].

The identified barriers and enablers were the input to the third step, where gap analysis was conducted and policy recommendations were formulated. The project team applied scenario technique [31, 32, 36, 38, 48, 55] to develop ideal future cross-border OOP scenarios in the five domains that were selected for the gap analysis, roadmapping and policy recommendations (i.e. education, healthcare, moving, social protection, and taxation). Scenarios are narrative textual descriptions (structured or unstructured), which are complemented with a rich picture to illustrate a perceived view or understanding of a specific topic [5, 31]. The future once-only principle scenarios in the cross-border context described how future interactions between governments and the corresponding stakeholders could look like, which tools, standards, and technologies could be used to share and reuse data, and what further soft enabling factors complemented a comprehensive view on the future OOP implementation.

The five future cross-border OOP scenarios were used in interactive workshops with the stakeholders to deliberate barriers and enablers, to understand the gaps, needs and benefits of implementing the OOP at large, and to formulate policy recommendations for the widest possible OOP implementation. A total of nine workshops were conducted in the period 2018–2019. Each workshop had around 15 to 30 participants and three to five scenarios were deliberated in respective group discussions. The participants came from academia, public administrations, businesses as well as students and NGOs acting as citizen representatives.

The results of the good practice analysis of OOP solutions are presented in the next two sections.

4 OOP Good Practice Examples in Europe

In the SCOOP4C project, 57 OOP cases and 34 OOP enablers were analyzed [50]. The next subsections provide an overview of the OOP cases and OOP enablers studied, along with an outline of examples of OOP cases in the five selected domains and of OOP enablers in the categories 'secure data exchange', 'OOP enabling infrastructure', as well as 'eID and trust services'.

4.1 OOP Cases

Table 1 provides an overview of the OOP good practice cases studied in the SCOOP4C project.[1] It is important to point out that the list of OOP good practices is by no means an exhaustive list of existing OOP cases in Europe. Instead and as mentioned in Sect. 3, the cases were identified either by steering board members or project members via searches and own contacts or were recorded by experts from the OOP cases via the online template.

To provide more detailed insights on OOP good practices, the following four OOP cases are exemplified from different domains (more detailed information is provided in [50, 54]):

Austrian Birth Registration and Child Benefit (ALF). Before modernizing the birth registration and child benefit service, parents of a newborn had to interact with six different public agencies to carry out up to nine different public services along the registration of a newborn and application for child benefit. These processes have been streamlined and integrated based on the once-only principle. With the new process of ALF [2], parents visit only the Civil Registry Office (one stop) and they need not to bring along any documents to evidence data that is already in the hands of public administration, except a personal identification (passport or personal ID card). In the Civil Registry Office, all data to record the newborn is collected and entered into the relevant interacting registers, such as the central civil register (ZPR), central citizenship register (ZSR) and central residence register (ZMR). After the recording of data on the newborn by the Civil Registry Office, a notification is sent to the Social Security Institution to trigger the issuance of the healthcare card (e-Card) for the newborn. The Social Security Institution generates the unique healthcare number and issues the e-Card, which is then automatically sent to the parents of the newborn (no stop). Furthermore, the unique healthcare number is sent to the Tax Authority, who also received a notification from the Civil Registry Office about the registration of a newborn. The two notifications trigger the next step, the establishment of a record for child benefit by the Tax Authority. If any data is missing, this is collected from the parents. However, if all data is available,

---

[1] See detailed descriptions of the OOP cases under https://scoop4c.eu/casetable.

Table 1. Overview of OOP cases studied in SCOOP4C

Domain (# of cases studied)	Examples of OOP cases studied in SCOOP4C (cases marked in italic are summarized below)
Citizenship, basic data and registration (18)	Bulgarian guide for administrative assistance and awareness (GAAA), Danish basic data program, several Estonian registration and basic data services (e-Census, Eesti.ee, Election information system, Internet voting, e-PRIA, Employment register, register of professions, Smart road system, Sports registry), French Dites-les-nous une fois, German refugee digitalization system, Hellenic Citizen Registry, Irish government portal Gov.ie, several Spanish registration and basic data services (Address change service, Verification system and data query (EPS), Via Oberta)
Healthcare (10)	Austrian electronic health records (ELGA), Bulgarian national council on prices and reimbursement of medical products, several *Estonian health services (Central health information system and patient portal*, Digital prescription, Doctor-doctor consultation, e-Ambulance and time-critical health data, Medical certificate, Medical digital image bank), Italian online service portal – healthcare booking system, e-Health service eZdravje in Slovenia
Education (8)	*Higher Education Institution Application Systems in the Netherlands (Studielink)*, Estonia (EHIS and SAIS), Ireland (Central Application Office), Portugal (LGDF), Spain (NISUE), UK (UCAS), and the European Student Card (ESC)
Taxation (6)	*Online tax filing systems* in Austria (FinanzOnline), Estonia (E-Tax), France, Germany (pre-filled tax return), *Greece (TAXISnet)* and UK (MTD)
Social protection (5)	*Austrian birth registration and child benefit (ALF)*, Estonian Parental Benefit, French Revenu de sulidarité active, Polish baby bonus Becikowe, Tell us once in UK
Mobility (3)	Austrian-German x-trans.eu, Tallinn public transport ticket system (Estonia), French application for parking vignette

(*continued*)

Table 1. (*continued*)

Domain (# of cases studied)	Examples of OOP cases studied in SCOOP4C (cases marked in italic are summarized below)
Others (7)	Several Estonian services (Consumer Service Environment Data System, e-File system, e-Notary, Sports Registry, Veterinary and Food Board), French Attestation Légale, French e-bourgogne-franche-comté GIP

the parents need no interaction with the Tax Authority in order to receive the child benefit on a monthly basis (no stop).

In order to make this OOP case work, the necessary political commitment and legal grounds (revision of the Austrian Act for family benefits, several legal acts on digital public services and basic enablers) have been put in place. Furthermore, the collaborative processes and interactions among the base registers have been standardized. A core enabler is the Portalverbund, an architecture for secured and trusted access to data across different registers and applications based on the secure identification of employees in public service through eID (see brief description in Subsect. 4.2).

Through 'ALF', substantial administrative burden reduction is achieved for parents, as they have only to go once to the Civil Registry Office to register the newborn and change the family status, they have not to bring along a number of evidences for the process, and they can receive the healthcare card and family allowance without having to fill any application upon the birth of a child. Key benefits for the public administrations are streamlined and automated processes, higher quality of data since the data is accessed at the authentic sources, and higher satisfaction of citizens overall through better and faster public services.

Dutch Higher Education Institution Application System (Studielink). Studielink [10] is the common registration and enrollment portal for all non-private higher education institutions (HEIs) in the Netherlands, which supports the exchange of data between the current or prospective students and the HEIs. To enroll to a HEI, the student first identifies him- or herself in Studielink through the Dutch eID (DigID). Subsequently, personal and educational data is retrieved through the application from relevant authentic sources such as the education register (maintained by the Dutch Education Executive Agency/Ministry of Education) and the personal data registers (municipal personal records database (GBA) run by the Dutch municipalities). The student then checks the retrieved information, adds new data on the intended study program, and finally applies to the study program. The HEIs can then retrieve the relevant applications and further process them.

Relevant enablers of the case are the political commitment and issuance of relevant legal regulations such as the Higher Education Act or the Personal Data Protection Act. Furthermore, an overall architecture concept and the Dutch System of Base Registries enables the secure data exchange across registers and domain-specific applications. The Dutch eID service DigID is another enabler to provide secure authentication of users.

Studielink offers significant burden reduction for students and higher education institutions. It also increases the quality of data, since the basic data is retrieved from the authentic sources while only new information is entered by the users.

Estonian Central Health Information System and Patient Portal (EHR). The EHR [11] is a central patient-oriented system in Estonia, where data about a person's health treatments is collected, such as a short overview about the visit, anamnesis, diagnoses, treatment, examinations and recommendations. The data is accessible for all clinicians who treat the patient; for doctors that need to see a patient's data – access is only possible with their personal ID-card; and for patients through the patient portal using their personal ID-cards to see their own data, to make declarations (e.g. organ donations), and to check their treatment bills, prescriptions and the logging of who has accessed the patient's data. The EHR is one of a number of healthcare systems in place in Estonia. It is linked through X-Road (see OOP enabler example outlined in the next subsection) to other patient and medical information systems like the Medical Images Bank, the Prescription Centre and healthcare provider systems.

The success of the OOP case builds on a number of enablers, such as legal acts and regulations to enable the OOP case, including relevant data security guidelines issued by the Estonian Data Protection Inspectorate. The relevant actors have been involved to define and harmonize the collaborative business processes such as agreed workflows in the procedures, standards, classifiers and domain-specific data models among the health professionals. Contractual agreements of all healthcare providers to participate in the OOP case and in the sharing and re-use of the patient data. As already pointed out before, xRoad is the core secure data exchange layer that enables confidential and legally binding data exchange in the OOP case. In addition, the Estonian Public Key Infrastructure and eID infrastructure (ISKE) provides – through IDcard, mobileID or digiID – secure and trusted access to the relevant data for patients, doctors and nurses. Semantic interoperability is ensured through the Estonian Catalogue of Public Sector Information (RIHA), which provides necessary metadata descriptions. To ensure access to the 'right' data, unique personal identification codes and unique company commercial registry codes have been established as well. Trust and transparency are established by enabling persons to view their prescriptions, summary reports, test results (except images) and the details of their children. The users can also see, who else has viewed their data in the systems. And they can decide to make their data accessible or inaccessible to doctors and other healthcare service providers, issue expressions of will (regarding organ donations, powers of attorney) and order electronic medical certificates.

The EHR case significantly reduces administrative burden for patients and the actors in the healthcare system, as all documents and data of a patient and his or her health history are available through the central system. With the central EHR system and its secure and trusted interconnectedness through xRoad, improved quality of medical service is provided, which in turn leads to higher satisfaction of citizens.

Greek Online Tax Filing System (TAXISnet). TAXISnet [29] is the integrated information system of the Hellenic tax system aiming to provide online electronic services to citizens and businesses through pre-filled forms and the collection of citizen data from employers (such as salary details), banks and other administrations to provide these data to other public authorities at a central point. The information system interconnects all tax departments in Greece with the central point and the respective databases, and it has probably the largest number of users of public sector information systems in Greece. TAXISnet offers personalized information to citizens and businesses through its portal, as well as by sending automated emails. The registration to the service is a simple procedure. After the registration to the service, citizens or businesses are informed regularly by SMS on the tax that they have to pay and by when the payments are due. Recent amendments of the TAXISnet solution towards further OOP implementations are the confirmation of a person's details, the tax registration data, certificates that a person or a company do not have any debts relevant to tax (relevant e.g. in public procurement procedures), certification for any debts of a person or a company to any public-sector organization, or the provision of vehicle owner details at a specific point of time.

A crucial enabler is the Interoperability Centre of the Ministry of Finance, which provides a set of web services to public administrations to get access to relevant data of citizens and businesses, which is in the hands of other public administrations in Greece.

The main benefits of this case are for citizens to receive proactive services and notifications on relevant taxes to be paid and other certifications needed in public services. Public administrations are supported in the execution of their tasks by web services to access relevant data from authentic sources.

4.2 OOP Enablers

In Table 2, the OOP good practice enablers studied in SCOOP4C[2] are grouped along six categories. Like for the OOP cases, this list does by no means provide an exhaustive list of existing OOP enablers in Europe. The enablers were either identified in the same way as the OOP cases (see indication at the beginning of Subsect. 4.1) or these were spotted along the data collection on OOP cases.

The following four examples provide more detailed insights into good practice enablers of secure data exchange and enabling infrastructure (more detailed information is provided in [50, 54]):

Dutch Basisregistraties. Basisregistraties [9] were established in the Netherlands to store all vital data about citizens, businesses and institutions in a centralized manner. In total, ten basis registries have been officially instated to implement the once-only principle in public service provisioning (addresses and buildings, geographical information and maps, topography, income registry for taxation, cadasters and real estate property, reference property values, environment and surface, citizens, companies, vehicles). These are mandatory data registration sources for all governmental institutions when executing their public duties. To enable the secure data exchange among these base registries and applications in the Netherlands, several core building blocks were set up as well: a) Digidelivery as the electronic delivery service enables public administrations and businesses to quickly and efficiently exchange data among key register clients in the shape of event messages; b) Digilink offers standards for interfaces, including agreements, for the exchange of data between public authorities. Digilink therewith enables to connect

---

[2] See detailed descriptions of the OOP enablers under https://scoop4c.eu/enablertable.

Table 2. Overview of examples of OOP enablers studied in SCOOP4C

Category (# of enablers studied)	Examples of OOP enablers studied in SCOOP4C (enablers marked in italic are summarized below)
Secure Data Exchange (12)	Belgian MAGDA, Czech Basic Registers, *Dutch Basisregistraties*, *Estonian X-Road*, European-wide ECRN, European-wide ECRIS, European-wide EESSI, European EMREX, European-wide EURCARIS, Spain's PID-SVD, Spain's SIR, Spain's SPD
Enabling Infrastructure (10)	*Network of public authorities in Austria (Portalverbund)*, European-wide BRIS, Greek's SYZEFXIS, Irish Government Network, Luxemburg's my Guichet, Portugal's iAP, Spanish SEDIPUALB@, Spanish InSide, Spanish CONSERVATIONISTS, *Spanish Red SARA*
eID and Trust Services (6)	PKI and ISKE in Estonia, PKI in Greece, Irish MyGovID, Irish Public Service Card, Spanish PKI Suite @firma
Interoperability Governance (3)	Greek and Spanish Interoperability Models, Argentinian Interoperability Model
Interoperability Assets (2)	German xAusländer, Irish Personal Public Service Number
Catalogue (1)	Estonian Catalogue of Public Sector Information (RIHA)

nearly all e-government building blocks set up in the Netherlands; c) Diginotification is a notification tool to guarantee the quality of data in the key registries to be up-to-date and reliable; d) NORA as the Netherlands Government Reference Architecture provides an overall framework and existing agreements for the Dutch governmental information management system to ensure smooth cooperation with other services, and optimal re-use of existing solutions; and finally e) a System Catalogue, which make the data in the base registries findable and reachable.

The use of the Basisregistraties in the Netherlands offers a variety of benefits including reduction of administrative burdens for citizens and businesses as they do not need to provide information again that is already in the hands of government. The government can operate more efficiently and improve quality of services that government organizations such as public health services or fire stations deliver.

Estonian X-Road. X-Road [12] is a technical and organizational environment enabling secure data exchange between various information systems in Estonia. Security is provided through authentication, multilevel authorization, a high-level log processing, as well as encrypted and time-stamped data traffic. Public and private sector institutions can connect their decentrally organized information systems with the central component X-Road. X-Road can be considered as a federation with the capability to provide secure Internet-based data exchange across different ecosystems. Every X-Road environment is managed by a competent organization (center) that defines the applied security policy and manages the information of its ecosystem members. The federation agreement entails the description of organizational and legal liabilities between the centers of different ecosystems, which allows databases to interact and make integrated e-services possible, and institutions not to be locked into any one type of database or software provider. Some underlying components of the X-Road enabler are a) the unique personal identification code that is needed to identify the right personal data from different registers; b) the unique company commercial registry code that is needed to identify the right business data from different registers; and c) the catalogue of services and data (RIHA), which provides metadata on registers and services to be findable and usable.

X-Road enables institutions to save resources and implement significantly more efficient services, since a cooperative and secure data exchange layer is provided to all members that have signed the agreement.

Network of Public Authorities in Austria (Portalverbund). The Austrian Portalverbund [1] enables different government portals to team up with each other to simplify the authentication of users that have already been authenticated via another trusted portal in the government network. This way, the portal group building block connects many applications from a single entry point (the starting portal of a user) and realizes the single sign on concept. Communication within the portal group is managed, both technically and organizationally, through the portal group protocol (PVP) and the use of security classes. Application providers determine which of their applications will be available over which portals. Keeping in accordance with all data protection regulations, they specify which administration units and employees are authorized to access which applications and define user roles with corresponding access rights.

The Portalverbund targets employees of public administrations and simplifies the access to the various authentic sources and e-government applications in the Austrian e-government applications with the purpose to simplify and enable the benefits of the OOP to be realized for citizens and businesses.

Spanish Red SARA. The Spanish Public Administration telecommunications networks are organized hierarchically based on the Spanish territorial sovereignty (network of municipalities of a certain region, network of regions, network of Ministries). Because governments need to interact and collaborate over the different federal levels, a secure and reliable interchange of information among all levels of government was set up, the Red SARA (or SARA network - System of applications and connections of public administrations) [51]. Red SARA is a set of telecommunications infrastructure and basic common services (such as e-signature validation, verification of identity and residence data, e-notification) that supports the interconnection and the interoperability of all existing Spanish Public Administration networks. It facilitates the sharing of information and services between public administrations over all federal levels in Spain and it interconnects to institutions in Europe and other European Member States through sTESTA [15].

The benefits of Red SARA are the independence of Spanish Public Administrations in their own infrastructure setup, while they can easily connect and interact with other institutions at the different federal levels over the commonly agreed interfaces and interoperability features. This way, the once-only principle can be implemented in public service provisioning, leading to simplification and reduction of administrative burdens for citizens and businesses, while at the same time maintaining the autonomy of government actors in the federal system.

5 Discussion and Recommendations from the Good Practices

The previous section outlined good practices of OOP cases and OOP enablers in European Member States. In order to consider an OOP case or OOP enabler a good practice and a success, the benefits of OOP implementations as well as the barriers and enablers in cross-border OOP public services need to be understood well. Both are synthesized and derived from the case studies and from literature analysis, and described in the following.

5.1 Benefits of OOP Implementation and the Need for OOP Enablers

As already outlined in Sect. 2 and along the description of OOP cases and enablers in the previous section, the once-only principle embodies a number of benefits to the actors involved. These are summarized below along the main benefits identified both in literature (see e.g. [6, 16, 20, 21, 24, 33, 34, 49, 54, 58]) and demonstrated in the OOP examples ALF, EHR, Studielink and TAXISnet outlined in Sect. 4. In addition to the benefits for targeted stakeholders, needed OOP enablers to realize the benefits are spotted.

Reduction of Administrative Burden. The once-only principle contributes to administrative burden reduction in various ways as:

a) citizens and businesses need not to provide the same data repeatedly along public service provisioning. To render the public service providers as data consumers to access data that they need in public service provisioning from data providers, relevant OOP enablers such as secure data exchange mechanisms, interoperability assets and enabling infrastructures need to be in place.

b) public service providers benefit from simplified, less cumbersome and more convenient procedures and pro-active public service offers alike, as they can access and re-use data from the authentic sources through secure enabling infrastructure.

Increased Transparency and Trust. By realizing the concept of consent for sharing and reusing data on respective data subjects (citizens or businesses), the once-only principle contributes to higher trust and transparency in public service, since data subjects can verify (e.g. through a user account and through particular logging mechanisms, etc.) the compliant use of their data and they can have better control over their data. This mechanism is e.g. implemented along the Estonian OOP infrastructure X-Road. In the TOOP project, such mechanism is conceptualized and implemented as well.

Increased Efficiency and Effectiveness. The wide implementation of the OOP contributes to increased efficiency and effectiveness of public administration through co-creation and collaboration between administrations by opening up, sharing and re-using knowledge and resources with the aim to unlock productivity improvements and foster the creation of more public value. Providing access to relevant data also enables public service providers to pro-actively offer public services to citizens as is demonstrated in the ALF OOP case outlined above. Along with the proactive service provisioning, the sharing and re-use of data across public service providers enables governments to fulfill legal obligations faster. Such efficiency gains are clearly recognizable in the OOP cases studied in SCOOP4C [49, 54] and exemplified in the OOP cases in Subsect. 4.1 above.

Higher Quality of Data. Another core benefit for public administrations in the OOP implementation is that enablers such as secure data exchange, eID and trust services as well as enabling infrastructures offer access to quality-assured authentic sources of data. In combination with the reduction of administrative burden and more efficient and effective process execution, public administration are facilitated to save costs and to reduce redundant and error-prone activities of repeated recording of data that is already in the hands of public administration, as the data is retrieved from the quality-assured authentic sources. In addition, the recording of new or revised data is done once. In many cases, this step is even assigned to the data subject (i.e. citizens and businesses) through online service portals.

5.2 Enablers as a Vehicle to Overcome Barriers of OOP Implementations

In order to realize the benefits of the once-only principle for citizens and businesses as well as for public service providers, a number of key enablers have to be in place. In the SCOOP4C project, we argue that barriers and enablers of OOP implementations are two sides of the same coin: while the barriers represent obstacles and hindrances that prevent the realization of the OOP in public service provisioning, the enablers help to overcome these barriers and to guarantee the widest possible success in leveraging the benefits of the once-only principle. In other words, governments need to put in place the respective enablers to ensure the successful and effective implementation of the once-only principle.

Along the good practice analysis and subsequent roadmapping activity in SCOOP4C, the subsequent enablers of OOP implementations have been identified and elaborated. Since barriers of OOP are considered the non-availability of enablers, only the positive side of the coin (i.e. existing enablers) is considered below. The categorization of enablers is on the one hand derived from the interoperability layers of the European Interoperability Framework and the conceptual model of public services in the EIF [14], the European Interoperability Reference Architecture (EIRA) [13]. On the other hand, further soft factors are grouped into relevant categories as outlined in Sect. 3.

The following core enablers of successful OOP implementations have been grouped along the interoperability layers and concepts of the public service conceptual model of the EIF:

Political Commitment. Political commitment is considered a pre-condition for successful OOP implementations and is particularly stressed at European level through strategic documents such as the EU eGovernment Action Plan 2016–2020 [16], the

Single Digital Market Strategy for Europe [17], the Single Digital Gateway Regulation [21] or the EIF [14]. Many EU Member State countries have corresponding digitalization strategies incorporating the once-only principle as a strategic priority. Integrating the implementation of the once-only principle in digitalization strategies at the different levels of Government in Europe is a key enabler. An essential aspect along such political commitments are the will and capacities of governments to finance, coordinate, implement, and monitor the realization of the once-only principle in public service provisioning. To boost innovation and to respect different maturity levels across Europe, the implementation of the OOP in public service may first be based on coalitions of the willing actors and therewith also boost competition in being the first and best practice.

Legal Frameworks. Legal frameworks are required to enable the sharing and reuse of data stored in government's base registries while at the same time ensuring data privacy and protection of citizen's rights. Hence, legal frameworks have to be scrutinized and adjusted to enable the once-only principle to be realized in public service provisioning. Particular areas, where regulations represent key enablers for the sharing and re-use of sensitive data, concern e.g. the many base registries of the public sector, secure data exchange mechanisms, eID and trust services, as well as data protection and data privacy. The European Union has provided such crucial legal enablers such as the General Data Protection Regulation [19] or the Single Digital Gateway Regulation [21]. The same applies to the Member State countries. For example, to enable the OOP solutions ALF, Studielink, EHR and TAXISnet presented in Sect. 4, necessary legislation has been put in place in Austria, Estonia, Greece and the Netherlands.

Organizational Commitment and Collaborative Business Processes. Besides the legal framework, organizational commitment and collaborative business processes have to be in place to enable governments to share citizens' (personal) data among public administrations in secured networks (i.e. sharing and re-using knowledge assets e.g. stored in base registries) and on the basis of standards. The OOP cases outlined in Sect. 4.1 build on such commonly agreed collaborative business processes. Another organizational enabler is multilateral agreements to collaborate as well as to use open standards and open specifications in the public service provisioning implementing the OOP. Such agreements should also be in place regarding the use of common technical infrastructure.

Ensuring Semantic Interoperability Through Common Data Exchange Standards, Common Vocabularies and Taxonomies. Data exchange across different institutions requires semantic enablers to be in place, such as standards for the data exchange, a common terminology, controlled vocabularies and agreed-upon code lists (e.g. as unique identifiers of data sets), or taxonomies to facilitate data exchange between different institutions. The secure data exchange enablers introduced in Sect. 4.2 above present such examples.

Technical Enablers such as Secure Networks and Infrastructure. Commonly used secure networks and infrastructure are key enablers for the interchange and re-use of citizens' data across the governments, including across borders. This includes commonly used services for electronic identification and for trust services (e.g. concept of active consent) as well as commonly used solutions for secure and trusted enabling infrastructure such as e-delivery building block. Examples from the SCOOP4C case study are described in Sect. 4.2.

Collaborative Governance Mechanisms. The implementation of the once-only principle demands different institutional actors to collaborate among different stakeholders. To facilitate the successful implementation of the once-only principle, appropriate collaborative governance models are needed, which clearly define the responsibilities and roles of actors on different levels of governance. Of particular relevance are interoperability governance and public service governance, which both need to be aligned as spotted in [13, 54, 57, 59].

Beyond the key enablers clustered on the basis of the EIF, the following crucial soft enabling factors have been identified and synthesized from the case study analysis:

Motivators, Benefits, and Public Value. Providing incentives, benefits, public value or convenience for citizens, businesses and governments to share and re-use data stored in public administrations' registries is the first soft key enabler to mention. The OOP case examples outlined in Sect. 4.1 demonstrate clearly these motivators and benefits to the relevant stakeholders. This contributes to better acceptance and use of the OOP solution.

Access to Authentic Sources Contributes to Improved Data Quality. The access to authentic data contributes to increased data quality in governmental registries. This enabler can be achieved through the implementation of enablers such as secure data exchange and enabling infrastructure and the necessary interoperability enablers outlined before and some examples provided in Sect. 4.2. Great examples that demonstrate the value-added of improved data quality realized through direct access to authentic sources are the OOP cases presented in Sect. 4.1.

Trust and Transparency. Trust and transparency mechanisms enable citizens to control and monitor by whom, when, and why their data is accessed. Such enabling building blocks are for example the concept of active consent for the sharing and re-use of sensitive or personal data of citizens and businesses or the access to the logging of who has accessed data on the data subject in a particular registry, by when and for what purpose. Such a service is e.g. provided via the X-Road enabler in Estonia (cf. enabler description in Sect. 4.2).

Data Protection and Privacy. The sharing and re-use of citizen data requires to respect privacy and ensure data protection. Hence, mechanisms for data protection need to be in place. Such mechanisms can be on the one hand relevant legislation as is outlined in the respective legal framework enabler above as well as technical building blocks such as eID and trust services such as the concept of the consent (see next enabler) or secure data exchange or infrastructure building blocks.

Socio-cultural Influence Factors. Socio-cultural aspects such as traditions of sharing or not sharing data among governments, ownership of data and citizens' obligations vs. freedom of deciding when and how to provide data to governments are central for gathering acceptance of the once-only principle by citizens and businesses. In some countries, the data stored only for special purposes means that this data is not usable beyond the given constitutional and legal frame, organizational settings and cultural restrictions, thus limiting the OOP implementation to the scope of the service and data. Such factors may vary across countries. However, they play a crucial role in the public service provisioning and in ensuring acceptance and trust of citizens and businesses in the public service.

Citizen-Centered Design. To correspond to the needs and expectations of citizens and other stakeholders in the OOP implementation in the best possible was, the relevant actors need to be involved in co-designing and co-developing of the OOP services, ensuring ease of use, convenience, and good user experience. The more citizen-centered the design of public services is, the more it enables the creation of better quality policy decisions and the offering of better services in the future.

It is important to note that the different enablers outlined above are not mutually exclusive. Instead, the enablers build upon one another and are therefore intertwined and mutually dependent. This means that just implementing one of the enablers is not sufficient for a successful implementation of OOP solutions.

6   Conclusions

This contribution investigated the implementation of the OOP across Europe by studying existing good practice cases and enablers in different Member States. First, an overview of relevant theoretical and political foundations was provided, followed by an outline of the research design, which employed literature analysis and case study research. The presentation of good practices is divided into OOP cases and OOP enablers. In the SCOOP4C project, 57 OOP cases and 34 OOP enablers were analysed. Four examples per group were briefly outlined in the paper to demonstrate how the OOP is realized and provides benefits to citizens and public sector actors.

Subsequently, a synthesis of benefits and key enablers to realize the once-only principle widely was presented. The benefits affiliated with OOP implementations in public service provisioning are a) reduction of administrative burden, b) increased trust and transparency, c) increased efficiency and effectiveness, and higher quality of data. Eleven key enablers of OOP implementations were spotted: 1) political commitment, 2) legal frameworks, 3) organizational commitment and collaborative business processes, 4) semantic interoperability through common data exchange standards, common vocabularies and taxonomies, 5) technical enablers such as secure networks and infrastructure, 6) collaborative governance mechanisms, 7) motivations, benefits, and public value, 8) Access to authentic sources to improve data quality, 9) trust and transparency, 10) data protection and privacy, and 11) citizen-centred design.

The research stressed that barriers and enablers of OOP implementations form linked concepts, i.e. a barrier indicates a lack (or absence) of what is, in the positive formulation, an enabler. For example, a barrier at political level was identified in SCOOP4C as the *"lack of political commitment to enforce and implement fully digital procedures in student exchange across Europe"* while the complementary enabler would be a *"strong political commitment to implement the digital procedures in student exchange services across Europe*" [49].

To sum up the findings from the OOP good practice analysis, the investigation has evidenced existing good practice cases and enablers in different Member States. However, the diffusion of OOP solutions is still scarce, especially at cross-border levels of OOP solutions. Further research and efforts from the side of government actors are needed to successfully implement the OOP across borders. The TOOP project provides a great federated architecture [28, 44] for enabling the provision of OOP solutions across borders. This architecture is picked up and further developed in the DE4ALL project [8]. However, as the analysis of good practices has shown, the success of the OOP implementation depends on many different enablers. Putting such enablers in place demands further considerable effort along a holistic perspective on public service design and implementation with the OOP.

Some further general insights from the above research can be summarized as follows:

- While strategic policies in Europe extensively promote digitalization, networked systems and interoperability, digital transformation in practice and with the OOP as underlying paradigm is considerably lagging behind these visions.
- While OOP visions are promoted to create awareness of the potentials and benefits, these activities are not necessarily reaching out to those that in the end have to implement the OOP solutions.
- In particular, top-down implementation of digitalization needs to urgently be complemented with bottom-up engagement of relevant stakeholders by employing e.g. co-creation concepts, stakeholder engagement and similar to involve the relevant stakeholders in such digital transformations.
- Attempts of bottom-up stakeholder engagement to realize interoperable cross-border public services need be complemented with qualitative research to systematically and rigorously understand barriers and challenges of actors in digital public service provisioning and to design OOP solutions that meet the users' expectations.

References

1. Austrian Portalverbund. https://neu.ref.wien.gv.at/at.gv.wien.ref-live/web/reference-server/ag-iz-portalverbund. Accessed 01 Sept 2020
2. Austria's Antraglose Familienbeihilfe. https://www.brz.gv.at/was-wir-tun/services-produkte/no-one-stop-shops/antraglose-familienbeihilfe.html. Accessed 01 Sept 2020
3. Brown, M., Brudney, J.: Achieving advanced electronic government services: an examination of obstacles and implications from an international perspective. In: Paper presented at the 6th National Public Management Research Conference, Bloomington, IN (2001)
4. Bellamy, C., Taylor, J.A.: Reinventing government in the information age [electronic resource]: international practice in IT-enabled public sector reform. Public Money Manag. 14(3), 59–62 (1994)
5. Carroll, J.: Scenario-Based Design: Envisioning Work and Technology in System Development. Wiley, New York (1995)

6. Cave, J., Botterman, M., Cavallini, S., Volpe, M.: EU-wide digital Once-Only Principle for citizens and businesses. Study for the European Commission (2017). https://ec.europa.eu/esf/transnationality/filedepot_download/1671/1692. Accessed 24 Oct 2020
7. Cordella, A., Bonina, C.M.: A public value perspective for ICT enabled public sector reforms: a theoretical reflection. Gov. Inf. Q. **29**(4), 512–520 (2012)
8. DE4ALL – Digital Europe for All. https://cordis.europa.eu/project/id/870635. Accessed 11 Oct 2020
9. Digital Government - Dutch Base Registries. https://www.nldigitalgovernment.nl/dossiers/base-registers-and-system-standards/. Accessed 30 Oct 2020
10. Dutch Studielink. https://www.studielink.nl/. Accessed 01 Oct 2020
11. Estonian central health information system and patient portal (EHR). https://www.digilugu.ee. Accessed 31 Oct 2020
12. Estonian X-Road. https://www.ria.ee/en/state-information-system/x-tee.html. Accessed 01 Oct 2020
13. European Commission: European Interoperability Reference Architecture and Cartography tool, ISA[2] - Interoperability solutions for public administrations, businesses and citizens. https://ec.europa.eu/isa2/solutions/eira_en. Accessed 24 Oct 2020
14. European Commission: New European Interoperability Framework - Promoting Seamless Services and Data Flows for European Public Administrations. Publications Office of the European Union, Luxemburg (2017)
15. European Commission - ISA[2]: Strengthening the EU's telecommunications backbone. https://ec.europa.eu/isa2/actions/strengthening-eu%E2%80%99s-telecommunications-backbone_en. Accessed 31 Oct 2020
16. European Union: EU eGovernment Action Plan 2016–2020 - Accelerating the Digital Transformation of Government. COM/2016/0179 final, Brussels (2016)
17. European Union: A Digital Single Market Strategy for Europe. COM (2015) 192 Final. https://eur-lex.europa.eu/legal-content/EN/TXT/?uri=celex%3A52015DC0192
18. European Union: Horizon 2020 funding programme: Europe in a changing world - Inclusive, innovative and reflective societies. http://ec.europa.eu/programmes/horizon2020/node/85. Accessed 04 Oct 2020
19. European Union: Regulation 2016/679 of the European parliament and the Council of the European Union: General Data Protection Regulation. Official Journal of the European Communities (2016). https://eur-lex.europa.eu/eli/reg/2016/679/oj
20. European Union: Tallinn Declaration on eGovernment at the Ministerial Meeting during Estonian Presidency of the Council of the EU (2017). https://ec.europa.eu/newsroom/document.cfm?doc_id=47559. Accessed 04 Oct 2020
21. European Union: Regulation 2018/1724 of the European Parliament and of the Council on establishing a single digital gateway to provide access to information, to procedures and to assistance and problem-solving services. Official Journal of the European Communities (2018). https://eur-lex.europa.eu/legal-content/EN/TXT/?uri=uriserv:OJ.L_.2018.295.01.0001.01.ENG.
22. Fang, Z.: E-government in digital era: concept, practice, and development. Int. J. Comput. Internet Manag. **10**(2), 1–22 (2002)
23. Gagnon, Y.-C.: The CASE STUDY as Research Method: A Practical Handbook. Presses de l'Université du Québec, Quebec City (2010)
24. Gallo, C., Giove, M., Millard, J., Valvik Thaarup, R. K.: Study on eGovernment and the Reduction of Administrative Burden. Final Report, European Commission, DG CNECT (2014). https://doi.org/10.2759/42896

25. Gil-Garcia, J.R., Guler, A., Pardo, T.A., Burke, G.B.: Characterizing the importance of clarity of roles and responsibilities in government inter-organizational collaboration and information sharing initiatives. Gov. Inf. Q. **36**(4), 101393 (2019). https://doi.org/10.1016/j.giq.2019.101393
26. Gil-Garcia, J.R., Martinez-Moyanoc, I.J.: Understanding the evolution of e-government: the influence of systems of rules on public sector dynamics. Gov. Inf. Q. **24**(2), 266–290 (2007)
27. Gil-Garcia, J.R., Sayogo, D.S.: Government inter-organizational information sharing initiatives: understanding the main determinants of success. Gov. Inf. Q. **33**(3), 572–582 (2016)
28. Grandy, E., et al.: Generic Federated OOP Architecture. TOOP Consortium (2018). http://www.toop.eu/sites/default/files/D22_Generic_Federated_OOP_Architecture_Final.pdf
29. Greek's TAXISnet. https://www.gsis.gr/. Accessed 31 Oct 2020
30. Janowski, T.: Digital government evolution: from transformation to contextualization. Gov. Inf. Q. **32**(3), 221–236 (2015)
31. Janssen, M., et al.: Scenario building for e-government in 2020: consolidating the results from regional workshops. In: Proceedings of the 40th Annual Hawaii International Conference on System Sciences (HICSS-40), IEEE Computer Society, Washington (DC), Digital Proceedings (2007)
32. Janssen, M., van der Duin, P., Wimmer, M.: Methodology for scenario building. In: Codagnone, C., Wimmer, M.A. (eds.): Roadmapping eGovernment Research. Visions and Measures towards Innovative Governments in 2020, pp. 21–27 (2007)
33. Kalvet, T., Toots, M., van Veenstra, A.F., Krimmer, R.: Cross-border e-government services in Europe: expected benefits, barriers and drivers of the once-only principle. In: Proceedings of the 11th International Conference on Theory and Practice of Electronic Governance (ICEGOV2018), pp. 69–72 (2018)
34. Krimmer, R., Kalvet, T., Toots, M., Cepilovs, A., Tambouris, E.: Exploring and demonstrating the once-only principle: a European perspective. In: Proceedings of the 18th Annual International Conference on Digital Government Research, pp. 546–551 (2017)
35. Lindgren, I., van Veenstra, A.F.: Digital government transformation: a case illustrating public e-service development as part of public sector transformation. In: Proceedings of the 19th Annual International Conference on Digital Government Research, Article No. 38 (2018). https://doi.org/10.1145/3209281.3209302
36. Lob, G., Costa, S., Nogueira, R., Antunes, P., Brito, A.: A scenario building methodology to support the definition of sustainable development strategies: the case of the Azores Region. In: 11th Annual International Sustainable Development Research Conference (2005)
37. Luna-Reyes, L.F., Mellouli, S., Bertot, J.C.: Key factors and processes for digital government success. Inf. Polity **18**(2), 101–105 (2013)
38. Majstorovic, D., Wimmer, M.: Future scenarios of ICT solutions for governance and policy modelling. In: Proceedings of ICEGOV 2014, ACM, Digital Proceedings (2014)
39. Milakovich, M.E.: Digital Governance: New Technologies for Improving Public Service and Participation, 1st edn. Routledge, New York (2012)
40. Müller-Bloch, C., Kranz, J.: A framework for rigorously identifying research gaps in qualitative literature reviews. In: Proceedings of Thirty-Sixth International Conference on Information Systems (2015)
41. OECD: Recommendation of the Council on Digital Government Strategies. Public Governance and Territorial Development Directorate (2014). https://doi.org/10.1007/s13398-014-0173-7.2
42. OECD: Data-Driven Innovation: Big Data for Growth and Well-Being. OECD Publishing, Paris (2015). https://doi.org/10.1787/9789264229358-en
43. Paré, G., Trudel, M.-C., Jaana, M., Kitsiou, S.: Synthesizing information systems knowledge: a typology of literature reviews. Inf. Manag. **52**(2), 183–199 (2015)

44. Pavleska, T., Aranha, H., Masi, M., Grandy, E., Sellitto, G.P.: Cybersecurity evaluation of enterprise architectures: the e-SENS case. Proc. PoEM **2019**, 226–241 (2019)
45. Pereira, G.V., Parycek, P., Falco, E., Kleinhans, R.: Smart governance in the context of smart cities: a literature review. Inf. Polity **23**(2), 143–162 (2018)
46. Pucihar, A., Bogataj, K., Wimmer, M.: Gap Analysis Methodology for Identifying Future ICT Related eGovernment Research Topics – Case of "Ontology and Semantic Web" in the Context of eGovernment. AIS Electronic Library (2007)
47. Rosenbaum, S.: Data governance and stewardship: designing data stewardship entities and advancing data access. Health Serv. Res. **45**(5), 1442–1455 (2010)
48. Rotmans, J., et al.: Visions for a sustainable Europe. Futures **32**, 809–831 (2000)
49. Roustaei, A., et al.: Gap analysis report of challenges, needs and benefits of the OOP4C analysis. SCOOP4C Consortium (2019). https://scoop4c.eu/sites/default/files/2019-06/SCO OP4C_D4.1_v1.1.pdf. Accessed 04 Oct 2020
50. SCOOP4C - Stakeholder Community for the Once-Only Principle for Citizens project. https:// scoop4c.eu/. Accessed 04 Oct 2020
51. Spanish Red SARA. https://administracionelectronica.gob.es/ctt/redsara?idioma=en. Accessed 05 Sept 2020
52. Stocksmeier, D., Wimmer, M.A., Führer, M., Essmeyer, K.: Once-only in Deutschland und Europa: Eine Roadmap grenzüberschreitender Vernetzung im Bereich Steuern. In: Digitalisierung von Staat und Verwaltung, 87–98 (2019)
53. TOOP – The Once-Only Principle project. https://toop.eu/. Accessed 11 Oct 2020
54. Vallner, U., et al.: State of play report of best practices. SCOOP4C Consortium (2017). https:// scoop4c.eu/sites/default/files/2018-01/SCOOP4C_D1.2_0.pdf. Accessed 01 Oct 2020
55. van Notten, P., Rotmans, J., van Asselt, M., Rothman, D.: An updated scenario typology. Futures **35**(5), 423–443 (2003)
56. Weerakkody, V., Janssen, M., Dwivedi, Y.K.: Transformational change and business process reengineering (BPR): lessons from the British and Dutch public sector. Gov. Inf. Q. **28**(3), 320–328 (2011)
57. Wimmer, M.A., Boneva, R., di Giacomo, D.: Interoperability governance: a definition and insights from case studies in Europe. In: Proceedings of the 19th Annual International Conference on Digital Government Research: Governance in the Data Age, ACM (2018). https:// doi.org/10.1145/3209281.3209306
58. Wimmer, M.A., Marinov, B.: SCOOP4C: reducing administrative burden for citizens through once-only - Vision & challenges. Jusletter IT (2017)
59. Wimmer, M.A., Neuroni, A.C., Frecè, J.T.: Approaches to good data governance in support of public sector transformation through once-only. In: Viale Pereira, G., et al. (eds.) EGOV 2020. LNCS, vol. 12219, pp. 210–222. Springer, Cham (2020). https://doi.org/10.1007/978-3-030-57599-1_16
60. Yildiz, M.: E-government research: reviewing the literature, limitations, and ways forward. Gov. Inf. Q. **24**(3), 646–665 (2007)
61. Yin, R.K.: Case Study Research and Applications: Design and Methods, 6th edn. Sage Publications Inc., New York (2018)

The Single Digital Gateway Regulation as an Enabler and Constraint of Once-Only in Europe

Hans Graux[(✉)]

Timelex Law Firm, Brussels, Belgium
`hans.graux@timelex.eu`

Abstract. The adoption of the Single Digital Gateway Regulation is a gamechanger in European e-government. For the first time, it creates a horizontal, non-sector specific legal framework for the direct exchange of digital evidence between public administrations in different Member States. However, these exchanges require public administrations to have a certain degree of trust in each other, which is built on a shared legal basis. The Single Digital Gateway Regulation achieves its goal of creating a legal basis and establishing trust, but also builds in a number of explicit and implicit legal constraints. These will help make the once-only principle in Europe a reality, but also enshrine limitations that will require revisions and expansions of the Regulation at some point in the future. This paper examines the genesis of the Regulation, its legal choices and priorities, the resulting implications and limitations, and potential challenges for the future.

Keywords: Single Digital Gateway Regulation · Legal framework · Trust

1 Introduction on Once-Only Legislation .

1.1 Legal Frameworks for Once-Only at the National Level

The once-only principle is not an entirely new concept, and already has a significant policy background in a number of Member States. In each country where the principle has been adopted at some level, legislation was also introduced in order to provide a clear legal basis and scoping of the principle and its effects. The need for such legislation is obvious: as described elsewhere in this book, the once-only principle fundamentally requires that certain information about a citizen or business can be transferred relatively seamlessly from one administration to another, in order to permit that information to be reused, thus relieving the citizen from a tedious burden while increasing efficiency and reducing errors.

These manifest benefits also imply a risk, however. Should the citizen or company be aware of the information exchange? What happens when the information contains errors? Which administrations are actually entitled to request information, under which conditions, and for which purposes? Which sources should administrations rely upon,

R. Krimmer et al. (Eds.): The Once-Only Principle, LNCS 12621, pp. 83–103, 2021.
https://doi.org/10.1007/978-3-030-79851-2_5

and to what extent can the information be expected to be accurate? All of these questions are critical, and answers can differ from country to country.

None the less, some characteristics recur quite frequently in Member State legislation. Typical examples of common requirements include notably:

- An explicit designation or description of authoritative sources (e.g. enumerated in the law or identified through subsequent formal decisions);
- An assertion that those sources are deemed the sole source of specific information (in order to avoid multiple and potentially conflicting databases being queried for the same data);
- A qualification of the information in those sources as benefiting from a presumption of legal accuracy;
- An explicit designation or description of public authorities which can request information from the authoritative sources;
- A legal obligation to request information from those sources – and not from the citizen or business concerned – whenever this is feasible;
- A legal obligation to notify the authoritative source if a gap or inaccuracy in the information is identified, so that the quality of data can be maintained and even improved over time, and to avoid misinformation from spreading.

While not universal, such obligations are generally fairly representative of the legal environment in which the once-only principle is implemented at any given administrative level (federal, national, or regional). The ultimate effect is the creation of a circle of trust between the designated public authorities, in which information can be exchanged with relative freedom without necessarily relying on the citizen or business as a carrier of their own data. As will be described in the following sections, recreating such a circle of trust is both the main objective and the main stumbling block for EU level legislation.

1.2 Scaling up the Law to Cross Border Once-Only

The Single Digital Gateway Regulation is a first attempt at building a European legislative framework for cross-border once-only services (among several other topics). The functional objective is described at a high level in recital (44) of the Regulation, which notes that *"The cross-border application of the 'once-only' principle should result in citizens and businesses not having to supply the same data to public authorities more than once, and that it should also be possible to use those data at the request of the user for the purposes of completing cross-border online procedures involving cross-border users."* In order to achieve this objective, the Regulation calls for the creation of a *"fully operational, safe and secure technical system for the automated cross-border exchange of evidence between the actors involved in the procedure, where this is explicitly requested by citizens and businesses"*.

The elaboration of the once-only principle in the Regulation, including its constraints and prerequisites, can be found mainly in Article 14 of the Regulation, which will be discussed in-depth below. However, it can already be noted that the approach of the Regulation differs significantly from the common elements found in national level legislation as summarised above. Notably, the Regulation does not designate authoritative sources, nor does it identify authorities that can request information from these sources. The Regulation also doesn't grant exchanged evidence any particular presumption of legal value, other than by noting that the evidence is "deemed to be authentic" – meaning that it should be considered to be originating from the competent authority, without however addressing whether that implies that it is adequate for the procedure at hand. And perhaps most critically: it emphatically places the users – citizens or businesses – at the centre of the once-only principle: as a general rule, evidence is exchanged using the once-only principle at the explicit request of the user.

All of these choices are the result of a delicate balancing exercise. The European Union has no prima facie competence to legislate administrative procedures horizontally, and it arguably would not be proportional to attempt to do so. Indeed, the formal legal basis of the Regulation is the protection of the free movement of citizens, based on Article 21(2) and Article 114(1) of the Treaty on the Functioning of the European Union (TFEU), as indicated in recital 6 of the Regulation.

The Regulation thus cannot directly envisage an overhaul of national public administration, which is one of the reasons why it would not be capable of designating competent authorities or of regulating the legal value of national evidence. None the less, the implementation of the once-only principle implies the creation of a circle of trust, at least to a sufficient extent to allow public administrations to exchange information without relying exclusively on the citizen or business as an intermediary.

At the national level, administrative proceedings can be directly regulated, and obligations – including the participation in a circle of trust - can be imposed directly on the administrations themselves. At the European level, the citizen or business must be at the centre, and therefore the Regulation is drafted in a user-centric manner: exchanges of evidence under the Regulation are generally driven by a user request, and imply prior verification of the evidence by the user. The user decides which exchanges can occur.

As will be examined in greater detail below, this has significant benefits, but also implies some constraints, both in terms of user friendliness and in terms of functionality. Mainly, the requirement in principle of a request and of verification of the evidence by the user ensures that no evidence can be exchanged under Article 14 without the user's awareness and approval. While the benefits of this approach are obvious, it also implies that the Regulation and its technical system will not be useful as devices for detecting malicious or unlawful behaviour: since the user will typically refuse to approve exchanges of evidence which will have negative consequences (e.g. documents proving that they are not or no longer eligible for a specific procedure or service), the Regulation will not be useful for public administrations as a mechanism for catching persons that attempt to circumvent legal requirements. In that sense, the Regulation serves the individual interests of the users more than the interests of the public administrations, or arguably even the public interest. Examples of these choices will be provided in the sections below.

2 The Single Digital Gateway Regulation – Concept and Choices

2.1 General Model for Trust Between Public Administrations Across Borders

Any implementation of the once-only principle implies the creation of a circle of trust between participation public authorities. After all, the principal operational requirement is that one public administration can request information pertaining to a citizen or business directly from another public administration, rather than from the citizen or business itself. While safeguards can and usually will be built in to avoid unlawful access to or use of the information, a mechanism to establish and maintain trust is necessary.

Within the Single Digital Gateway Regulation, this is done through a combination of elements. Firstly, as already noted above, Article 14 requires that the exchanges of evidence occur via a single technical system, which must be *"established by the Commission in cooperation with the Member States"*. The development, availability, maintenance, supervision, monitoring and security management of the technical system is a split responsibility of the Commission and Member States, who are each responsible for their respective parts of the technical system (Article 14.11). Since Member States are also explicitly required to "integrate the fully operational technical system as part of the procedures" covered by the Regulation (Article 14.7), the phrasing of the law strongly suggests a federated or at least strongly decentralized model – although this terminology is not used in the Regulation itself - in which each Member States retains a clear degree of control over their national administrative activities, with the Commission operating a smaller central component of the system that will be responsible for interconnecting the national nodes.

Thus, the technical model which is suggested by the Regulation already ensures that each Member State maintains control over national components of the infrastructure. Of course, in order for once-only exchanges to be viable, a more critical question is the trust in the infrastructure of *other* Member States, and in their compliance with the requirements of the Regulation. To some extent this is addressed by the Regulation's reliance on technical and functional "building blocks", which are already in use across the Member States and which offer basic capabilities such as electronic identification (the eID building block) and exchange of documents (eDelivery building block). As the recitals note, *"those building blocks consist of technical specifications, sample software and supporting services, and aim to ensure interoperability between the existing information and communication technology (ICT) systems in different Member States so that citizens, businesses and administrations, wherever they are in the Union, can benefit from seamless digital public services"*. On the basis that Member States could be trusted not to modify these building blocks in a manner that undermines their legal value, this already forms a part of the puzzle.

The building blocks are far from sufficient to bring about the entire technical system, and new components – which can form a Once-Only building block in its own right – can be governed by a new implementing act that sets out the technical and operational specifications of the technical system as a whole, as envisaged by Article 14.9.

However, this approach only touches on the trustworthiness of the technical infrastructure. Apart from this issue, the Regulation also imposes a number of functional and design constraints on the way the once-only principle can operate, including the role of the user, constraints on the use cases and evidences, and procedural safeguards. These will be discussed in the sections below.

2.2 Drawing the Lines: A Closed Model for Once-Only

One of the principal elements to be regulated in any legal framework pertaining to the once-only principle is the scoping of the use cases in which it can or must be applied. At the national level, this is commonly done by identifying the relevant authoritative sources and the public authorities that should rely on them, rather than opting for the definition of specific procedures. At the European level however, that approach would not be feasible, since neither the information sources nor public authorities are organised in a harmonised and homogeneous manner across the EU. In other words, it would not be possible to designate the evidences and the databases covered by the Regulation, or to specify the authorities, since those evidences, databases and authorities may not exist in some Member States, or at least be so incomparably different as to make a regulatory scoping meaningless.

For that reason, the European legislator opted for a different approach. In order to make sure that the Regulation contained appropriate constraints on the cases in which the once-only principle could be applied, even though neither evidences nor authorities can be clearly described, it opted for an exhaustive enumeration of the procedures in which the technical system could be used to support once-only exchanges.

More specifically, article 14 of the SDGR requires that this system supports the exchange of evidence necessary for the completion of the procedures listed in annex II of the SDGR, as well as procedures governed by the Directive on the recognition of professional qualifications, the Directive on services in the internal market, the Directive on public procurement, and the Directive on procurement by entities operating in the water, energy, transport and postal services sectors. Given that the entire list focuses on procedures which are either harmonised through EU level Directives or (in the case of Annex II) which are focused on universal high level "life events" such as birth, changing residence, or retiring, these procedures should indeed exist in all Member States, even if the competent authorities and evidence for each of the procedures might vary significantly.

While the approach has the benefit of feasibility, the downside is the fact that it is a 'closed list' approach, which does not allow new use cases or new procedures to be added without an amendment of the Regulation itself. It would of course also be feasible for future legislative initiatives to explicitly reference the use of the technical system envisaged by Article 14, but in the absence of new regulatory interventions, the growth potential of the number of procedures is inherently limited. This is a constraint that directly results from the impossibility to directly regulate authoritative sources and public authorities at the European level, but the unfortunate outcome is a lack of flexibility when new once-only needs will be identified. The TOOP pilot project already encountered this in one of its use cases, focusing on the exchange of evidences in a maritime environment: while this would be a good target for EU level once-only procedures, it is not included in the Regulation's closed list, and therefore would not be able to make use of the technical system under Article 14.

The scoping of exchanges of evidence is thus limited to specific procedures enumerated in the Regulation. A secondary but related issue is whether, once a public authority has received evidence in accordance with the Regulation through the technical system, they can share it with additional authorities within their own country.

The Regulation does not appear to comprehensively address this question. Article 14 does contain a purpose limitation principle, which notes that "The evidence made available to the requesting competent authority shall be limited to what has been requested and shall only be used by that authority for the purpose of the procedure for which the evidence was exchanged" (Article 14.8).

However, the use of the evidence "for the purpose of the procedure" should arguably also include any use of that evidence which is mandatory under national law as a result of that procedure, and which may also involve further use of that evidence. It is likely that some Member States will have their own once-only principles, governed by national law, under which they share data (including evidence) with other public administrations, or under which they are required to retain evidences after receiving them under the SDGR. There seems to be no prima facie reason why the SDGR would invalidate such national laws.

By way of example: after an exchange of evidence under Article 14, the evidence may need to be kept in an official archive under national archiving laws under national legal frameworks. Such uses however are subject only to national laws, which are not affected by the Regulation. As recital (26) to the SDGR notes, "This Regulation should also not affect the procedural workflows within and between the competent authorities, the 'back office', whether digitalised or not". Otherwise, use of the technical system would make it impossible for receiving competent authorities to respect national laws, or at least require them to create exceptions in existing laws to the effect that evidence may be reused whenever their laws require it, except if it reached their competent authorities through the technical system under the Regulation. That approach would likely be unworkable in practice. Thus, it seems reasonable to argue that the Regulation's requirement to only use evidence for the purpose of the procedure for which the evidence was exchanged should not affect further uses that are mandatory under national law. lease note that the first paragraph of a section or subsection is not indented. The first paragraphs that follows a table, figure, equation etc. does not have an indent, either.

2.3   User Centricity as the Principal Driver

It has already been stressed in the sections above that the Regulation takes a user-oriented perspective on the once-only principle, by introducing a general requirement that the technical system "shall enable the processing of requests for evidence at the explicit request of the user" (14.3 (a)). Moreover, it adds that the "use of the technical system shall not be obligatory for users and shall only be permitted at their explicit request, unless otherwise provided under Union or national law" (14.4). Finally, the Regulation requires that the technical system "shall enable the possibility for the user to preview the evidence to be used by the requesting competent authority and to choose whether or not to proceed with the exchange of evidence" (14.3 (f)). Thus, three clear elements of user centricity are enshrined in the text: the explicit request, the preview, and the optionality of using the system.

The Explicit Request

Requirements for the validity of an explicit request are outlined in the Regulation, which stresses that it must be "an explicit, freely given, specific, informed and unambiguous request of the user concerned", as a result of which consuming authorities must "request evidence directly from competent authorities issuing evidence in other Member States through the technical system" (article 14.7 SDGR). The technical system for the cross-border exchange of evidence must thus support a mechanism for the user to express an explicit request that meets the requirements above.

The phrasing of these requirements for an explicit request is nearly identical to the definition of a 'consent' in the General Data Protection Regulation. None the less, for reasons that will be outlined below, the concepts should not be conflated: the expression 'consent' does not occur in the SDGR, and the notion of 'consent' should not be used as a reference to the explicit request requirement of article 14 of the SDGR.

This approach puts the user in control over the evidence exchange, which has both benefits and downsides. The benefit (and goal of this requirement) is that the user is protected against potentially unlawful exchanges of evidence without their knowledge. The downside is that the user must in principle be involved in authorising an exchange. A transfer that would be beneficial for competent authorities (or for the public interest) may be defensible from a public policy perspective even without the request (or even knowledge) of the user, and it can even be considered an application of a broader inter-pretation of the once-only principle; but the SDGR does not allow such exchanges in principle, subject to the exceptions discussed below. By way of a practical example: the technical system can be used under the SDGR to allow the user to provide evidence that they are eligible for a particular service or benefit at the time when they apply for it. The system however cannot be used to allow the competent authority to continue to obtain evidence afterwards whether these requirements are still met, unless the user chooses to cooperate.

There are some theories on how the concept of a 'request' could be interpreted to none the less accommodate such models. One might e.g. consider the case where a user explicitly requests that a certain administration obtains certain evidences for a specific procedure, and that it asks that it keeps these up to date (including through future requests) for a specified period of time. In this case too, the exchanges are arguably based on an explicit request, the scoping of which could be clearly approved by the user. While each subsequent exchange (resulting from the initial request) is not the result of an entirely new request, there is no part of the Regulation's phrasing that suggests that individual requests for individual exchanges would be necessary.

None the less, there are some constraints that impede an easy adoption of such mod-els as a part under Article 14. Firstly, there is the consideration that the original request would at any rate need to be particularly clear and explicit on the scoping of the request, and in particular on the possibility of future exchanges, including purpose limitation and temporal limitation. A situation where a competent authority can request evidences with-out any limitation to specific administrative procedures or for an indeterminate period of time would not be compatible with the SDGR. Secondly, the Regulation also contains a preview requirement as will be examined below: the user must be able to preview each subsequent evidence exchange and be permitted to decide whether to proceed with it.

This latter element inherently requires user involvement, so that automated exchanges without user involvement are unlikely to comply with Article 14.

There are exceptions to the request requirement. As the Regulation notes, the "use of the technical system [...] shall only be permitted at their explicit request, unless otherwise provided under Union or national law" (14.4 SDGR). This exception could be applied to evidences which are publicly available to anyone without any constraints (e.g. via public websites, open web services, etc.). In such cases, it seems reasonable to argue that automated cross-border exchange without a request is also allowed. Secondly, it could also be reasonably applied to evidences which are available to be exchanged between designated competent authorities within the EU (without constraint to one or several specific Member States). Company information that can be exchanged between business registers via the BRIS network seem to be an example, since the BRIS legislation allows competent authorities to exchange information directly in the circumstances covered by that legislation (without the request by the user). In such cases it seems reasonable to argue that automated cross-border exchange without request is allowed via the technical system as well.

It is worth noting that national or European law could also have the inverse impact: rather than just eliminating any need for an explicit request (and permitting exchanges even without users explicitly requesting it), it would also be possible for such laws to mandate use of the technical system – not only eliminating the requirement of a request, but even invalidating the possibility of choosing alternative means of submission of evidence. In other words, future evolutions in European or national law can significantly impact the scoping of the use of the technical system.

The Preview Requirement
According to the Single Digital Gateway Regulation, the envisaged technical system "*shall enable the possibility for the user to preview the evidence to be used by the requesting competent authority and to choose whether or not to proceed with the exchange of evidence*" (14.3 (f) SDGR). Recital 47 clarifies that the user can exercise that right not to proceed "*in cases where the user, after previewing the evidence to be exchanged, discovers that the information is inaccurate, out-of-date, or goes beyond what is necessary for the procedure in question.*"

The technical system must thus support a mechanism of preview by the user of the evidence, and a mechanism of approval of the exchange after observing the preview (thus also preventing the exchange by refusing to approve it). However, the wording of the preview mechanism in the SDGR clearly indicates that the preview is only a *possibility* that must be afforded to the user, not that the user has to be required to actually use (observe) the preview.

The preview mechanism aims to support the accuracy and relevance of the data exchanged and strengthens control by the user over data exchanged through the technical system, allowing them to exercise some control over the consequences of their use of the system.

The English language version of the SDGR does not state explicitly when the preview should take place; it merely notes that the technical system should "enable the possibility for the user to preview the evidence to be used by the requesting competent authority and to choose whether or not to proceed with the exchange of evidence". Given this phrasing, the most rational interpretation is that the preview possibility is offered to the user *before* the exchange of evidence to the receiving authority occurs. A broader interpretation, where the receiving authority first receives the evidence and then allows the user to preview it and to block any use of the data, arguably raises compliance challenges with the phrasing of the SDGR. Other language versions of the SDGR are more explicit than the English phrasing in requiring a preview before the exchange occurs. E.g. in German, the Regulation requires the technical system *"dem Nutzer die Möglichkeit bieten, die von der anfordernden zuständigen Behörde zu verwendenden Nachweise vorab einzusehen und zu entscheiden"* – *vorab* indicating that the preview occurs before the exchange.

From a functional perspective, the principal objective is at any rate that the evidence can only be used for a preview, and not for the actual procedure itself, until the evidence exchange has been approved during the preview (or until the user declines the possibility to preview).

Similar to the explicit request, the SDGR indicates that the possibility of a preview is not required when "automated cross-border data exchange without such preview is allowed under applicable Union or national law" (14.5 SDGR). Again, the exception could plausibly be applied to evidences which are publicly available to anyone without any constraints, and to evidences which are available to be exchanged between designated competent authorities within the EU.

One additional complexity is the issue of which 'national law' determines whether a preview can be omitted or not. The simplest interpretation is that the main relevant question is whether the evidence is publicly available without constraints – and therefore that only the national laws of the data providing Member State govern the preview exception. However, a much stricter interpretation could be applied as well, in which the omission of a preview is governed by any national laws determining the rules behind a specific procedure. In that interpretation, the national laws of the data consuming Member State are equally relevant – i.e. if an evidence is freely available in Member State A, but Member State B does not recognise the free availability of that type of evidences in a specific procedure, Member State B might insist on previews, arguing that its own laws are not complied with if no preview was available. This is an open issue at present.

Finally, recital (47) of the SDGR also indicates that "the data included in the preview should not be stored longer than is technically necessary". Given the reference to technical necessity, this constraint seems to target only the storage required for the preview functionality, and not any storage that precedes or follows the preview (e.g. retention in the sending Member State for accountability purposes, or retention in the receiving Member State for the purposes of administrative follow-up of the service requested by the user).

In addition, the reference to "data included in the preview" seems to suggest that it is principally the evidence's content that may not be retained longer than necessary, which is reasonable from a data protection and confidentiality perspective. No part of this provision would seem to suggest that an audit trial is impermissible, provided that the audit trail doesn't include the "data included in the preview". In other words, an audit trail could contain any metadata related to the preview process, as well as e.g. hashed values of the evidence file in order to determine afterwards (in case of disputes) whether a specific file was exchanged, provided that the evidence itself and its contents are not retained.

Based on that understanding, the main implication seems to be that the technical system must include a function that ensures that an automated deletion of the evidence should occur after the user decides whether or not to transfer the evidence. This deletion (from static storage devices or from dynamic memory) should be verifiable through an appropriate log or audit trail. No centralised storage of the evidence is permissible under the SDGR.

Freedom to Choose

As a third pillar to the SDGR's user centricity (in addition to the user request and the preview requirement), Recital 47 of the SDGR indicates that the use of the technical system should be voluntary, and that other means of submitting evidence should remain available to users. This principle is repeated in Article 14.4, which notes that "*The use of the technical system shall not be obligatory for users and shall only be permitted at their explicit request, unless otherwise provided under Union or national law. The users shall be permitted to submit evidence by means other than the technical system and directly to the requesting competent authority*".

In other words, users can never be forced to use the technical system. This does not imply that the use of electronic communications cannot be made compulsory under national law; this is a matter of national sovereignty. However, if users do not wish to use the technical system, they must be provided with alternatives, which may be digital or analogue, as deemed permissible by the national laws governing the procedure.

2.4   Data Protection as a General Consideration Behind the SDGR

Applicability of Data Protection Law

A general concern in relation to the once-only principle is compliance with the EU's fundamental right to data protection, as enshrined in article 8 of the EU Charter of Fundamental Rights, and as governed principally by the General Data Protection Regulation. While not all evidences exchanged via the technical system will by definition qualified as personal data, it is clear that most evidences will contain at least some personal data, and that the requirement of human involvement (through the user) in any evidence exchange implies that at least some personal data processing is required for any application of the once-only principle as envisaged under Article 14. After all, the user will be identified, and information about the time, source and destination of the exchange will need to be generated and logged, as well as the nature of the evidence. Collectively, this already entails a processing of personal data.

Legal Basis for the Processing of Personal Data

The explicit request requirement to some extent helps to support compliance with key data protection principles under EU law, in particular the requirement to have a legal basis for a transfer of evidences containing personal data. The SDGR comments on this relationship explicitly, noting that "Where the exchange of evidence includes personal data, the request should be considered to be explicit if it contains a freely given, specific, informed and unambiguous indication of the individual's wish to have the relevant personal data exchanged, either by statement or by affirmative action. If the user is not the person concerned by the data, the online procedure should not affect his or her rights under Regulation (EU) 2016/679".

This assertion is short, but contains a few critical pointers for the interpretation of the relationship between request and consent. Notably, it recognises that not all evidences will include personal data. This is of course dependent on the procedure and on the evidences required. Furthermore, the recital's meaning should not be misunderstood as saying that a request under the SDGR is identical to consent under the GDPR. It notes only that, if evidences contain personal data and a consent meeting the requirement of the GDPR is obtained for the exchange, then the consent requirement also satisfies the requirement of the explicit request. It however does not indicate that a consent meeting the requirements of the GDPR is always required, nor that every request under the SDGR satisfies the requirements of a consent under the GDPR.

To understand the exact relationship between the request and a consent, it is important to understand that any exchange (or other form of processing) of personal data through the technical system must comply with the requirements of the GDPR. A central challenge in any SDGR procedure – among other data protection challenges – is ensuring that there is a legal basis for the transfer of evidence, assuming that the evidence indeed contains personal data. It would be tempting to assume that the explicit request of the user to transfer any personal data constitutes a consent under the GDPR, and therefore that it is sufficient as a legal basis in all cases. None the less, this would be incorrect for several reasons.

Firstly, a consent under the GDPR must be given by the data subject, i.e. the person whose data will be processed. This is sometimes not possible in specific procedures, where the user may not be the (only) person whose personal data will be processed – consider e.g. an accounting person using the SDG to transfer personal data relating to the management of a company: the accounting person cannot by definition provide consent on behalf of the management.

Secondly, consent under the GDPR must be freely given. It has been a long standing interpretation of European data protection law – and this point has been recently affirmed in official guidance from European data protection authorities – that freely given consent is not possible when there is a clear imbalance of power between the data controller (the party asking for the consent) and the data subject (the party giving their consent). The aforementioned Guidelines take a very strict approach on this point, and stress that "it is unlikely that public authorities can rely on consent for processing as whenever the controller is a public authority, there is often a clear imbalance of power in the relationship between the controller and the data subject. It is also clear in most cases that the data subject will have no realistic alternatives to accepting the processing (terms) of this controller. The EDPB considers that there are other lawful bases that are, in principle, more appropriate to the activity of public authorities". While this position appears strict, it is not illogical: in the case of e.g. moving one's home to a different Member State, there is hardly any freedom left: a citizen either consents, or is unable to move homes. In these circumstances, there is little choice in reality, and therefore no way to provide a consent satisfying the requirements of the GDPR.

Similarly and perhaps less intuitively, the same Guidelines note that "an imbalance of power also occurs in the employment context. Given the dependency that results from the employer/employee relationship, it is unlikely that the data subject is able to deny his/her employer consent to data processing without experiencing the fear or real risk of detrimental effects as a result of a refusal. It is unlikely that an employee would be able to respond freely to a request for consent from his/her employer to, for example, activate monitoring systems such as camera observation in a workplace, or to fill out assessment forms, without feeling any pressure to consent. Therefore, the EDPB deems it problematic for employers to process personal data of current or future employees on the basis of consent as it is unlikely to be freely given. For the majority of such data processing at work, the lawful basis cannot and should not be the consent of the employees (Article 6(1)(a)) due to the nature of the relationship between employer and employee".

In both cases – public authorities and employees – consent is not entirely impossible if there is indeed no imbalance of power, but it is generally not the favoured legal basis for the processing of personal data under European data protection law. However, this is not an insurmountable problem in practice, since the GDPR does not require consent by definition, but rather a legal basis, for which consent is only one available option. The SDGR similarly does not mention consent at all – nor any other legal basis under the GDPR – thus leaving multiple justifications open. As the European Data Protection Supervisor also noted in its Opinion 8/2017 on the proposal for the SDGR, "the three most relevant legal grounds for implementing the 'once-only' principle are consent, legal obligation and public task/official authority. Depending on the circumstances, one or another of these legal bases could be the most appropriate choice. As a general rule of thumb, for the case of any recurring and structural data sharing, the EDPS recommends - in order to ensure legal certainty- that whenever possible, further processing of personal data based on the once-only principle be specified in a legislative instrument, which provide appropriate safeguards to ensure compliance with data protection law, including the principle of purpose limitation and ensuring data subjects' rights".

Thus, it is clear that consent in the sense of the GDPR is not a requirement for the exchange of evidence, and that the procedural prerequisite of the SDGR of an explicit request should not be conflated with a GDPR consent requirement: the explicit request obligation may apply even in cases where there is no personal data involved, and inversely a legal basis for the exchange of evidence must exist even when there is an exception to the explicit request requirement. The two obligations – explicit request and legal basis – exist side by side, and are separate.

In some procedures, the choice for a GDPR consent as a legal basis for the exchange of evidence is plausible, but in many (including those where consent is not possible) a different legal basis will need to be relied upon. While the choice can be different from use case to use case, the legal basis will generally be the legal obligation for the competent authorities to transfer evidences under EU or national law; or the legal obligation for the competent authorities to transfer evidences as a part of the performance of a task carried out in the public interest or in the exercise of official authority vested in the controller. To the extent that the SDGR creates the obligation for competent authorities to cooperate in such exchanges, an appropriate legal basis under the GDPR is thus available.

Once-only and Further Processing of Personal Data

The once-only principle relies essentially on the reuse of data previously created, collected or stored by public administrations in relation to citizens and businesses; indeed, such reuse is even its sole purpose. Where the information exchanged through the application of the once-only principle includes personal data, issues concerning 'further processing' as described under the GDPR must be addressed. The notion of further processing, which is processing of personal data beyond the initial purpose for which it was collected, is tied to the principle of purpose limitation.

Under the GDPR, purpose limitation is a fundamental data protection principle according to which data is collected for specified, explicit and legitimate purposes and may not be further processed in a manner that is incompatible with those purposes (Article 5.1 GDPR). There are exceptions, when the data subjects consented to the further processing or when or when it constitutes a necessary and proportionate measure in a democratic society to safeguards certain of its fundamental elements (such as listed in article 23 of the GDPR). As highlighted by the European Data Protection Board, easing administrative burdens on individuals or organisations is one of the primary aims of the once-only principle, and is undoubtedly of public interest. None the less, processing of personal data for other purposes should be allowed only where the processing is compatible with the purposes for which the personal data were initially collected (Recital (25) GDPR).

The compatibility of purposes must be assessed based on the link between the new purposes, the context of the processing, the nature of the data concerned, the possible consequences of the processing and the existence of appropriate safeguards (Article 6.4 GDPR). In the case of further processing through the technical system set up in compliance with the SDGR, the compatibility of purposes is largely governed by the legislator at EU level: the existence of the SDGR and its explicit requirement to apply the once-only principle in the listed procedures, under the safeguards stated in the SDGR, fundamentally implies that the further processing required by the SDGR is considered as compatible with the original purposes by the legislator. Of course, compliance with the safeguards of the SDGR is critical in this assessment, and notably the obligation in principle to only use the technical system at the explicit request of the user, or when required under Union or national legislation.

On this basis, the further processing of personal data under the SDGR must prima facie be deemed as compatible with the original purposes.

For the avoidance of doubt, it is clear that the SDGR also contains a purpose limitation principle, which notes explicitly that "The evidence made available to the requesting competent authority shall be limited to what has been requested and shall only be used by that authority for the purpose of the procedure for which the evidence was exchanged" (Article 14.8). However, it would appear logical that use of the evidence "for the purpose of the procedure" must include any use that's mandatory under national law as a result of that procedure. Otherwise, use of the SDGR would make it impossible for receiving competent authorities to respect national laws, such as archiving laws, since these too are essentially a form of further processing.

3 Challenges and Ambiguities

3.1 Reliance on Further Implementation

The analysis above has already shown that there are some ambiguities still on the exact interpretation of the SDGR, and the way the technical system will need to be implemented centrally and at the Member State level. Many of these are expected to be resolved through the adoption of one or more implementing acts by the European Commission, which should be in place by 12 June 2021, as required by Article 14.9 of the SDGR. These acts should set out the technical and operational specifications of the technical system.

In the sections below, we will briefly examine some further points of contention, which will likely be at least partially mitigated by the implementing acts.

3.2 Requirements for the User

As has been noted in the introduction above, the Regulation's approach is user centric in principle, since exchanges of evidence must be triggered by an explicit request from the user (subject to certain exceptions). Users can be either natural persons or businesses, since users are defined explicitly in the Regulation as "either a citizen of the Union, a natural person residing in a Member State or a legal person having its registered office in a Member State, and who accesses the information, the procedures, or the assistance or problem-solving services, referred to in Article 2(2), through the gateway".

The scoping is thus relatively broad, and it is worth noting that citizenhood (to be understood as having the nationality of a Member State) is not a prerequisite for eligibility to use the technical system. For a natural person, it is sufficient to have a residence in a Member State. Legal persons on similarly are required to have at least a registered office in a Member State.

While this approach is succinct and pragmatic, it also hides a significant degree of complexities that still need to be resolved, both technically and legally. The complexity stems from the fact that the Regulation envisages that the covered procedures can be completed in a fully online manner (Article 6), meaning that:

(a) *the identification of users, the provision of information and supporting evidence, signature and final submission can all be carried out electronically at a distance, through a service channel which enables users to fulfil the requirements related to the procedure in a user-friendly and structured way;*

(b) *users are provided with an automatic acknowledgement of receipt, unless the output of the procedure is delivered immediately;*

(c) *the output of the procedure is delivered electronically, or where necessary to comply with applicable Union or national law, delivered by physical means; and*

(d) *users are provided with an electronic notification of completion of the procedure.*

Thus, an important legal prerequisite is that users – natural and legal persons – can be identified electronically, that they can obtain the relevant evidence electronically, and that they can submit it electronically. This is not a trivial issue in practice. An important pre-existing input on this topic is the existence of the eIDAS Regulation(EU) No 910/2014, which regulates the recognition of national means of electronic identification by public authorities in cross border transactions, and also provides a legal framework for electronic signatures and electronic seals that may be used to authenticate evidences. However, there are several challenges on this point.

Firstly, the Single Digital Gateway Regulation does not contain a requirement to use means of electronic identification which are subject to the terms of the eIDAS Regulation. Recital (70) does note that "Member States are encouraged to increase the security of transactions and to ensure a sufficient level of confidence in electronic means by using the eIDAS framework laid down by Regulation (EU) No 910/2014 and in particular adequate assurance levels. Member States can take measures in accordance with Union law to safeguard cybersecurity and to prevent identity fraud or other forms of fraud". However, this is merely an encouragement, not an obligation.

While use of electronic identities that are recognised under the eIDAS Regulation – meaning that Member States have completed a notification procedure for these identities – is a partial solution, it does not resolve all challenges. At the time of writing, 14 Member States have a notified eID scheme – which is a substantial but not universal coverage. Furthermore, completing the notification process hardly resolves all legal challenges. The eIDAS Regulation recognises three tiers of quality of eID schemes (referred to as levels of assurance): low, substantial or high. There is no consensus at this stage which level of assurance should be adequate to permit identification within the technical system. While virtually all notified eID schemes achieve a 'high' level of assurance (meaning that they should open all relevant doors), there are some exceptions.

Secondly, even if all Member States would have a notified eID at the high level of assurance, that would still not comprehensively resolve all challenges for identifying users. Specifically for legal persons (i.e. companies or organisations represented by a specific natural person), there is no unambiguous legal framework yet for establishing the right of the natural person in any given procedure to represent the legal person in a given procedure. In simpler terms: neither the legislation nor the available infrastructure is currently capable of creating complete legal certainty on whether a specific person trying to access a procedure on behalf of a company is legally permitted to represent that company, or to obtain evidence for that company, or to submit it on that company's behalf. While pilot level solutions exist for this problem, the legal framework (and notably the eIDAS Regulation) has not yet been revised to create certainty on this point.

Thirdly, in order to resolve this problem, one should also take into account the potential multitude and variety of participants in an evidence exchange under the Single Digital Gateway Regulation. Insofar as a user interacts with a public authority targeted by the eIDAS Regulation, acceptance of a notified means of identification should be legally certain. However, evidences may be obtained from entities that do not normally interact with citizens in e-government procedures, or that may not unambiguously qualify as public authorities who would be obliged to accept notified electronic means of identification under the eIDAS Regulation (e.g. universities, who may need to provide electronic diploma's as a part of an Article 14 procedure). Therefore, even the universal applicability of the eIDAS Regulation would not comprehensively solve the identification and authentication challenge: the evidence providers may not currently support notified means of electronic identification, and moreover their own approach to user identification may not be technically capable of linking users unambiguously to an eIDAS notified eID.

Ultimately, this is largely a question of the extent to which competent authorities are willing to trust each other's procedures for the identification of users. If this trust is low, then a strict application of the eIDAS Regulation may be advisable, e.g. by requiring that evidences must be retrieved based on identification procedures using a high level of assurance under the eIDAS Regulation, and that proof of the use of such means of identification is presented. If trust is high, then other means of electronic identification could be permitted as well. Choices on this point, which are partially political and partially driven by objective risk assessment, will need to be made by the implementing acts.

3.3 Requirements for Competent Authorities

As noted in the introduction, a principal difference between national level once-only legislation and the SDGR is that national legislation can directly target specifically identified competent authorities, for the simple reason that they are known or at least identifiable under national law. The same is not true at the EU level, where administrations can differ widely from Member State to Member State, in terms of their designation, competences and capabilities.

For that reason, the SDGR applies a very open model, which focuses on high level identification of covered procedures, and succinctly notes that competent authorities comprise "any Member State authority or body established at national, regional or local level with specific responsibilities relating to the information, procedures, assistance and problem-solving services covered by this Regulation" (Article 3 (4)).

In other words, the relevant authorities are those entities which are tasked with specific responsibilities in relation to the covered procedures. In practical terms, this approach leaves Member States the greatest possible flexibility (and corresponding responsibility) in identifying entities which are affected by the SDGR. The consequence of this approach is also that a 'competent authority' is not necessarily a traditional public sector body. If a private sector entity is a body charged with these tasks, it will be qualified as a competent authority under the SDGR as well, and Member States will need to take measures to ensure that such entities can also provide evidences or accept them in the covered procedures.

Finally, it is worth underlining that the SDGR's provisions on the once-only principle as such do not require digitization of evidences and the underlying procedures. Article 14.2 notes that "where competent authorities lawfully issue, in their own Member State and in an electronic format that allows automated exchange, evidence that is relevant for the online procedures referred to in paragraph 1, they shall also make such evidence available to requesting competent authorities from other Member States in an electronic format that allows automated exchange".

The phrasing ("where" they issue) indicates that the clause is conditional: the authorities must also make evidence available in the context of the SDGR where it is already issued – if it is not issued in such a format, or if the issued evidence is not relevant to the online procedures, then there is no obligation for a Member State to move to such a format. More simply put: Article 14 does not create a legal obligation to issue electronic evidence at.

For completeness sake however, it should be recognized that Article 6 of the SDGR does contain an obligation for Member States to ensure that some procedures are offered fully online, which may result in evidences becoming available in an electronic format if the procedures require evidences; but the SDGR does not contain a direct legal obligation for Member States to introduce new types of evidences, or to provide electronic versions of them.

3.4   Requirements for Evidence

As noted above, the only evidences that must be made available for exchange within the scope of the SDGR are those which are already issued "in an electronic format that allows automated exchange". If such evidences are available, they must also be made available in the same format.

This raises a key issue: when exactly can evidence be considered to be "in an electronic format that allows automated exchange"? More specifically, does this description imply that the evidence must be formatted in a semantically meaningful way – i.e. must it be structured in a way that allows the evidence to also be interpreted and processed automatically, at least to some extent, by the receiving competent authority? Or from the opposite perspective: does it imply that unstructured evidence, such as a graphic image (a bitmap, JPEG, or PDF scan without a semantic structure), should not be considered to be evidence falling within the scope of Article 14?

The concept of evidence "in an electronic format that allows automated exchange" can be interpreted and scoped in many ways. Generally speaking, "evidence" is a fluid concept, that should not be simply equated to standardised formal documents, comparable to the traditional way of working in an analogue environment (e.g. through standardised birth certificates, statements of domicile, extracts from criminal registers, etc.). In a digital environment, a much more granular approach is possible.

Increasingly, evidences are no longer supplied as static documents. Rather, evidences are nowadays often available as the result of a dynamic process, consisting of a concrete response – sometimes as simple as a yes/no assertion – to a specific question. For instance, to prove that someone has permission to drive a certain type of car, it is not necessary to transfer comprehensive driver's license records. It suffices to query a register whether a specific person is allowed to drive. If the register only answers „yes" or „no", the 'evidence' is a minimal but perfectly suitable assertion, that would optimally preserve privacy.

There is still some discussion at present to what extent fully unstructured electronic evidences would satisfy the requirements of the SDGR. Based on the lack of constraints on this point in the SGDR, it seems that evidence requesting competent authorities cannot reject evidence in an unstructured format. It is the issuing Member State that determines which evidence is lawfully issued and how, in accordance with its own national laws. There is no legal basis for a receiving Member State (or a receiving competent authority) to reject evidence because it does not meet its formatting/structure expectations. For completeness, it can be noted that a receiving Member State may require additional documentation to be provided, such as translations of the evidence.

Since this means that semantic information may be missing from the evidence, it is all the more important for the technical system to ensure that at least sufficient metadata or some other form of semantic context is included during the exchange, to allow the receiving competent authority to interpret the nature and content of the evidence. As a result, the technical system should be designed in a way that allows this metadata or semantic context to be discovered during an evidence exchange, either because the metadata or semantic context is embedded in the evidence itself (which would be the optimal scenario), or because the exchange is accompanied by metadata that contains the relevant semantic context and corresponding information in the evidence.

There is one further layer of complexity relating to evidence in the SDGR. Article 14.8 requires that evidences must be "limited to what has been requested", which raises some concerns on the common practice of providing standardized evidentiary documents that contain substantially more information than required. By way of example, if a competent authority wishes to receive evidence of the date and location of birth, it may receive a birth certificate that contains not only those data points, but also information which is not strictly needed (e.g. identity of the attesting doctor or public official, identity numbers, identity of the parents, etc.). This is of course suboptimal from a data protection perspective, since more data is exposed than would be strictly necessary.

None the less, if such documents are the available and relevant evidences in the issuing country, it seems that they satisfy the requirements of the SDGR, even though they are arguably a practice that's subject to significant improvement.

3.5   Requirements for Data Flows

As an application of the once-only principle, Article 14 requires that the technical system allows the automated exchange of evidence between competent authorities in different Member States – a flow which therefore goes from administration to administration. Similarly, it notes that the authorities must "make such evidence available to requesting competent authorities from other Member States in an electronic format that allows auto-mated exchange". These provisions strongly suggest a direct exchange, where evidence is requested by one competent authority from another, and provided by that competent authority in response.

None the less, as the sections above in relation to request and preview have illustrated, the reality is not so straightforward: while one competent authority may request evidence from another, that request must in principle be preceded by a request from the user. It is presently still an open question whether the evidence issuing authority may insist on proof of the original request from the user, or whether it is simply required to trust that the requesting competent authority has met all applicable requirements. This issue too will presumably be addressed in the implementing acts.

Similarly, the preview requirement indicates that evidence does not simply flow from one competent authority to another upon request: it must be made available for preview to the user, which implies that it is transferred first to the user (possibly merely as a visual representation rather than as a comprehensive file). Since the communication to the user for the purposes of a preview will typically be needed, it also seems defensible that the evidence is not transferred directly from one authority to another, but rather that it passes through the user, e.g. via a controlled end user environment. This approach can be in line with the once-only principle, provided that it is organized in a clear data flow that allows the user to continue his or her administrative procedure seamlessly – in other words, provided that the implementation does not simply result in the user receiving their evidence and then being left to their own devices.

In ideal circumstances, relevant evidence will be immediately available upon request. However, there are situations where evidence will need to be collected or created upon request, e.g. because the relevant evidence is only available on paper and requires digitization. This implies an interrupted procedure, where a user initiates a procedure and evidence is requested, but the procedures is thereafter halted temporarily – potentially for hours or days – while electronic evidence is created. This is a challenge for the vision of the SDGR, due to the preview requirement – evidence that does not yet exist cannot be previewed, meaning that the session will need to be interrupted. This is not legally problematic under the SDGR, since it contains no requirement that evidences must be available instantaneously or that procedures must be completed immediately. However, from an infrastructural perspective it does create problems: since users cannot remain logged into a session for days, such interrupted procedures imply the creation of some form of personal information management system where procedures can be put on hold until all information requirements were met.

As a final challenge in implementing smooth data flows, there is also the problem that some evidence may not be available for free. In SDGR procedures, it is possible that a user has to pay to obtain certain evidences from an issuing authority. By way of examples, an extract from a business register may not be free, or even a birth certificate could in theory require a charge covering the administrative cost born by the authority.

The SDGR does not affect this ability to charge. It contains a section requiring Member States to ensure that electronic payments are possible for the completion of online procedures, namely Article 13.2 (e), which notes that "where the completion of a procedure requires a payment, users are able to pay any fees online through widely available cross-border payment services, without discrimination based on the place of establishment of the payment service provider, the place of issue of the payment instrument or the location of the payment account within the Union". However, this provision clearly is applicable to the payment by the user of a fee to the competent authority requesting evidences for the cost of the administrative process. It does not address the payment of a fee to the competent authority providing evidences (the data provider).

It appears that the SDGR is silent on the issue of payment to evidence providers, and therefore that there is no formal legal obligation for Member States or their authorities to modify or eliminate their charging policies in the context of the SDGR. In other words, if the issuing competent authority already charges a fee to the user for evidences outside of the context of the SDGR, they can also do so for procedures covered by the SDGR.

4 Concluding Notes and a Perspective on the Future

4.1 The SDGR as a First Step into a European Once-Only Framework

As this contribution hopes to illustrate, the SDGR is a milestone achievement for European e-government. It is the first attempt to create a legal framework for cross-border once-only functionality, and successfully defuses many of the inevitable challenges that arise at this scope, such as the need for user control (through the request and preview requirement), the difficulty of identifying competent authorities and relevant evidences (by focusing on enumerated procedures rather than on the entities and documentation behind them), and the freedom of the user to elect *not* to use the system if that is their preference.

None the less, the SDGR is not without its challenges. Its closed list of procedures means that it has limited flexibility to grow without further regulatory intervention. Its insistence on user control ensures that the once-only principle cannot be applied to enable verifications or recurring exchanges without user approval, even when this would be manifestly in the public interest. And there are very many topics – user authentication needs, semantic structure of evidence, interrupted procedures, the right for competent authorities to check each other's work, and payment for evidences, to name but a few – which are left open to further implementation and interpretation.

As such, the SDGR is truly the first step in this evolution: it is ambitious and challenging in its own right, but unlikely to be the conclusion of the once-only model.

4.2 Once-Only as an Evolving Story of Trust

To at least some extent, the constraints built into the SDGR are merely indicative of the current technical state of play, and of the need for Member States to establish a first measure of experience in direct evidence exchanges before engaging in even more ambitious variations on this theme. Even if the implementation of the SDGR as envisaged in Article 14 is fully successful, revisions of the functional model and the legal framework are inevitable.

Beyond extensions of the number of procedures to be covered, it is likely that at least some Member States will want to examine the possibility of direct exchanges of certain data *without* a prior request from the user – as is already permitted under many national once-only laws – including through data subscription models where any changes in the data are automatically communicated. Inversely, some Member States will want to work in an even more user centric manner, where citizens and companies have their own decentralized but protected personal data spaces, in which they can store and reuse evidences as they please, including by providing them to any desired recipients, rather than just those enumerated under European once-only law.

These approaches are neither inevitable, and nor are they necessarily superior to those of the SDGR. Rather, they are indicative of a different trust model, and of an evolving perspective on an ideal e-government or even on an ideal information society. Future trends are hard to predict, but in all likelihood, the SDGR will not prove to be the end station for European once-only legislation.

References

1. Author, F.: Article title. J. **2**(5), 99–110 (2016)
2. Author, F., Author, S.: Title of a proceedings paper. In: Editor, F., Editor, S. (eds.) CONFERENCE 2016, LNCS, vol. 9999, pp. 1–13. Springer, Heidelberg (2016)
3. Author, F., Author, S., Author, T.: Book title, 2nd edn. Publisher, Location (1999)

4. Author, F.: Contribution title. In: 9th International Proceedings on Proceedings, pp. 1–2. Publisher, Location (2010)
5. LNCS Homepage. http://www.springer.com/lncs, Accessed 21 Nov 2016

Legal Basis and Regulatory Applications of the Once-Only Principle: The Italian Case

Francesco Gorgerino[✉] [ID]

Università degli Studi di Torino, Turin, Italy
francesco.gorgerino@unito.it

Abstract. This study presents how the OOP is related to the constitutional and institutional principles concerning the good performance and impartiality of public authorities and the protection of citizens' rights against the action of public administration, with special regard to the Italian regulatory framework. The national path towards the implementation of the principle is examined, starting from the obligation of the use of self-certifications in place of certificates and the automatic acquisition of data and documents in administrative procedures down to the digitalization of administrations and the interoperability of public databases. A specific paragraph is devoted to the OOP in public procurement, as crucial for development of the European digital single market.

Keywords: Once-only principle · Interoperability · Public administration

1 Introduction

The once-only principle (OOP), states that "public administrations should collect information from citizens and businesses only once and then, respecting regulations and other constraints, this information may be shared". In other words, the OOP consists in the prohibition or, at least, in the limitation for public administrations to request documents and information that are already in their possession, with the consequent obligation to share data they contain, nowadays through IT systems interoperability [1–3].

Already in 2009, a declaration of this content was signed by the Ministers of the EU Member States: "we will use eGovernment to reduce administrative burdens, partly by redesigning administrative processes in order to make them more efficient. We will exchange experience and jointly investigate how public administrations can reduce the frequency with which citizens and businesses have to resubmit information to appropriate authorities" [4].

In 2015, the once-only principle was indicated as a pillar of the Digital Single Market Strategy for Europe launched by the European Commission, with the decision to undertake a pilot project to explore the possibilities of setting up a secure IT solution to achieve the objective of the widespread application on the continent of the principle, since only in (optimistic!) 48% of the cases "the public administration uses the information on citizens or businesses it already has, avoiding to ask again" [5].

R. Krimmer et al. (Eds.): The Once-Only Principle, LNCS 12621, pp. 104–125, 2021.
https://doi.org/10.1007/978-3-030-79851-2_6

Although it is recognized that Member States are digitising their public administrations to save time, reduce costs, increase transparency, and improve both data quality and the delivery of public services, the Commission has confirmed that digital public services are not yet a reality in the European Union, therefore a coordinated approach is necessary at all levels, when legislation is prepared, when public administrations organise their business processes, when information is managed and when IT systems are developed to implement public services. Otherwise the existing digital fragmentation will be intensified, which would endanger the offering of connected public services across the EU [6, 7].

In this context, this study will therefore deal with the Italian legal experience of implementing the OOP. First, it will seek to show that the once-only principle is strictly related to the constitutional principles of the Italian legal system in the field of public administration and constitutes a natural development of them.

Secondly, that many regulatory applications of the OOP can already be found in the internal legal system, starting from the non-recent rules concerning self-certifications. In this sector, the Italian legal system has gone from authorizing the use of self-certifications to complete de-certification and ex officio acquisition of data and documents by public entities.

In more recent times, copious legislation has developed regarding the digitization of administrative procedures, with the attempt to make interconnected public databases. It will therefore appear evident that the country is still lacking in terms coordination, the IT governance being divided between central and local authorities.

Finally, particular attention will be dedicated to the area of public procurement, also indicated by the European Commission, at the start of its Communication on the European Interoperability Framework, as the sector which accounts for over a quarter of total employment and contributes to approximately a fifth of the EU's GDP, and therefore plays a key role in the digital single market as a regulator, services provider and employer [6], especially in critical times, as in the current recovery period after the Covid-19 pandemic.

2 The Constitutional Basis of the OOP in Italy, as a Fundamental Rule of Administrative Activity and Organization

In the Italian legal system, the OOP reflects some general principles concerning organization and administrative activity: the rational organization and the correct performance of the administrative function is aimed at the protection of the position of private individuals [8, 9]. It is well known that procedural complications lend themselves to illegal negotiations [10–12] and they could represent a risk for impartiality and thus, organizational measures, in addition to behavioural ones, are indicated as fundamental to prevent corruption in public administrations [13].

Many studies have described the administrative function as constituted by organizational elements (function conceived as competence, office: from the Latin meaning of "officium", "munus") intrinsically connected with dynamic action (function as public purpose and function as carrying out of targeted activity) [14, 15].

The once-only principle can play an essential role in regulating the organization of bodies, as much as the dynamic development of their action from a service perspective [16–19]. OOP is aimed at increasing service levels, reducing costs, simplifying, but also improving the integrity of the administration and more fully satisfying the needs of citizens. It is therefore in close correlation with the institutional principle of functionality of public entities.

A general "right to good administration" is today declared by the Charter of Fundamental Rights of the European Union (having the same legal value as the Treaties: Art. 6 T.E.U.). If the art. 41 of this Charter literally refers to the need for administrative decisions to be taken impartially, fairly and within a reasonable time, many have provided a broad interpretation of it. This includes the duty of loyalty and the spirit of collaboration of the administrations with citizens, according to an approach of "administrative simplicity" which responds to the needs of substantial legality: burdens that are not strictly indispensable for the administration to carry out its service function should not be imposed on the citizen [20–22].

The principle of good administration (more than the right[1], or at least a duty[2]) is included in the Italian Constitution in the cardinal principles of the rule of law, impartiality and good performance (Art. 97 of the Constitution), as well as in the fundamental principles of the democratic State (art. 2 and 3 of the Constitution). In addition, numerous "programmatic rules" place proactive tasks on the Republic (from its highest institutions - the Parliament and the Government, as well as, on the implementation level, its executive institutions - the administrative offices)[3] to favour the implementation of the principle.

The criteria of economy, effectiveness and efficiency, set out in the general law on the administrative procedure are based on these constitutional rules, in addition to the prohibition of unjustified aggravation of the procedure[4]. and they represent an expression

---

[1] If considered as a right, it would necessarily correspond - in Italian law - to an action that can be brought before a judge. The principle of good administration includes, however, rules substantial and procedural, not all executable, to which administrative activity should conform in a modern democratic system of law [22].

[2] It should also be remembered the theories regarding a duty of good administration, including those operative rules which, although not always expressed, are not less relevant and no less binding for the administration, because imposed by the real and actual need to draw from the goal imposed by law [23]. The authors describe these "extra legem" rules (good administration directives) as flexible elements which represent an immanent necessity in this system, due to the flexibility necessary for administrative action in relation to the purposes to be achieved, and for the ineptitude of the written norm to adequately foresee all the situations that are determined in order for the purposes themselves. The Italian administrative justice traditionally sanctions the violation of this "ius non scriptum" (unwritten law) which guides the action of the public administration through judgment on excess power [24].

[3] Italian scholars refer to the programmatic rules of the Constitution as a "promised revolution", still to be implemented (as directives) with regulatory activity. In this sense, the discipline of public administration cannot be derived from Articles 97 and 98 only, but from the entire Constitution [25–28].

[4] Art. 1, par. 2 of the Law no. 241 of 1990, according to which the public administration cannot aggravate the procedure except for extraordinary and motivated needs imposed by the conduct of the proceeding.

of the institutional principles of proportionality[5] and reasonableness (attributable to the theories of procedural rationality) of public action [29, 30].

According to scholars, the prohibition of aggravation – as one of the principles of the "minimum procedure" [31] – constitutes a fairness or good faith canon, whose normative explanation is to prevent any harassment in contact between public authority and citizens, with the aim of guaranteeing the values of the person safeguarded at the constitutional level (Art. 2 and 3 of the Constitution) and, at the same time, enhance the spirit of collaboration that must connote the activity of the public official (Art. 98 of the Constitution) [32].

The EU legal framework and the Italian constitutional principles therefore represent a solid basis from which to derive the rule of legal civilization, according to which users (citizens and other public offices) must not be repeatedly requested by the administration to provide data already produced to it. In other words, the once-only principle, as a fundamental rule of simplification, responding to a public and private interest of good administration [9, 30], tends to avoid duplication of requests for unnecessary and overabundant documentary mailings, which represent inefficient and uneconomical operations for the administration and which generate intolerance and distrust in citizens, often causing them harm.

In literature, the principle recalls the famous novel "The Castle" by Franz Kafka, in which the irrational management of documents by public servants causes an extreme discouragement in citizens who meet them: "The woman opened the cupboard at once, while K. and the mayor watched. It was stuffed with papers, and when it was opened two large bundles of files fell out, tied up as you might tie up bundles of firewood. The woman flinched in alarm. 'Try lower down, lower down,' said the mayor, directing operations from his bed. The woman, gathering up the files in her arms, obediently cleared everything out of the cupboard to get to the papers at the bottom. The room was already half full of papers. [...] 'I don't think the files are going to be found,' said K. 'Not found?' cried the mayor. 'Mizzi, please search a little faster! For a start, however, I can tell you the story without files..." [33].

In the Italian experience, the formalism of the procedures is often justified also by the lack of mutual trust that characterizes the relationship between citizens and public administrations. The former are inclined to exploit the shortcomings of the offices to their advantage (for example, the high rate of non-veracity of the self-certifications, which is also favored by the absence of controls); the latter are often not very credible as regards the information provided and inclined to disregard the credit lines generated. The same legislator tends to set rigid and binding rules (for example in terms of conflict of interest) that seem to convey the idea that the public administration cannot be trusted [34].

In fact, the rules on administrative action and organization (such as the prohibition of procedural aggravation and therefore the once-only principle) are set to protect the

---

[5] The proportionality principle is stated by Art. 5 of the T.E.U. and from its Protocol no. 2 on the application of the principles of subsidiarity and proportionality. Here we can summarize it according to the liberal formula, which in Italy can be traced back to the studies of the early nineteenth century by Gian Domenico Romagnosi, of the "minimum means", that is the pursuit of the public interest with the least possible sacrifice of the interests of citizens.

dignity of the individual and to guarantee his full development (see Art. 3, par. 1 of the Constitution), not only as mechanisms for increasing functionality and administrative efficiency, according to the logic of good performance (Art. 97 of the Constitution) [32]. Thus, they assume a double role, of organizational and functional principles with which the public entity ("ex parte principis") must comply, but also of protection of citizens' rights towards power ("ex parte civis") [22, 35]. Conversely, acts of maladministration constitute a potential violation of the fundamental rights of the individual and the constitutional principle of solidarity (Art. 2 of the Constitution) [36].

3   A First Regulatory Application: Self-certifications and Ex Officio Acquisition of Data and Documents

In Italy, a first, temperate, application of the once-only principle can be found in the self-certification legislation. Since the reform of 1968[6], it has been possible to prove with declarations, also contextual to the application, signed by the interested party in place of the normal certificates, the date and place of birth, residence, citizenship, the enjoyment of political rights, the state of celibate, married or widowed, family status, existence in life, birth of son, death of spouse, ascendant or descendant, position for the purposes of military obligations and registration in registers or lists kept by the public administration[7]. The law also introduced temporarily substitutive declarations, substitutive declarations of the deed of notoriety and proof of date and place of birth, residence, unmarried, married or widowed state and any other state or personal quality by showing identity documents[8] [37]. Previously, the legislation already provided that the requirements of citizenship, good conduct and the absence of criminal records were ascertained ex officio by the administration which must issue the provision. On the other hand, the administration could not request documents or certificates from the private individual concerning facts and circumstances that were attested in documents already in its possession or that it itself was required to certify[9].

From a legal point of view, self-certifications can be associated to the scheme of liberalization from administrative authorizations. In the past, certifications represented the only suitable tool to create legal certainty and, therefore, to legitimize the activities and behaviours that in this declaration found a prerequisite. Through self-certification, the public title is replaced by an act formed independently by the citizen concerned, through a private declaration, which is recognized as having the same validity and effectiveness as the certification act issued by the public authority [38].

Although self-certification does not imply the total exclusion of sending information already held by the administration, nevertheless it has represented a significant simplification and lightening of the burden to present documents [39], especially when the automatic exchange of content between the various "static" archives of public administrations was not yet possible, unlike "dynamic" archives of today's databases [40].

---

[6] Law of 4 January 1968, no. 15, which states rules on administrative documentation and on the legalization and authentication of signatures.

[7] Art. 2 of the Law no. 15 of 1968.

[8] Respectively, Articles 3, 4, 5 of the Law no. 15 of 1968.

[9] Art. 2 of the Presidential Decree of 2 August 1957, no. 678.

Following further reforms, the legislation was taken up, reordered and expanded by the Consolidated Act of the laws and regulations of 2000 on administrative documentation [41] which provided for the general prohibition for public administrations to issue and request the production of certificates [42] accompanied by the obligation to automatically acquire the information subject to substitute declarations as well as all data and documents that are already in their possession[10]. Especially the original version of Art. 43 of the Act presented a structure very close to the European definition of the once-only principle[11] [43].

The binding force of these rules lies, moreover, in the presence of specific sanctions for officials who do not accept self-certifications or who, on the contrary, request and receive certificates[12], in addition to the limitation of the validity and usability of certificates issued by the public administration only in relations between private subjects[13].

In this regard, however, the consequence of the spontaneous presentation by the citizen of certificates for the initiation of an administrative proceeding is not clear. If the rule on decertification is interpreted rigorously, it could lead to the result - quite contrary to the idea of simplification - of invalidity of the decision adopted by the proceeding administration based on the illegitimately produced certificate. This conclusion has been discarded, since the rules on decertification are primarily aimed at protecting the user who submits the application in order to reduce the bureaucratic burden on him [43].

With the 2005 reform, it was also included in the general law on the administrative procedure the obligation of ex officio acquisition of the documents necessary for the investigation certifying deeds, facts, qualities and subjective states, when they are in the possession of the proceeding administration or which are held, institutionally, by

---

[10] Art. 43, par. 1 of the Presidential Decree of 28 December 2000, no. 445, as amended by Art. 15 of the Law of 12 November 2011, no. 183, which states that public administrations and managers of public services are required to acquire ex officio the information which is the subject of the substitutive declarations referred to in articles 46 and 47 of the same Decree, as well as all data and documents held by public administrations, upon indication by the interested party, of the essential elements for finding the information or data requested, or to accept the substitute declaration produced by the interested party.

[11] Art. 43, par. 1 of the Presidential Decree no. 445 of 2000, in its original version, stated that public administrations and managers of public services could not request deeds or certificates relating to states, personal qualities and facts listed in art. 46 of the same Decree, or which in any case they were required to certify. In place of these deeds or certificates, the subjects indicated were required to acquire the relevant information ex officio, upon indication, by the interested party, of the competent administration and of the elements essential for the retrieval of the information or of the requested data, or to accept the substitute declaration produced by the interested party.

[12] Art. 74 of the Presidential Decree no. 445 of 2000, which punishes as a violation of official duties the non-acceptance of the substitute declarations of certification or deed of notoriety made pursuant to the provisions of the Decree, the request and acceptance of certificates or notarial deeds; the refusal by the employee in charge of accepting the attestation of states, personal qualities and facts through the presentation of an identification document; the request and production, respectively by civil status officers and health directors, of the certificate of assistance at birth for the purpose of training the birth certificate; the issue of certificates that do not comply with the provisions of Art. 40, par. 2, of the same Decree.

[13] Art. 40, par. 1 of the Presidential Decree no. 445 of 2000.

other public administrations [44]. The law only allows the proceeding administration, collaborating with private citizens, to request from interested parties the elements which are strictly necessary for the search for documents[14]. On the other hand, the law allows the suspension of the deadline for the conclusion of the procedure only for the acquisition of information or certifications relating to facts, states or qualities not attested in documents already in possession of the administration itself or not directly obtainable from other public administrations[15].

The ex officio assessment, expression of the non-aggravation and economy principles, as an ordinary and prevalent method for the acquisition of evidence by the administrations, represents a fundamental instrument, which simplifies to the widest possible extent, up to practically eliminating them, the obligations to provide certain data to the administration, while ensuring that the data acquired are fully reliable [42]. Rare judgments of administrative justice on this subject have underlined the relationship between the rules on the ex officio assessment and the principles of non-aggravation and cost-effectiveness, as well as the principle of "informality", initially present in the draft law on administrative procedure prepared by the Commission chaired by Mario Nigro [45, 46].

If effectively respected, the obligation to acquire ex officio data and documents would represent the overcoming of both certifications and self-certifications and substitute declarations, as perfect applications of the once-only principle, with the further positive effect of the greater degree of certainty for the administration as the certification cycle would be completely exhausted within the public organization [38].

4 The OOP and Public Systems Interoperability

The practical application of self-certification and ex officio document acquisition necessarily requires efficient systems of communication and exchange of information between paper archives and databases [47]. In fact, there are many public and private interests which are compared with reference to administrative data: the interest of the proceeding administration in the safe storage of its documents, the interest of other authorities in acquiring public information quickly and efficiently, the citizen's interest in avoiding providing administrations with duplicate information for different administrative procedures, but to provide data only once for the entire administrative system interconnected on the network [48].

According to the definition given by the European Commission, when we talk about interconnected networks we indicate a (computer) system within which two or more terminals are able to communicate and therefore exchange information between themselves in an automated way, thus allowing access to data stored on a system other than the one requesting the information itself [5].

By applying this paradigm within administrations, a public entity could have access to information held by another one without the need - at least technical - for any interaction between officials. It would be enough for the proceeding office to request, through its own

---

[14] Art. 18, par. 2 of the Law no. 241 of 1990, as amended by Art. 3 of the Law-Decree of 14 March 2005, no. 35.

[15] Art. 2, par. 7 of the Law no. 241 of 1990.

computer system, the data it needs, and it could automatically retrieve the information requested by the system made available by another public administration [40].

Thus, launching a strategy to implement interoperability, the European Commission proposed it as a key factor in making a digital transformation possible, that allows administrative entities to electronically exchange, amongst themselves and with citizens and businesses, meaningful information in ways that are understood by all parties. It includes the four fundamental aspects that impact the delivery of digital public services: legal issues (legal interoperability), by ensuring that legislation does not impose unjustified barriers to the reuse of data in different policy areas; organisational aspects (organisational interoperability), by requesting formal agreements on the conditions applicable to cross-organisational interactions; data/semantic concerns (semantic interoperability), by ensuring the use of common descriptions of exchanged data; and technical challenges (technical interoperability), by setting up the necessary information systems environment to allow an uninterrupted flow of bits and bytes [6, 7].

In order to reach the effective possibility for citizens, institutions and companies to provide data only once to the administration that needs to have it, also according to the Italian Court of Auditors it is therefore necessary to apply an "organic approach" [49], which involves the creation of information systems able to guarantee interoperability, that is the effective and automated exchange of data and information, both internally between offices of the same administration, and externally between different public entities [50].

The possibility of correlating the collected data multiplying the information capacity of the consultations and the possibility of exchanges between different databases are considered features of the electronic processing systems that bring undeniable advantages for an orderly and efficient performance of administrative activity. The easiest access to information, the reduction of costs and times, the elimination of duplications of data collections, the uniformity of the techniques that can be adopted and the simplification of the controls that the public administration could carry out on a large scale thanks to the existence of the databases, constitute great advantages of any technically organized documentation [51].

Interoperability is defined by the Italian legislator as characteristic of an information system, whose interfaces are public and open, to interact automatically with other information systems for the exchange of information and the provision of services[16]. It constitutes an indispensable prerequisite for promoting and accelerating the circulation of public evidences without resorting to the traditional instrument of certificates [42]. The simplification of the document burdens is therefore closely related to the rules on digitization, starting from the general provision according to which public administrations use in internal relations, in those with other administrations and with private individuals information and communication technology, ensuring the interoperability of the systems and the integration of service processes between the various administrations in compliance with the Guidelines[17] [47].

---

[16] Art. 1, par. 1, lett. dd of the Legislative Decree of 7 March 2005, no. 82, Digital Administration Code, added by Art. 1, par. 1, lett. g of the Legislative Decree of 26 August 2016, no. 179.

[17] Art. 12, par. 2 of the Legislative Decree no. 82 of 2005.

In organizing their own activity autonomously, the same administrations are required to use information and communication technologies to achieve the objectives of efficiency, effectiveness, economy, impartiality, transparency, simplification and participation in compliance with the principles of equality and non-discrimination, as well as for the effective recognition of the rights of citizens and businesses in accordance with the objectives indicated in the three-year Plan for information technology in the public administration[18]. One of the three fundamental «paradigms» of the 2019–2021 Plan is precisely the once-only principle, according to which public administrations must avoid asking citizens and businesses for information already provided [52]. For public procurement the interoperability of the platforms is indicated as a key factor to guarantee quality, uniqueness and certainty of data [53, 54].

In this context, information technology has moved from a simple tool to support procedures to an enabling factor for innovation and development, with a strategic role in contemporary society: the once-only principle makes it possible to rethink the control and monitoring processes using all the potential offered by ICT technologies [49].

Data governance aimed at guaranteeing uniformity in management through a common system design, is therefore essential for full interoperability, "the key to a holistic approach" (as we said, technical and organizational but, above all, semantic interoperability which requires a common language that allows systems to communicate with each other) [7, 50, 55]. The Italian Constitution, as amended in 2001, takes due consideration of this aspect, entrusting the legislative and IT information coordination of state, regional and local administration data to the exclusive legislative competence of the State[19] [48, 56].

Unfortunately, it must be noted that in the Italian administrative system, characterized by sections of accentuated centralism and sections of strong decentralization [48], this essential function of coordination has so far been carried out in an at least fluctuating manner – so that it has been described as a "harnessed giant" [57]. The evolution of governance in the field of public IT has been widely described, with continuous transformations in terms of the subjects involved and related institutional structures, competences and assigned resources, organizational models adopted. It can provide useful elements to understand the public response to the evolving market of citizens and businesses [49].

Since the nineties, the need for a unitary direction to improve innovation in the public sector was evident. In 1993 an Authority for Information Technology in the Public Administration (AIPA) was established[20], which became in 2003 the National Center for IT in the Public Administration (CNIPA). From 1 January 2004, the CNIPA incorporated the Technical Center for the RUPA (Unitary Network of Public Administration).

In the years 2001–2006 a Minister for Innovation and Technologies was appointed, with authority for the coordination and direction of the Government policy in matters of development of ICT and, at the same time, set up a Department for the Innovation of Public Administration. In the years 2008–2011, the Innovation and Technologies Department was entrusted to the Minister for the Public Administration.

---

[18] Art. 12, par. 1 of the Legislative Decree no. 82 of 2005.

[19] Art. 117, par. 1, lett. r of the Constitution.

[20] In implementation of the Legislative Decree of 12 February 1993, no. 39.

In 2009 CNIPA was transformed into DigitPA, a public body charged with design, technical and operational functions, and with the mission of contributing to the creation of value for citizens and businesses through the implementation of the digital administration.

Subsequently, within the framework of the strategies outlined by the European Digital Agenda, in 2012 the establishment of a "Control Room" for the implementation of the Italian Digital Agenda[21] was provided. The Agency for Digital Italy (AgID)[22] was also established, to support the implementation of the Digital Agenda and therefore to direct the innovative digital evolution. AgID took over the functions of DigitPA and the Innovation and Technologies Department.

In 2016, the "Control room" was replaced by an Extraordinary Commissioner for the implementation of the Digital Agenda, with operational coordination functions of public entities operating in the field of ICT[23]. The powers of the Extraordinary Commissioner were joined by a "Digital Transformation Team", composed of selected experts also outside the public administration. The Commissioner and the Team ended their mandate in 2019.

In this long wake of reforms, lastly, a Minister for Innovation and Technologies was appointed to the new Government. At the same time, from 1 January 2020, the Department for Digital Transformation[24] was restored, as a general structure of the Prime Minister's Office, aimed at ensuring, also through technological-interoperable architectural choices, the necessary operational coordination between the State administrations involved, in various capacities, in the pursuit of the Government's objectives regarding innovation and digitalisation. The new Department makes use of the experts who already formed the Digital Transformation Team.

Despite the effort of continuous improvement and reorganization, the need to overcome the fragmentation and overlaps of governance in this field remains, given that other institution such as the Department of the Public Function, the Ministry of Economy and Finance, the Ministry for Economic Development, the AgID, the National Anti-Corruption Authority (A.N.AC.), the Guarantors for the protection of personal data continue to maintain relevant data coordination functions in their sectors of activity.

Recent reforms to the Digital Administration Code have required the conclusion of framework agreements in order to share data between certifying bodies, other public administrations and private individuals, in the absence of which the Government can intervene by establishing a deadline within which administrations they make the data available, accessible and usable. Failure to fulfil the obligation to share data is sanctioned as failure to achieve a specific result by the managers responsible for the structures and leads to reductions in the remuneration[25].

---

[21] Art. 47 of the Law of 4 April 2012, no. 35.

[22] Law-Decree of 22 June 2012, no. 83.

[23] Legislative Decree no. 179 of 2016.

[24] Decree of the Prime Minister (d.P.C.M.) of 19 June 2019.

[25] Art. 50, par. 2-ter, of the Legislative Decree no. 82 of 2005, introduced by the Law-Decree 19 May 2020, no. 34; Art. 50, par. 3-ter, of the Legislative Decree no. 82 of 2005, introduced by the Law-Decree 16 July 2020, no. 76, converted by Law 11 September 2020, no. 120.

For years the legislator has issued numerous tools to try to implement interoperability between public databases. At European level the Commission has established and periodically updates a European Interoperability Framework, as a commonly agreed approach to the delivery of European public services in an interoperable manner, which defines basic interoperability guidelines in the form of common principles, models and recommendations [3]. As it is not possible to review all the tools provided in specific sectors here (a focus on public procurement will be carried out in the following paragraph), we can however identify two main interoperability systems envisaged at a general organization level of public administrations by the Digital Administration Code.

From a technical point of view, the first infrastructure that addressed the interoperability needs was the RUPA, created by AIPA, later replaced by the Public Connectivity System (SPC) which defines both the enterprise architecture of the Italian PA (i.e. the reference system for linking inter-administrative operational processes with the information systems that support them) both the subsidiary, coordination and governance actions[26] [58, 59]. It was further developed in 2016, when it was clarified in the Digital Administration Code that the SPC is established as a set of technological infrastructures and technical rules that ensures interoperability between the information systems of public administrations, allows the information and IT coordination of data between central administrations, regional and local and between them and the systems of the European Union and is open for accession by public service operators and private entities[27] [50].

The SPC is thus a tool aimed at overcoming the barriers between administrations, with a view to full decertification, to make it possible to fully share and acquire data ex officio: the law establishes that exchanges of IT documents carried out within the framework of the SPC, created through the application cooperation and in compliance with the related safety technical procedures and rules, constitute valid documentary transmission for all legal purposes[28].

A further important tool aimed at promoting the knowledge and use of the information assets held, for institutional purposes, by administrations and managers of public services, as well as for the sharing of data between the subjects who have the right to access it for the purpose of simplifying administrative requirements of citizens and businesses, is the National Digital Data Platform (PDND) governed by Art. 50-ter of the Digital Administration Code, recently reformulated by the Law-Decree for simplification and digital innovation[29].

Promoted by the Prime Minister's Office, it consists of a technological infrastructure that makes it possible to interoperate information systems and public databases, through accreditation, identification and management of the authorization levels of the subjects authorized to operate on it, as well as the collection and storage of information relating to

---

[26] Introduced in the Digital Administration Code (Articles 72 et seq. of the Legislative Decree no. 82 of 2005) by the Legislative Decree of 4 April 2006, no. 159.

[27] Art. 73, par. 1, of the Legislative Decree no. 82 of 2005, as amended by the Legislative Decree no. 179 of 2016.

[28] Art. 76 of the Legislative Decree no. 82 of 2005.

[29] Art. 50-ter, par. 1 of the Legislative Decree no. 82 of 2005, as amended by the Law-Decree no. 76 of 2020.

accesses and transactions made through it[30]. It was first developed by the Digital Transformation Team as Data and Analytics Framework (DAF); since 2019 it was entrusted to the new public company, PagoPA Spa[31]. The Department for Digital Transformation has the task of supervising the strategic objectives of the PagoPA company [60].

The new regulation provides that, in the first application phase, the PDND ensures priority interoperability with the information system of the Indicator of the Equivalent Economic Situation (ISEE), with the National Registry of the Resident Population (ANPR) and with the Revenue Agency databases. The AgID is in charge of adopting guidelines for the definition of technological standards and safety, accessibility, availability and interoperability criteria for platform management[32].

The Law-Decree for simplification and digital innovation of 2020 has also introduced a National Data Strategy, to be adopted with a Decree of the Prime Minister, which identifies the types, limits, purposes and methods of making available aggregated and anonymised public data[33].

5   The OOP in Public Procurement

The Digital Single Market Strategy for Europe launched by the European Commission in 2015 already indicated the need to apply the once-only principle in public procurement, which represents about 19% of the Union's GDP. Given the few and fragmented possibilities of contact between public administration, citizens and businesses, the Commission estimated the economies of scale brought about by the electronic reform of public contracts at 50 billion euros per year. Therefore, the objectives of administrative simplification and efficiency by digitizing public procurement appear immediately closely related: "The Commission will present a new e-Government Action Plan 2016–2020 which will include (i) making the interconnection of business registers a reality by 2017, (ii) launching in 2016 an initiative with the Member States to pilot the 'Once-Only' principle; (iii) extending and integrating European and national portals to work towards a 'Single Digital Gateway' to create a user friendly information system for citizens and business and (iv) accelerating Member States' transition towards full e-procurement and interoperable e-signatures" [5].

In this sense, the potential in terms of economic benefits of digitalisation of public administrations has been highlighted for a long time, if it is conceived not so much as a simple transposition of papery procedures into computerised (which would involve a mere transfer of the criticalities of the former in the latter), but as an opportunity to radically reorganize and simplify the same [34, 53]: in particular the digitalisation of the public procurement sector [61, 62] can play a strategic role for the economic and social increase especially in critical times, for instance capturing the effects of structural renewal of the impact of the Covid-19 emergency [63].

---

[30] Art. 50-ter, par. 2 of the Legislative Decree no. 82 of 2005.

[31] Law-Decree of 14 December 2018, no. 135.

[32] Art. 50-ter, par. 2 of the Legislative Decree no. 82 of 2005, as amended by the Law-Decree no. 76 of 2020.

[33] Art. 50-ter, par. 4 of the Legislative Decree no. 82 of 2005, as amended by the Law-Decree no. 76 of 2020.

In addition, the OECD has suggested the digitalization of public procurement for numerous other reasons, in terms of improving efficiency, transparency and anti-corruption [64]. In particular, the OECD highlights the purposes of e-procurement to increase "transparency, facilitate access to public tenders, reduce direct interaction between procurement officials and companies, increasing outreach and competition, and allow for easier detection of irregularities and corruption, such as bid rigging schemes. The digitalisation of procurement processes strengthens internal anti-corruption controls and detection of integrity breaches, and it provides audit services trails that may facilitate investigation activities" [65].

With reference to cross-border trade, the once-only principle also appears as one of the main reasons for the European Union's decision to establish a single digital gateway to reduce bureaucratic burdens towards all Member States, with the aim of simplifying administrative procedures for citizens and businesses within the single market [66, 67]. Already the Directive 2014/24/EU of the European Parliament and of the Council of 26 February 2014 on public procurement referred at least implicitly to the OOP, providing for the establishment of the single European tender document [67].

With the Union Action Plan for e-Government 2016–2020, the Commission programmed to gradually introduce the 'digital by default' and 'once-only' principles, eInvoicing and eProcurement and to assess the implication of a possible implementation of the 'no legacy' (action no. 6); to launch a pilot on the once-only principle for business (action no. 13); to assess the possibility of applying the once-only principle for citizens in a cross-border context (action no. 18) [68].

At the beginning of 2020, the Italian Government has repeatedly stated that it intends to focus on the once-only principle for a strong simplification of bureaucracy in the post-emergency phase [69].

According to European Commission, "reliable data are essential to prepare appropriate policy responses. The digital transformation, the growing wealth of data in general and the availability of open data standards offer opportunities to create better analytics for needs-driven policy-making and warning systems to signal and tackle corruption in public procurement. [...] Access to public procurement data should enable the dialogue with civil society and holds governments more accountable. [...] To this end, setting up publicly accessible contract registers is strongly recommended, providing transparency on awarded contracts and their amendments. [...] New digital technologies offer great opportunities to streamline and simplify the procurement process through the roll-out of electronic public procurement. [...] However, the full benefits of e-procurement will only be captured if the whole public procurement process undergoes digital transformation". Its Communication on public procurement includes among the specific actions: new procurement standard forms to improve the collection of data; publicly accessible contract registers; implementation of the European Single Procurement Document, the once-only principle and electronic invoicing in the Member States [62].

In response to these European requests, the once-only principle was recently introduced in the Italian Public Contracts Code, which defines it as the principle according to which each data is provided only once to a single information system, and cannot be requested by other systems or databases, but is made available by the receiving information system. This principle applies to data relating to the planning of works, services and supplies, as well as to all the procedures for awarding and implementing public contracts subject to the Code, and to those excluded from it, in whole or in part, whenever reporting obligations to a database are imposed by the same Code[34]. From the linguistic point of view, the Council of State made some comments on the draft of this Decree, which initially reported the principle of "univocità" of sending data. It seemed preferable instead to refer to the principle of "unicità" of sending data, since it is a quantitative (one-time sending) and non-qualitative (sending data with unambiguous meaning) requirement for the dispatch [70]. This appears a logical consequence: evidently, in order to have unequivocal data, it is primarily essential to have a unique transmission of them.

The regulatory definition was introduced with the aim of significantly reducing the administrative burden for entities generally subject to the so-called "statistical harassment", or to the uncoordinated request for data by various administrations [71], and therefore primarily to avoid duplication of mailings by the contracting authorities - especially for the officials responsible for the procedure - to whom a considerable amount of information and publication obligations are imposed for each award procedure started (and, for some kinds of contract) concluded and executed.

Unfortunately, today there is no complete and organic recognition of the information obligations imposed on the contracting authorities. The direct channel for sending data to A.N.AC. is SIMOG (Tender Monitoring Identification System) and SmartCIG (simplified channel for low-value contracts) [72]. At the same time, in absence of coordination between these two information systems, the publication of the data is mandatory (in part coinciding with those of SIMOG and SmartCIG) on the websites of the contracting authorities [73]. Other types of data must be transmitted to other central authorities such as the Ministry of Economy and Finance and the Ministry of Infrastructure and Transport. Recently A.N.AC. asked for a complete rationalization of the rules on administrative transparency in public contracts [54].

In order to prevent this principle from remaining a "chimera" [74] it is important, first of all, the complete digitization of the documentation relating to public contracts for the production, from the beginning of each procedure, of digital native data, which feeds the sector databases exhaustively and correctly. Numerous provisions of the Public Contracts Code already lay in this direction (Articles 44, 212 and Art. 213 which we will examine below)[35], although they have not yet been fully implemented, in addition

---

[34] Art. 3, par. 1, lett. ggggg-bis of the Legislative Decree of 18 April 2016, no. 50, Public Contracts Code, added by Art. 4 of the Legislative Decree of 19 April 2017, no. 56.

[35] Art. 44 of the Legislative Decree no. 50 of 2016 states that within one year from the date of entry into force of the same Decree, by Decree of the Minister for Simplification and Public Administration, in consultation with the Minister of Infrastructure and Transport and the Minister of Economy and Finance, after consulting the Agency for Digital Italy (AGID) as well as the Privacy Authority, the procedures for digitizing the procedures of all public contracts should have been defined, also through the interconnection for interoperability of data of public administrations. Best practices should also be defined regarding organizational and work methodologies, programming and planning methodologies, also referring to the identification of relevant data, their collection, management and processing, IT, telematic and technological support solutions. Art. 212, par. 1, lett. d, of the same Decree orders the creation of a control body in the Prime Minister's Office to promote the creation, in collaboration with the competent subjects, of a national plan on the subject of electronic purchase procedures, in order to spread the use of IT tools and to digitize the stages of the purchase process.

to the recent European Regulation which, starting from 2023, require the adoption of standard digital forms for the above-threshold assignments. The Recital no. 8 of this Regulation states that "notices are electronic files rather than paper documents. In order to comply with the 'once only' principle in e-government, and thus reduce administrative burden and increase data reliability, and to facilitate voluntary publication of notices whose value is below the EU threshold or which are based on framework agreements, such standard forms should be established that can be automatically filled-in with information from previous notices, technical specifications, tenders, contracts, national administrative registries and other sources of data. Ultimately, such forms should no longer need to be filled-in manually, but should be automatically generated by software systems" [75]. The goal, recalled by the National Anti-Corruption Authority, is therefore to achieve an automatic interconnection between all the publication platforms of the documents (European, national and of the individual contracting authorities) and the central databases [54].

Since 2010 the National Public Contracts Database (BDNCP), managed by A.N.AC., was established as a specific tool for interoperability in this sector[36]. The institutional purpose of BDNCP [76] is indicated in the collection of all the data relating to public contracts contained in the existing databases, also at a territorial level, in order to guarantee unified accessibility, transparency, publicity and traceability of the tender procedures and their preparatory and subsequent phases[37].

For public works, the law also provides for the conclusion of agreements between the public entities managing databases on how to collect and exchange information, to ensure compliance with the once-only principle and reducing administrative burdens[38]. In implementation of the Decree, A.N.AC. and the Ministry of Economy and Finance

---

[36] Art. 62-bis of the Legislative Decree no. 82 of 2005, added by Art. 44 of the Legislative Decree of 30 December 2010, no. 235 introduced the National Public Contracts Database (BDNCP) managed by the National Anti-corruption Authority, to facilitate the reduction of administrative burdens deriving from information obligations and to ensure the effectiveness, transparency and real-time control of administrative action for the allocation of public expenditure on works, services and supplies, also in order to respect legality and the correct action of the public administration and to prevent corruption.

[37] Art. 213, par. 8, of the Legislative Decree no. 50 of 2016.

[38] Art. 213, par. 8, of the Legislative Decree no. 50 of 2016 lays down for public works that A.N.AC., the Ministry of Economy and Finance and the Ministry of Infrastructure and Transport, the Prime Minister's Office and the Regions and Autonomous Provinces as managers of the computerized systems referred to in Art. 29, par. 4 of the same Decree conclude an agreement on the methods for collecting and exchanging information within the National Public Contracts Database and other relevant databases, in order to ensure compliance with the once-only principle and the reduction of administrative burdens for the effective monitoring from planning to construction of the works and the traceability of the related financial flows or the agreement of the fulfilments in terms of preventive transparency. It also states that, without prejudice to the autonomy of the National Database of Economic Operators referred to in Art. 81 of the same Code, A.N.AC. and the Ministry of Infrastructure and Transport agree on the methods for exchanging information to guarantee the function of preventing corruption and protecting the legality of the Authority and at the same time avoid overlapping of competences and optimize the use of data in the interest of the use of the same by businesses and contracting authorities.

concluded a Framework Agreement on 19 December 2018 for the exchange of knowledge, data, analysis methodologies and good practices and for the full deployment of institutional synergies.

Since the establishment of the new National Anti-Corruption Authority in 2014, the management and analysis of the databases it owns has appeared among its most important functions for the prevention and contrast of corruption and the promotion of efficiency [77–80]. On 18 October 2018 the BNDCP won the first prize in the Better Governance through Procurement Digitalization competition, National Contract Register category, having successfully assessed its scope, given that "there are essentially no value thresholds for being included" and its interoperability with other systems: "6 different systems send data to the Italian contract register and 10 systems take data from the contract register and use it elsewhere" [81]. Moreover, some criticisms of the setting up and management of the same database have been raised, especially from the point of view of accessibility to its data, but also of the lack of coordination with other information systems [82].

The Digital Administration Code places the BDNCP among the Databases of National Interest[39], unitary information systems that consider the different institutional and territorial levels and that guarantee the alignment of information and access to the same by public administrations concerned. These information systems must adhere to the minimum characteristics of security, accessibility and interoperability[40]. The information contained therein must be made available by the administrations that manage it according to the safety and management standards and criteria defined in the Guidelines, also through the National Digital Data Platform (PDND)[41]. According to scholars, the organizational rules on Databases of National Interest, although of a sectorial nature and above all referring to the central administration, represent the first and most relevant nucleus of provisions that pertain to the constitutional principle of IT coordination [56].

In this context, the once-only principle refers to the exchange of data especially between administrations, in order to simplify the flow of information that contracting authorities must send to the various agencies responsible for controlling and monitoring public procurement. In the absence of a total centralization of the cognitive function of the State - the Regions and autonomous Provinces, maintain the competence of monitoring the planning, entrusting and execution of contracts of regional importance or territorial entities[42] - as mentioned, coordination is essential and therefore interoperability between local and central databases[43].

---

[39] Art. 60, par. 3-bis, lett. c of the Legislative Decree no. 82 of 2005.

[40] Art. 60, par. 2 of the Legislative Decree no. 82 of 2005.

[41] Art. 60, par. 2-bis of the Legislative Decree no. 82 of 2005, as amended by the Law-Decree no. 76 of 2020.

[42] Art. 29, par. 3 of the Legislative Decree no. 50 of 2016.

[43] Art. 29, par. 4 of the Legislative Decree no. 50 of 2016, according to which for contracts and public investments of local or regional competence, the contracting authorities provide for the fulfilment of the information and advertising obligations set out in the same Decree, through the regional computerized systems and the e-procurement telematic platforms interconnected to them, ensuring the exchange of information and interoperability, with the databases of A.N.AC., the Ministry of Economy and Finance and the Ministry of Infrastructure and Transport.

For this reason the Public Contracts Code provides that between A.N.AC., the Ministry of Economy and Finance, the Ministry of Infrastructure and Transport and the Conference of Regions and Autonomous Provinces a general protocol is concluded to define the interoperability rules and the methods for exchanging data and documents between the respective databases, in compliance with the once-only principle[44]. The Protocol has not yet been adopted, although the desire to collaborate has been expressed in order to rationalize and simplify the obligations within the Conference of Regions and Autonomous Provinces [83]. The major problems of the system of regional observatories on public contracts have been recently highlighted by A.N.AC [54].

The law entrusts A.N.AC. with the important role of coordinating data: on the one hand, the Authority has to identify information on the public procurement subject to the publication obligation and the related transmission methods pursuant to the anticorruption legislation[45] and Public Contracts Code[46]; on the other hand, it defines the functioning of the Observatory for public contracts, as well as the mandatory information, terms and forms of communication that contracting authorities and contracting entities are required to transmit[47].

In exercising these responsibilities, A.N.AC. asked the legislator, in order to avoid overlapping of information burdens on the contracting authorities and to homogenize the system for acquiring information data from the BDNCP, considering that much of the information relating to the contractual changes referred to in Art. 106 of the Legislative Decree no. 50 of 2016 are already acquired by the Public Contracts Observatory pursuant to Art. 213, par. 9 of the same Code, to replace the precise indications on how to communicate such data and related documents[48]. This is to allow the same Authority to indicate the relevant information and the related transmission methods, in order to better organize the information flows with a view to complete digitalization and to manage the supervision of the variants in a more efficient manner by requiring only the transmission of the data necessary to process certain anomaly indices [84]. Further proposals for simplification and coordination of legislation addressed to Parliament and Government have been formulated by A.N.AC after the Covid-19 emergency [54].

---

[44] Art. 29, par. 4-bis of the Legislative Decree no. 50 of 2016.

[45] Art. 1, par. 32 of the Law of 6 November 2012, no. 190 states that with reference to every public procurement procedure, the contracting authorities are required to publish on their institutional websites: the proposing structure; the subject of the call; the list of operators invited to submit offers; the contractor; the award amount; the completion times of the work, service or supply; the amount of the amounts paid. Administrations transmit this information in digital format to A.N.AC., which publishes them on its website in a section freely with - available to all citizens, catalogued according to the type of contracting authority and by region. The Authority identifies with its resolution the relevant information and the related transmission methods.

[46] According to the art. 29, par. 1 of Legislative Decree no. 50 of 2016, all the documents of the contracting authorities relating to the planning of works, services and supplies, as well as to the procedures for the award of public service contracts, supplies and works, public planning competitions, ideas and concessions, must be published and updated on the profile of the client, in the "Transparent Administration" section with the application of the provisions of Legislative Decree 14 March 2013, no. 33.

[47] Art. 213, par. 9 of Legislative Decree no. 50 of 2016.

[48] Art. 106, par. 8 and par. 14.

Parallel to the BDNCP, the Public Contracts Code also establishes the National Economic Operators Database (BDOE) as an information tool which, if operational, would constitute a significant concentration of data in order to simplify and significantly reduce the time required to verify the requirements of the economic operators participating in the tender procedures[49]. Since this Code rule has never been implemented, various hypotheses have been put forward for the relaunch of the previous information management system for the documentation relating to the qualification of economic operators (AVCpass, held transiently by A.N.AC.[50]) [85], in order to achieve the automatic acquisition of proof documents with important benefits in terms of speed, efficiency of procedures and once-only principle for companies and contracting authorities [53, 54].

References

1. Position Paper on Definition of OOP and Situation in Europe, submitted to the European Commission on 30 April 2017
2. Krimmer, R., Kalvet, T., Toots, M., Cepilovs, A., Tambouris, A.: Exploring and demonstrating the once-only principle: a European perspective. In: 18th Annual International Conference on Digital Government Research, pp. 546–551. ACM (2017). https://doi.org/10.1145/3085228. 3085235
3. See more widely the chapter of this book: The OOP – definition & objectives (EU policies, European landscape & TOOP context)
4. Ministerial Declaration on e-Government, signed in Malmo (Sweden) on 19 November 2009
5. European Commission. Communication to the European Parliament, the Council, the European Economic and Social Committee and the Committee of the Regions, 6 May 2015, COM (2015) 192, A Digital Single Market Strategy for Europe (2015)
6. European Commission, Communication to the European Parliament, the Council, the European Economic and Social Committee and the Committee of the Regions, 23 March 2017, COM (2017) 134 European Interoperability Framework – Implementation Strategy.
7. European Commission. Communication to the European Parliament, the Council, the European Economic and Social Committee and the Committee of the Regions, 23 March 2017, COM (2017) 134 European Interoperability Framework – Implementation Strategy, Annex 2 (2017)
8. Nigro, M.: Studi sulla funzione organizzatrice della pubblica amministrazione. Giuffrè, Milano (1966)
9. Ferrara, R.: L'interesse pubblico al buon andamento delle pubbliche amministrazioni: tra forma e sostanza. Dir. e proc. amm. **1**, 31–81 (2010)

---

[49] Art. 81, par. 1 of Legislative Decree no. 50 of 2016 provides that the documentation proving the possession of the general, technical-professional and economic and financial requirements, for participation in the public procurement procedures and for the control during the execution of the contract of the permanence of these requirements, is acquired exclusively through the centralized database managed by the Ministry of Infrastructure and Transport, called the National Economic Operators Database.

[50] Art. 216, par. 13 of Legislative Decree no. 50 of 2016 and Art. 6-bis of the Legislative Decree no. 163 of April 12, 2016 which provided that from 1 July 2014, the documentation proving the possession of the general, technical-organizational and economic-financial requirements for participation in the public procurement procedures has been acquired exclusively through the National Public Contracts Database.

10. Costantino, F.: Semplificazione e lotta alla corruzione nella legge 241 del 1990. Dir. amm. **4**, 623–682 (2016)
11. Report to the President of the Italian Chamber of Deputies of the Study Committee on Corruption Prevention led by Sabino Cassese, 23 October 1996
12. Vannucci, A.: Come combattere la corruzione in Italia? Quad. Sociol. **14**, 121–144 (1997). https://doi.org/10.4000/qds.1539
13. Italian National Anticorruption Plan 2019, adopted with Resolution of A.N.AC. of 13 November 2019, no. 1064 (2019)
14. Modugno, F.: Funzione. In: Enc. dir., vol. 18, pp. 301–313. Giuffrè, Milano (1969)
15. Benvenuti, F.: Funzione, I) Teoria generale. In: Enc. giur., vol. 14, pp. 1–3. Treccani, Roma (1989)
16. Benvenuti, F.: Eccesso di potere amministrativo per vizio della funzione. Rass. dir. pub. **1**, 1–47 (1950)
17. Benvenuti, F.: Funzione amministrativa, procedimento, processo. Riv. trim. dir. pubbl., pp. 118–145 (1952)
18. Ottaviano, V.: Studi sul merito degli atti amministrativi. Ann. dir. comp. **22**, 308–433 (1948)
19. Casetta, E.: Attività e atto amministrativo. Riv. trim. dir. pubb., pp. 293–336 (1957)
20. Zito, A.: Il "diritto ad una buona amministrazione" nella Carta dei diritti fondamentali dell'Unione europea e nel diritto interno. Riv. it. dir. pub. com., pp. 425–444 (2002)
21. Sorace, D.: La buona amministrazione e la qualità della vita, nel 60° anniversario della Costituzione. In: http://www.costituzionalismo.it (2008)
22. Celone, C.: Il diritto alla buona amministrazione tra ordinamento europeo ed italiano. Dir. econ. **3**, pp. 669–704 (2016)
23. Resta, R.: L'onere di buona amministrazione. In: Scritti giuridici in onore di Santi Romano, pp. 105–140. Cedam, Padova (1939)
24. Cavallo Perin, R.: Potere di ordinanza e principio di legalità. Giuffrè, Milano (1990)
25. Esposito, C.: Riforma dell'amministrazione e diritti costituzionali dei cittadini. Jus **3**, 355–368 (1952)
26. Calamandrei, P.: Costruire la democrazia (Premesse alla Costituente). In: Id.: Opere giuridiche. Volume III. Diritto e processo costituzionale, pp. 127–214. Roma Tre Press, Roma (2019)
27. Calamandrei, P.: Cenni introduttivi sulla Costituente e i suoi lavori. In: Id.: Opere giuridiche. Volume III. Diritto e processo costituzionale, pp. 288–336. Roma Tre Press, Roma (2019)
28. Calamandrei, P.: Incoscienza costituzionale. In: Id.: Opere giuridiche. Volume III. Diritto e processo costituzionale, pp. 470–480. Roma Tre Press, Roma (2019)
29. Galetta, D.-U.: Il principio di proporzionalità fra diritto nazionale e diritto europeo (e con uno sguardo anche al di là dei confini dell'Unione Europea. www.giustizia-amministrativa.it
30. Ferrara, R.: Introduzione al diritto amministrativo: le pubbliche amministrazioni nell'era della globalizzazione. Laterza, Roma-Bari (2014)
31. De Leonardis, F.: I principi generali dell'azione amministrativa. In: Romano, A. (ed.) L'azione amministrativa, pp. 2–133. Giappichelli, Torino (2016)
32. Tarullo, S.: Il divieto di aggravamento del procedimento amministrativo quale dovere codificato di correttezza amministrativa. Dir. amm. **2**, 437–516 (2008)
33. Kafka, F., Bell, A.: The Castle. Oxford University Press, Oxford (2009). (translate)
34. Clarich, M.: Riforme amministrative e sviluppo economico. Riv. trim. dir. pubbl. **1**, 159–188 (2020)
35. Cassese, S.: Il diritto alla buona amministrazione. Relazione alla Giornata sul diritto alla buona amministrazione per il 25° anniversario della legge sul Síndic de Greuges della Catalogna, Barcellona, 27 March 2009

36. Racca, G.M., Cavallo Perin, R.: Curruption as a violation of fundamental rights: reputation risk as a deterrent against the lack of loyalty. In: Racca, G.M., Yukins, C.R. (eds.) Integrity and Efficiency in Sustainable Public Contracts: Balancing Corruption Concerns in Public Procurement Internationally, pp. 23–48. Bruylant, Bruxelles (2014)

37. Barbiero, A., Garuti, M.: Autocertificazione. Definizioni, regole e strumenti. Azienditalia. **4**, 3–16 (1999)

38. Gardini, G.: Autocertificazione. In: Digesto delle discipline pubblicistiche, Aggiornamento, pp. 107–121. UTET, Torino (2005)

39. Lazzara, P.: Le dichiarazioni sostitutive di certificazione. In: Romano, A. (ed.) L'azione amministrativa, pp. 572–583. Giappichelli, Torino (2016)

40. Carullo, G.: Big Data e pubblica amministrazione nell'era delle banche dati interconnesse. Concorrenza e mercato **1**, 181–204 (2016)

41. Bombardelli, M.: Il testo unico delle disposizioni sulla documentazione amministrativa. Giornale dir. amm. **7**, 664–674 (2001)

42. Bombardelli, M.: Divieto di utilizzare certificati nei rapporti con le P.A. In: Garofoli, R., Treu, T. (eds.) Il libro dell'anno del diritto, pp. 201–206. Treccani, Roma (2013)

43. Tentoni, F.: Semplificazione documentale, un "cantiere" sempre aperto. Azienditalia **4**, 312–317 (2012)

44. Amorosino, S.: La semplificazione amministrativa e le recenti modifiche normative alla disciplina generale del procedimento. Foro amm. TAR **7–8**, 2635–2651 (2005)

45. Arsì, M.: L'obbligo d'acquisizione d'ufficio di atti e documenti. Giornale dir. amm. **12**, 1133–1136 (1996)

46. Cafagno, M.: Il principio di non aggravamento del procedimento. In: Renna, M., Saitta, F. (eds.) Studi sui principi del diritto amministrativo, pp. 493–508. Giuffrè, Milano (2012)

47. Macrì, I.: I dati delle pubbliche amministrazioni fra adempimenti e opportunità. Azienditalia **7**, 533–539 (2012)

48. Merloni, F.: Coordinamento e governo dei dati nel pluralismo amministrativo. In: Ponti, B. (eds.) Il regime dei dati pubblici. Esperienze europee e ordinamento nazionale, pp. 153–180. Maggioli Editore, Santarcangelo di Romagna (2008)

49. Corte dei conti, Sezioni riunite in sede di controllo, Referto in materia di informatica pubblica, approved on 18 October 2019

50. Carullo, G.: Gestione, fruizione e diffusione dei dati dell'amministrazione digitale e funzione amministrativa. Giappichelli, Torino (2017)

51. Loiodice, A.: Informatica, banche di dati e diritto all'informazione. Inform. dir. **1**, 118–159 (1975)

52. Agenzia per l'Italia Digitale (AgID), Piano triennale per l'informatica nella Pubblica amministrazione 2019–2021

53. Donato, L., Mariconda, M., Mirrone, M.: La digitalizzazione possibile degli appalti pubblici. L'analisi della Banca d'Italia per l'Anac sulle prospettive dell'e-procurement. Astrid Rassegna. **8**, 1–31 (2020)

54. A.N.AC.: Strategie e azioni per l'effettiva semplificazione e trasparenza nei contratti pubblici attraverso la completa digitalizzazione: le proposte dell'Autorità, document approved on 27 May 2020

55. European Commission. Communication to the European Parliament, the Council, the European Economic and Social Committee and the Committee of the Regions, 26 September 2003, COM (2003) 567 on eGovernment

56. Cardarelli, F.: Amministrazione digitale, trasparenza e principio di legalità. Dir. inf., pp. 227–272 (2015)

57. Carloni, E.: Algoritmi su carta. Politiche di digitalizzazione e trasformazione digitale delle amministrazioni. Dir. pubbl. **2**, 363–391 (2019). https://doi.org/10.1438/94607

58. Arpaia, C.M., Ferro, P., Giuzio, W., Ivaldi, G., Monacelli, D.: L'e-Government in Italia: situazione attuale, problemi e prospettive. Questioni di Economia e Finanza (Occasional papers), vol. 309. Banca d'Italia, Roma (2016)

59. Santucci, G., Minasi, P.: Il Sistema pubblico di connettività (Spc) quale strumento di governance, razionalizzazione e valorizzazione delle basi di dati pubbliche. In: Leggere il cambiamento del Paese. Atti della Nona Conferenza Nazionale di Statistica, pp. 191–198. Istat, Roma (2010)

60. Ministro per l'Innovazione Tecnologica e la Digitalizzazione, Piattaforma Digitale Nazionale Dati. https://innovazione.gov.it/it/progetti/pdnd/ Accessed 24 July 2020

61. Communication of the European Commission to the European Parliament, the Council, the European Economic and Social Committee and the Committee of the Regions, 20 April 2012, COM (2012) 179, A strategy for e-Procurement

62. Communication of the European Commission to the European Parliament, the Council, the European Economic and Social Committee and the Committee of the Regions, 3 October 2017, COM (2017) 572, Making Public Procurement Work in and for Europe

63. Donato, L.: Gli appalti pubblici nel guado tra anticorruzione e semplificazione. In: Donato, L. (eds.) Gli appalti pubblici tra istanze di semplificazione e normativa anticorruzione. Alla ricerca di un equilibrio tra legalità ed efficienza. Quaderni di ricerca giuridica del Servizio Legale, vol. 89, pp. 9–40. Banca d'Italia, Roma (2020)

64. OECD. Recommendation of the Council on Public Procurement (2005)

65. OECD. Preventing Corruption in Public Procurement (2016)

66. Regulation (EU) no. 2018/1724 of the European Parliament and of the Council of 2 October 2018 Establishing a Single Digital Gateway to Provide Access to Information, to Procedures and to Assistance and Problem-Solving Services and Amending Regulation (EU) no. 1024/2012

67. Monica, A.: Lo sportello digitale unico: uno strumento che può unire cittadini e amministrazioni europee. Riv. it. dir. pubbl. com. 3, 477–496 (2019)

68. Communication of the European Commission to the European Parliament, the Council, the European Economic and Social Committee and the Committee of the Regions of 9 April 2016, COM (2016) 179, EU eGovernment Action Plan 2016–2020, Accelerating the Digital Transformation of Government

69. Response of 16 April 2020 by the Minister of Public Administration to the urgent interpellation of the Hon. Giacomelli et al., no. 2–715

70. Consiglio di Stato, Commissione speciale, Parere no. 782 of 22 March 2017

71. Illustrative Report of the Legislative Decree no. 56 of 2017

72. Resolution of A.N.AC. n. 556 of 31 May 2017, which updates the Guidelines on the traceability of financial flows pursuant to Article 3 of the Law of 13 August 2010, no. 136

73. Resolution of A.N.AC. n. 39 of 20 January 2016

74. Croce, G.: Trasmissione dati e rendicontazione … la chimera del principio di unicità dell'invio dei dati. In: In pillole, 17 February 2020. www.mediappalti.it

75. Commission Implementing Regulation (EU) 2019/1780 of 23 September 2019 establishing standard forms for the publication of notices in the field of public procurement and repealing Implementing Regulation (EU) 2015/1986 ('eForms')

76. Ferrara, R.: Premessa ad uno studio sulle banche dati della pubblica amministrazione: fra regole della concorrenza e tutela della persona. Dir. amm. 4, 555–585 (1997)

77. Racca, G.M.: Dall'Autorità sui contratti all'Autorità Nazionale Anticorruzione: il cambiamento del sistema. Dir. amm. 2–3, 345–387 (2015)

78. A.N.AC., Annual Report 2018, 6 June 2019, chapter 3 on corruption risk indicators

79. Sbicca, F., Marino, G. (eds.): Efficienza dei contratti pubblici e sviluppo di indicatori di rischio corruttivo. A.N.AC., Roma (2018)

80. A.N.AC.:Final report of the PON Program "Governance e Assistenza Tecnica 2007–2013". Analisi istruttoria per l'individuazione di indicatori di rischio corruzione e di prevenzione e contrasto nelle amministrazioni pubbliche coinvolte nella politica di coesione (2017)
81. https://ec.europa.eu/growth/content/european-commission-award-better-governance-thr ough-procurement-digitalisation. Accessed 23 June 2020
82. Addante, F.: Anac, poco trasparente la banca dati contratti pubblici: ecco perché. June 29, 2018, available at https://www.agendadigitale.eu/procurement/poco-trasparente-la-banca- dati-dei-contratti-pubblici-anac-ecco-perche/. Accessed 23 June 2020
83. Conferenza delle Regioni e delle Province Autonome, Ordine del giorno sulla rete degli Osservatori regionali/provinciali dei contratti pubblici, 24 October 2019
84. A.N.AC., Reporting Act of 13 February 2019, no. 4
85. Resolution of A.N.AC. no. 157 of February 17, 2016

TOOP Trust Architecture

Luca Boldrin[1] , Giovanni Paolo Sellitto[2(✉)], and Jaak Tepandi[3]

[1] InfoCert, Rome, Italy
`luca.boldrin@infocert.it`
[2] ANAC, Rome, Italy
`g.sellitto@anticorruzione.it`
[3] Information Systems Group, Tallinn University of Technology, Tallinn, Estonia
`jaak.tepandi@taltech.ee`

Abstract. While information security nowadays represents a core concern for any organization, Trust Management is usually less elaborated and is only important when two or more organizations cooperate towards a common objective. The overall Once-Only Principle Project (TOOP) architecture relies on the concept of trusted sources of information and on the existence of a secure exchange channel between the Data Providers and the Data Consumers in this interaction framework. Trust and information security are two cross-cutting concerns of paramount importance. These two concerns are overlapping, but not identical and they span all of the interoperability layers, from the legal down to the technical, passing through organizational and semantic layers. While information security aims at the preservation of confidentiality, integrity and availability of information, trust establishment guarantees that the origin and the destination of the data and documents are authentic (authenticity) and trustworthy (trustworthiness), and that data and documents are secured against any modification by untrusted parties (integrity). In this chapter, the TOOP Trust Architecture is presented, starting from a simple abstract model of interaction between two agents down to the detailed end-to-end trust establishment architecture, modeled onto the Toop Reference Architecture presented in the previous chapter.

Keywords: Security · Trust · Enterprise Architecture

1 Introduction

In the logic of the "once only principle" there is one single entity which is entitled to provide evidence in support of a specific claim, therefore TOOP significantly relies upon trusted and managed sources of information, which in many cases are also called Base Registries. 'Base registry' refers to a trusted and authentic source of information under the control of a public administration or of an organisation entitled by a law provision. According to the European Interoperability Framework 2.0, base registries are 'reliable sources of basic information on items such as persons, companies, vehicles, licences, buildings, locations and roads' and are 'authentic and authoritative, and form, separately or in combination, the cornerstone of public services' [6]. In the context

R. Krimmer et al. (Eds.): The Once-Only Principle, LNCS 12621, pp. 126–140, 2021.
https://doi.org/10.1007/978-3-030-79851-2_7

of a cross-border architecture, spanning different policy domains, it is of paramount importance to guarantee trust establishment between the parties that interact to provide the Once-Only Principle (OOP) service. Therefore trust establishment complements the usual information security management concerns. Information security and trust establishment represent two overlapping, but not identical concerns and they span all of the interoperability layers, from the legal down to the technical, passing through organizational and semantic layers.

The standard ISO/IEC 27000:2018 [1] defines information security as preservation of confidentiality, integrity and availability of information; in addition, other properties, such as authenticity, trustworthiness, accountability, non-repudiation, traceability, and reliability can be involved. Trust establishment guarantees that the origin and the destination of the data and documents are authentic (authenticity) and trustworthy (trustworthiness), while security ensures that data and documents are protected against any modification by untrusted parties (integrity) [2–4]. The implementation of trust relies on the Regulation (EU) N°910/2014 on electronic identification and trust services for electronic transactions in the internal market (hereafter the eIDAS Regulation).

As an example of the differences between the concepts of security and trust, security usually does not involve trustworthiness of the data origin (this is not the same as authenticity - property that an entity is what it claims to be). On the other side, trust usually does not involve availability, reliability, and all aspects of confidentiality. Additional constituents of trust management - accountability, non-repudiation, traceability, and confidentiality[1] can be supported by maintaining processing logs and other controls, encrypting data and documents during the transmission, etc. In general, a Security Architecture involves the general approach to security and controls not directly related to trust, while Trust Architecture includes controls and procedures associated with establishment of trust. Privacy, which is one of the main concerns when handling pieces of information about natural personae, can be handled in the context of trust and security, introducing the concept of consent. In addition, trust requires a clear definition of roles and reliable identities of the entities assigned to those roles.

The Trust Architecture as devised in the TOOP Reference Architecture focuses on the trust establishment between the actors involved in an OOP System to provide guarantees on the origin, destination, authenticity (property that the entity providing the data is what it claims to be), trustworthiness (property that the entity providing the data can be relied on as honest or truthful), and integrity of information that is exchanged between the actors. This architecture makes a distinction between the TOOP specific and non-specific requirements, trust relationships, and controls related to trust establishment.

The rest of this Chapter is structured as follows: in Sect. 2 we present an overview of the trust concept and related literature. In Sect. 3 an overview of solutions for establishing trust is presented. The more specific TOOP requirements and solutions are discussed in Sect. 4, which introduces the concept of End-to-End Trust and in Sect. 5, where the TOOP reference Trust Architecture is presented. In the final Sect. 6, we draw some conclusions and discuss the points that are still open.

---

[1] Here Confidentiality is intended as a component of trust management not as a security related feature.

2   Overview of the Trust Concept

Trust in the digital domain has been widely addressed in the literature as a border territory between philosophy, management, law, information technology and sociology (see for example [5] for a literature review). A computational definition of trust was devised by Marsh[2], who gave a formal model for representing trust in mathematical terms.

For our purposes we take a simplified and pragmatic view, which is however consistent with ISO/IEC 27000-series and aligned with the "trust service" concept introduced by EU Regulation [eIDAS]. In this setting, we are dealing with two parties: a sender of data and a recipient of data.

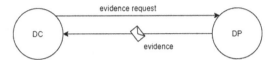

In order to identify the actors involved in trust establishment and the pieces of information that they exchange, which in turn represent the assets to be protected, we can refer to an abstract[3] trust establishment process, considering a simple interaction model between a Data Consumer (DC) and a Data Provider (DP). Taking into account the overall architecture of the EU digital Service infrastructure that connects the Data Provider and the Data Consumer, the interaction can be abstracted as a communication through two access points and therefore we must consider the exchange of information between DP/DC and their respective access points (APs), where the information is the DP/DC identity, the source is respectively DP/DC and the consumer is the Access Point (AP) that must identify DP/DC.

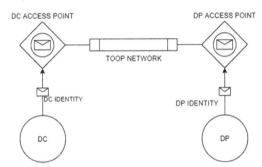

Once the DP and DC have been recognized by their respective Access Points, the Access Points must establish a channel and the communication is between Access Points: the information exchanged is the Access Point Identity Claim and the response relay confirmation.

We have here that AP1 (Source) sends an AP1 Identity Claim (Information) to AP2 (Consumer), AP2 (Source) sends an AP2 Identity Claim (Information) to AP1

---

[2] Marsh, Stephen. 1994. "Formalising Trust as a Computational Concept".

[3] In this case, the term "abstract" refers to the absence of any reference in this model to a specific technology or standard to support the trust establishment process. The technical solutions will be examined in the following paragraph.

(Consumer) and in response AP2 (Source) sends a relay confirmation (Information) to AP1(Consumer).

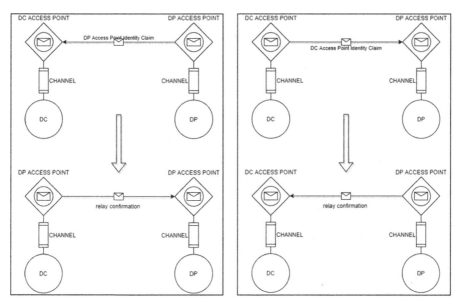

These interactions lead to the creation of a secure and trusted channel between the Data Consumer and the Data Provider: the channel will be used by these two nodes to communicate.

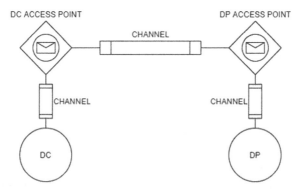

After the channel is established, the User (Source), which is the Data Subject or acts on behalf of the Data Subject must send the Consent (Information) to the Data Provider (Consumer). The user Consent (Information) is also sent by the Data Consumer vouching for the user (Source) to the Data Provider (Consumer) that in response, as Source, will send the DP Identity (Information) to the User (Consumer).

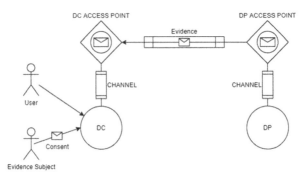

It is worth noting that this approach embraces the fundamental issue of "identification of the sender" as a special case of trust establishment. In this case, the original trust question specifies: "how can the recipient assume that the sender is the one he/she claims to be?". The data provided by the sender therefore consists in an "identity claim" i.e., a set of attributes which allows the recipient to have a partial/total knowledge on the real world identity of the sender. The trust establishment process supports the recipient in validating that data, therefore acquiring some confidence on the identity of the sender.

3   Solutions to Establish Trust

The basic trust establishment process is presented here in an abstract and simplified manner, without referencing any specific organizational, legal or technical solution or standard. It is essentially an organizational process, which shall be supported by technical (digital in the XXI century) solutions to establish and maintain security and trust. In the case of the exchange of an evidence from DP to DC, DC needs to trust the evidence provided by DP. While this is certainly an over-simplification, the main approaches to the establishment of digital trust[4] fall into the following classes:

- *trust by history*: the data is assumed to be true because it comes from a sender which proved honest in previous interactions. This method implies that the recipient has the means to identify the sender through multiple transactions.
- *trust by reputation*: the data is assumed to be true because the sender's trustworthiness is vouched for by other actors. This method implies that there is a reliable way to collect feedback by (possibly many) other parties.
- *trust by liability*: the data is assumed to be true because there is a way of enforcing liability on the provided data. This method implies the knowledge of the real-world identity of the issuer of the data (which may differ from the sender) as well as a way to verify who is entitled to provide some type of data (a criminal record certificate can only be attested by the appropriate law enforcement agency).

The main concern of the TOOP Trust Architecture is to ensure that any sociotechnical system compliant with TOOP Reference Architecture (TOOPRA), in addition to the

---

[4] For a deeper analysis see Luhmann, Niklas. 2000. Familiarity, Confidence, Trust: Problems and Alternatives.

main concern (the Once only Principle), will also preserve trust and the related security features, by default and by design. Ensuring trust by design entails a well-thought mix of the three approaches to guarantee that trust will be preserved over the entire lifecycle of the TOOPRA compliant socio-technical system.

The scenario addressed by TOOPRA can involve organizations that could have had no previous interaction, therefore the preferred choice is trust by liability, possibly in conjunction with trust by reputation, which makes it possible to assume trust in some well-known data providers established or appointed as the trustable data sources by law (a Ministry, etc.). Controls related to trust management not specific to TOOPRA must still be implemented.

Additionally, most of the trust scenarios managed in TOOP rely on trust by liability, supported by some existing general purpose trust-enabling tools:

- **electronic identity (eID)**: this term identifies the digital identities provided by national electronic identity systems which are mutually recognized across EU countries by virtue of eIDAS Regulation [eIDAS] and the associated Implementation Acts (IA 1501/2015, IA 1502/2015, IA 1984/2015]. The eID building block also comprises the technological infrastructure which has been set up in order to support cross-border electronic identity interoperability (the so called "eIDAS network").
- **electronic delivery (eDelivery)**: this term identifies "a service that makes it possible to transmit data between parties by electronic means and provides evidence relating to the handling of the transmitted data, including proof of sending and receiving the data, and that protects transmitted data against the risk of loss, theft, damage or any unauthorised alterations" [eIDAS art 3 (33)]. Such services are offered by third parties in compliance with eIDAS regulation on Trust Service Providers, and provide legal value as established in [eIDAS art. 43, 44].
- **electronic signature/seal (eSignature/eSeal)**: this term identifies the tools and services to support non-repudiability of data, based on "certificates" issued by a Certification Authority.

These services are provided by Trust Service Providers, and provide legal value as established in [eIDAS art. 25, 35]. While the regulation is technologically neutral, public administrations are bound to accept specific formats for signatures[5], which are defined by the European Telecommunications Standards Institute (ETSI)[6] in the following specifications, namely the baseline specification for Advanced Electronic Signature

---

[5] Ruled by the Commission implementing Decision (EU) 2015/1506 of 8 September 2015 laying down specifications relating to formats of advanced electronic signatures and advanced seals to be recognised by public sector bodies: https://eur-lex.europa.eu/legal-content/EN/TXT/PDF/? uri=CELEX:32015D1506.

[6] ETSI is an independent, not-for-profit, standardization organization in the information and communications technology industry fulfilling European and global market needs. ETSI supports the development and testing of standards for ICT-enabled systems, applications and services.

of XML[7], CMS[8] and PDF[9] documents and a specification for a digital Container[10], to bind together one or more signed objects with their advanced electronic signatures or time-stamp tokens.

Electronic delivery services (e-Delivery Building Block) are not bound to specific technological implementations. TOOP adopts as much as possible the building blocks provided by the Connecting Europe Facility (CEF) Digital Service Infrastructure (DSI), specifically:

- CEF eSignature building block[11], which provides off-the-shelf components to implement eIDAS compliant advanced/qualified digital signature.
- CEF eID Building Block[12], granting cross-border authentication for TOOP-enabled services through national eIDAS Nodes.
- CEF eDelivery[13] building block, which allows to create a network of nodes for secure digital data exchange and the creation of a safe and interoperable channel to transfer documents and data between organizations ensuring data integrity and confidentiality in every transmission through the use of digital signatures and encryption.

These Building Blocks enable legal assurance and accountability in the exchange of data and documents. As an example, eDelivery mandates that the recipient of a message must send a digitally signed acknowledgement of receipt for every message received.

4   Establishing the End-to-End Trust

The overall Trust and Security architecture of TOOP relies heavily on a set of building blocks which ensure, in the technology layer, the possibility to create a distributed network of trusted partners. This particular architecture enables a community-based approach to digital trust, based on the existence of a network of trusted nodes (Access Points), which provide the capability to establish a secure and trusted channel between different public and private organizations. The Technology layer is complemented by the Organizational layer and the Legal layer, where the governance model is specified respectively in terms of Business Interoperability specifications, which are agreements between the organizations participating in the community, and with regulations or laws that establish the Owners of the Trusted Data Sources, i.e. the organizations in charge of the governance of the Base Registries.

The resulting end-to-end trust view between the DP and DC is specific to the OOP Reference Architecture (TOOPRA). It is depicted on the following diagram, involving the Data Consumer (Competent Authority acting as a Data Consumer) certificate used for sealing the TOOP Data Request.

---

[7] XML Advanced Electronic Signature (XAdES), specification ETSI TS 103171.

[8] PDF Advanced Electronic SignaturePAdES - ETSI TS 103172.

[9] CMS Advanced Electronic Signature CAdES - ETSI TS 103173.

[10] Associate Signature Container (ASiC) Baseline Profile - ETSI TS 103174.

[11] https://ec.europa.eu/cefdigital/wiki/display/CEFDIGITAL/eSignature.

[12] https://ec.europa.eu/cefdigital/wiki/display/CEFDIGITAL/eID.

[13] https://ec.europa.eu/cefdigital/wiki/display/CEFDIGITAL/eDelivery.

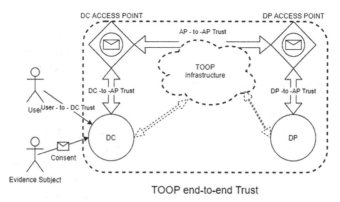

TOOP end-to-end Trust

In addition to the TOOPRA specific trust relationships, an OOP system involves trust relationships not specific to TOOPRA. For example, trusting the Data Consumer to Access Point and Access Point to Data Provider communications, Routing Metadata Discovery data, eIDAS Node data, DNS Server data, AS4 Message Service data, and Central Trust List server data is not dependent on TOOPRA. These relationships are represented in the TOOP Reference Architecture diagrams by pointing to a (cloud) TOOP infrastructure, nevertheless they must be trusted by the stakeholders.

The brokered trust through the Access Point gateways is depicted on the following diagram. It relies on the use of the Access Point Provider certificates from both the Data Provider and the Data Consumer Member States and involves verification of the Data Provider and Data Consumer, sealing the AS4 Message using the Access Point Provider certificate, as well as verification of the seal of the AS4 Message.

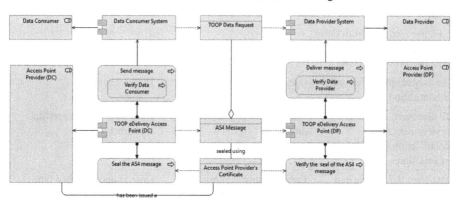

All the assets identified above, as well as the relationships (communications involving data belonging to these assets), need to be trusted.

Trusting the Assets
In trusting the assets, the main emphasis is on the authenticity and trustworthiness of the data sources, as well as integrity of data processing within the stakeholders, e.g., data owners, maintaining the assets.

The user identification and authentication data, request data, and consent data are created during the evidence exchange between the Data Consumer and the Data Provider.

The mechanisms for trusting both these assets and their relationships must be provided. Quality of other information assets involved in TOOPRA is the responsibility of the respective data owners and thus outside the TOOPRA scope; this applies also to the authenticity and trustworthiness aspects of data assets. Thus in TOOPRA only mechanisms for trusting the relationships between these assets are provided.

Trusting the Relationships

In trusting the relationships, the main emphasis is on the integrity of data - the stakeholders need to be sure that the assets have not been modified by untrusted parties.

The following table presents a list of main TOOPRA specific trust relationships. The trust establishment relies significantly on the eIDAS Regulation. Taking into account the potentially critical nature of transactions, the general requirement is that the trust services are qualified. Special cases need to be considered on a case by case basis.

Table 1. List of main TOOPRA specific trust relationships

Information asset (data)	Source	Destination
User request to retrieve evidence User consent	User	Data consumer
User identity User consent between DC and DP Evidence Request from DC to DP Evidence retrieved from DP Evidence processed by DP Evidence provided to DC	Data provider/data consumer	Data consumer/data provider
The user identification and authentication	User	Data consumer
DP discovery data, data services directory Identification of public organisations	Data consumer/data services directory	Data services directory/data consumer
Data from the criteria and evidence type rule base required evidence identification data	Data consumer/criteria and evidence type rule base	Criteria and evidence type rule base/data consumer
Semantic mediation data	Data consumer/ontology repository	Ontology repository/data consumer

For all of the information assets exchanged in the interactions reported in Table 1, the trust establishment solutions usually comprise trust services (e.g., qualified electronic signatures, qualified electronic registered delivery services, qualified electronic seals, or transactions secured by qualified certificates for website authentication) according to the eIDAS Regulation as mechanisms that ensure secure and protected data exchange in public services. In addition, we can provide other relevant general and TOOP specific trust and integrity related controls indicated in the next section.

5 The TOOPRA Trust Architecture

Trust establishment guarantees that the origin and the destination of the data and documents are authentic and trustworthy, and that data and documents are secured against any modification by untrusted parties. Trust management can also involve authorization, accountability, non-repudiation, traceability, as well as confidentiality as a component of trust management.

The preceding sections have detailed the methods to set up a secure and trusted channel between a DP and a DC. Based on these considerations, the current section presents the steps needed to establish trust.

From the architecture development point of view, the TOOP security and trust architectures have been designed adopting the ISO/IEC 27000-series of standards. The overview standard of this series, ISO/IEC 27000:2018, proposes the notion of an Information Security Management System (ISMS), consisting of the policies, procedures, guidelines, and associated resources and activities, collectively managed by an organization to protect its information assets.

The following steps are needed to establish, monitor, maintain, and improve an ISMS:

- identify information assets;
- identify associated information security requirements;
- assess and treat information security risks;
- select and implement relevant controls to manage unacceptable risks;
- manage the ISMS - in particular, monitor, maintain and improve its effectiveness.

These steps are detailed below.

Assets

The trust architecture is developed based on information assets subject to trust management. All these assets need to be trusted - for example, the stakeholders need to be sure that the assets have not been modified by untrusted parties.

Based on the Business Architecture, Information System Architecture, and Technology Architecture views, the following information assets are identified.

Various data related to the users must be trusted, such as the User identification and authentication data, the User identity data, the User request data to retrieve evidence, and the User consent data.

To find data providers and retrieve evidence, the data from the Criteria and Evidence Type Rule Base, the required evidence identification data, the data on the request for evidence from DC to DP, the Data Provider Discovery data, data from the Data Services Directory, the identification data of Public Organisations, and the semantic mediation data need to be trusted as well.

Various other kinds of data, such as data about the User consent exchanged between the DC and DP, data of the evidence retrieved from the Data Provider, data of processing the evidence retrieved from the Data Provider, data of the evidence provided to the Data Consumer, and the evidence exchange data are needed and must be trusted.

Finally, various kinds of technical data must be trusted to provide an OOP service: routing Metadata Discovery data, including data in the SMP and BDXL, eIDAS Node data, DNS Server data, and AS4 Message Service data.

Requirements

The following TOOP specific requirements related to trust establishment have been reported.

- The authenticity of the data transmitted by the DP must be trusted by the DC
- The transmission of an Evidence from DP to DC must guarantee the integrity of the exchanged Evidence
- The Data Provider is responsible for transmitting the requested Evidence in accordance with the confidentiality and integrity requirements
- Any exchange of evidence organised under the OOP must be possible to verify by competent authorities in case of disputes (including the identification of the sending and receiving competent authorities, the time of the exchange, and the integrity/authenticity of the exchanged data itself)
- The technical system shall in particular ensure the confidentiality and integrity of the evidence
- A common security and privacy framework must be defined and processes for public services must be established to ensure secure and trustworthy data exchange between public administrations and in interactions with citizens and businesses
- Trust services must be used according to the Regulation on eID and Trust Services as mechanisms that ensure secure and protected data exchange in public services
- A level of security appropriate to the risk, including inter alia as appropriate the ability to ensure the ongoing integrity of processing systems and services, must be ensured by the competent authorities and any other participants in the evidence exchange mechanism
- The user must have the possibility to preview the evidence to be used by the DC, and check the validity of the retrieved information

Risks

Assessment and treating of specific trust related risks deals with the authenticity and trustworthiness aspects of creating and exchanging data.

All the assets identified above, as well as the relationships (communications involving data belonging to these assets), need to be trusted. In trusting the assets, the main emphasis is on the authenticity and trustworthiness of the data sources, as well as integrity of data processing within the stakeholders, e.g., data owners, maintaining the assets.

The user identification and authentication data, request data, and consent data are created during the evidence exchange between the Data Consumer and the Data Provider.

Quality of other information assets involved in TOOPRA is the responsibility of the respective data owners and thus outside the TOOPRA scope.

The highest trust related risks concern data of the evidence (data in transit) in Single Digital Gateway Regulation (SDGR) domain: data related to both citizens and businesses as stated in the SDGR.

Also significant are risks related to the data of the evidence (data in transit) in TOOP domain: information related to business activities and on cross-border sharing of this information.

The User request data, response data, consent data, activity log data need to be trusted as well. Integrity of information assets related to central services and components: the Criterion & Evidence Type Rule Base, Data Services Directory, Ontology Repository, SMP, BDXL must be preserved.

A risk treatment decision must be made with respect to all risks. The stakeholders should establish criteria for determining which risks can be accepted. Options for risk treatment include applying controls to reduce the risks, accepting the risks that satisfy the criteria for risk acceptance, avoiding risks, as well as sharing the risks to other parties, for example to insurers or suppliers. These options depend on the legislation and organisational policies of particular information system stakeholders. Therefore they must be further specified in the system initialization and development processes.

Controls

Establishment of trust depends both on the assets and communications created specifically for a TOOPRA based system, as well as on supporting assets and communications that exist independently of such a system. The following organisational and technical controls must be taken into account to ensure appropriate level of trust related to both TOOPRA specific and non-specific components and relationships, independently of who implements them:

- use of trust services according to the eIDAS Regulation as mechanisms that ensure secure and protected data exchange in public services;
- ensuring that the competent authorities and any other participants in the evidence exchange mechanism implement appropriate technical and organisational measures to ensure a level of security appropriate to the risk, including as appropriate the ability to ensure the ongoing integrity of processing systems and services;
- ensuring that all the information assets identified in the above sections can be trusted.

The relevant general trust and integrity related controls include as appropriate classification of information in terms of integrity, usage of public key cryptography and digital signatures, issuing public key certificates by a recognized certification authority, appropriate handling of public and private keys, suitable authentication processes, using trusted third parties to provide application services, segregation of networks based on trust levels, ensuring trustworthiness of personnel working with the system, use of cryptographic techniques to protect integrity and authenticity of information, providing protection from malware, providing adequate backup facilities, establishing network controls to safeguard integrity of data passing over public networks or over wireless networks, applying appropriate logging and monitoring to enable recording and detection of actions that may affect information security, enforcing formal change control procedures to ensure the integrity of systems, applications and data, introducing incident response measures related to loss of integrity, and other.

A process must be introduced for regularly testing, assessing and evaluating the effectiveness of technical and organisational measures for ensuring the security of the processing.

The technical controls must ensure that the authenticity of the data transmitted by the DP is trusted by the DC, that the transmission of an evidence from DP to DC will guarantee the integrity of the exchanged evidence, and that the Data Provider acknowledges the responsibility for transmitting the requested evidence in accordance with the confidentiality and integrity requirements.

The following building blocks, standards and interfaces need to be supported to achieve the appropriate trust level:

- ETSI ASiC Specifications: Electronic Signatures and Infrastructures (ESI), ASiC Baseline Profile Technical Specification and Electronic Signatures and Infrastructures (ESI); Associated Signature Containers (ASiC) Technical Specification;
- the CEF eSignature and eID Building Blocks;
- the CEF eDelivery AS4 profile for message exchange;
- the CEF eDelivery profile of the BDXL specification;
- the OASIS Service Metadata Publishing 1.0(BDXR SMP) specification;
- the CEF eIDAS Profile.

Management of the ISMS
The stakeholders of an information system based on the Once-Only Principle need to maintain and improve the ISMS. This is done by monitoring and assessing performance against organizational policies and objectives, and reporting the results to management for review. The review evaluates whether the ISMS includes specified controls that are suitable to treat risks within the ISMS scope. Based on the records of these monitored areas, it provides suggestions for corrective, preventive and improvement actions.

All TOOP specific data, as well as associated systems and communications, must be monitored. Regular testing, assessing and evaluating the effectiveness of technical and organisational measures is needed for ensuring the security of the processing.

6   Conclusion

Trust between the users, data subjects, data providers, data consumers, and other stakeholders involved in an OOP system is of vital importance. Without digital trust, the stakeholders will not use services of an OOP system.

Digital trust can be established by liability (there is a way of enforcing liability on the provided data), reputation (the sender's trustworthiness is vouched for by other actors), construction (the system is designed and developed to preserve trust), and /or history (the sender has proved honest in previous interactions). For real-life applications, all these aspects are important.

From the legal and organizational point of view, the OOP is mainly interested in the concept of trust between Organizations and the legal interoperability between different policy domains. The achievement of these two objectives is deeply rooted in the Semantic and Technical layer, where the means to ensure the semantic equivalence for the evidence that are exchanged between DP and DC and their integrity and availability must be ensured.

From a technical point of view, the establishment of trust between organizations, be them public or private, and the possibility for citizens and business to re-use some documents across different contexts, possibly cross-border (as postulated by the OOP) requires a framework for the mutual recognition of key enablers across borders, such as electronic identification, electronic documents, electronic signatures and electronic delivery services, and for interoperable e-government services across the European Union.

Trust by construction also assumes the chain of trust: trusted source, trusted communications, trusted intermediate nodes, and trusted processing in the nodes.

In turn, the technical framework can hold only if some organizational and legal basis for collaboration between different entities exist and if the exchanged information maintains its meaning or can gain some meaning also in a different organizational context.

The diffusion of mutually recognised electronic identification means will facilitate cross-border provision of numerous services in the internal market and enable businesses to operate on a cross-border basis without facing many obstacles in interactions with public authorities, facilitating the adoption of the OOP.

Finally, without a history of successful use of different OOP systems, the users, organisations, and governments will not trust them. The TOOP Reference Architecture gives a tool for more efficient development of such systems and for design of trust as a component in their construction.

References

1. ISO/IEC 27000:2018. Information technology — Security techniques — Information security management systems — Overview and vocabulary
2. Cofta, P.: Trust, Complexity and Control: Confidence in a Convergent World. John Wiley I and Sons (2007)
3. Raj, G., Sarfaraz, M., Singh, D.: Survey on trust establishment in cloud computing. In: 2014 5th International Conference - Confluence the Next Generation Information Technology Summit (Confluence), pp. 215–220 (2014)
4. Winslett, M., et al.: Negotiating trust in the web. IEEE Internet Comput. 6(6), 30–37 (2002)
5. Taddeo, M.: Defining trust and e-trust. Int. J. Technol. Hum. Interact. 5, 23–35 (2011). https://doi.org/10.4018/jthi.2009040102
6. European Interoperability Framework 2.0

The Technical Challenges in OOP Application Across the European Union and the TOOP OOP Architecture

Jaak Tepandi[1], Carmen Rotuna[2], Giovanni Paolo Sellitto[3], Sander Fieten[4], and Andriana Prentza[5(✉)]

[1] Information Systems Group, Tallinn University of Technology, Tallinn, Estonia
[2] ICI BUCHAREST, Bucharest, Romania
[3] ANAC, Rome, Italy
[4] Chasquis, Leiden, Netherlands
[5] Department of Digital Systems, University of Piraeus, 18532 Piraeus, Greece
aprentza@unipi.gr

Abstract. The Once-Only Principle requires the public administrations to ensure that citizens and businesses supply the same information only once to the Public Administration as a whole. Widespread use of the Once-Only Principle has the potential to simplify citizens' life, make businesses more efficient, and reduce administrative burden in the European Union. The Once-Only Principle project (TOOP) is an initiative, financed by the EU Program Horizon 2020, to explore the possibility to enable the cross-border application of the Once-Only Principle by demonstrating it in practice, through the development of selected piloting applications for specific real-world use cases, enabling the connection of different registries and architectures in different countries for better exchange of information across public administrations. These piloting ICT systems are designed as a result of a pan-European collaboration and they adopt a federated model, to allow for a high degree of independence between the participating parties in the development of their own solutions. The main challenge in the implementation of an OOP solution is the diversity of organizations, procedures, data, and services on all four main levels of interoperability: legal, organizational, semantic, and technical. To address this challenge, TOOP is developing and testing the TOOP Reference Architecture (TOOPRA) to assist organizations in the cross-border implementation of the OOP. The paper outlines the TOOPRA users, principles, and requirements, presents an overview of the architecture development, describes the main views of TOOPRA, discusses architecture profiling, and analyses the TOOPRA sustainability issues.

Keywords: eGovernment · Interoperability · Reference Architecture

1 Introduction

The Once-Only Principle (OOP) requires the public administrations to ensure that citizens and businesses supply the same information only once to the Public Administration

© The Author(s) 2021
R. Krimmer et al. (Eds.): The Once-Only Principle, LNCS 12621, pp. 141–163, 2021.
https://doi.org/10.1007/978-3-030-79851-2_8

as a whole. A widespread use of OOP has the potential to simplify citizens' life, make businesses more efficient, and reduce administrative burden in the European Union (EU). The practical application of the OOP requires the set-up of a complex legal, organizational and technical environment to ensure that the information exchanged between public administrations maintains its original validity and meaning even if its expression is changed when used in a different place or context. All these conditions are usually referred to as levels of interoperability between organizations and at the EU level they are clearly explained in the European Interoperability Framework (EIF) [1] and defined in the European Interoperability Reference Architecture (EIRA) [2].

The Once-Only Principle project (TOOP) represents an initiative – financed by the EU Program Horizon 2020 – to explore the possibility to enable the cross-border application of OOP by demonstrating it in practice, through the development of some Information and Communication Technology (ICT) systems to pilot its application to specific real-world use cases, enabling the connection of different registries and architectures in different countries for better exchange of information across public administrations. These piloting ICT systems are designed as a result of a pan-European collaboration and they adopt a federated model, to allow for a high degree of independence between the participating parties in the development of their own solutions.

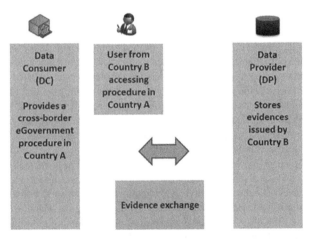

Fig. 1. A high-level illustration of an OOP exchange.

From a high-level point of view (see Fig. 1), an OOP exchange does not deviate much from the usual interaction between a Data Consumer (DC), where the User accesses a digital public service, and a Data Provider (DP), who acts on behalf of the User. The difference is precisely in the Once Only principle that requires that the Data Provider is the one that from a legal point of view is recognized as trusted, reusable and authoritative source of data for the User (a Base Register, in the European Interoperability Framework terminology).

The main challenge in the implementation of an OOP solution is the diversity of organizations, procedures, data, and services on all four main levels of interoperability: legal, organizational, semantic, and technical [3]. To address this challenge, TOOP is developing and testing the TOOP Reference Architecture (TOOPRA) to assist organizations in the cross-border implementation of the OOP.

An enterprise architecture is typically developed because there are concerns that need to be addressed by the business and Information Technology (IT) systems within an organization. The role of the architect is to address these concerns [4].

A Reference Architecture is a set of standardized Enterprise Architectures that provides a frame of reference for a particular domain, sector, or field of interest [5]. The TOOPRA is driven by the users, architecture principles, and Architecturally Significant Requirements (ASRs). The Architecturally Significant Requirements are "those requirements that have a measurable impact on a software system's architecture" [6]. The architecture is described on four architecture layers (business, data, application, technology), organized in multiple architecture views according to The Open Group Architecture Framework (TOGAF) [7].

One of the main difficulties in designing TOOPRA was related to changing principles and requirements. Therefore, TOOPRA was developed by combining top-down and bottom-up approaches considering also new requirements emerging from the Single Digital Gateway Regulation (SDGR) [8] among others. These issues are presented throughout the paper.

The next section outlines the TOOPRA users, principles, and requirements. An overview of the architecture development is presented in the third section. Main views of TOOPRA are described in the fourth section. The fifth section covers architecture profiling. TOOPRA sustainability issues are analyzed in the sixth section and main conclusions are presented in the last section of the chapter.

2   The TOOPRA Users, Principles, and Requirements

The TOOPRA is intended to provide support in the cross-border implementation of OOP, thus helping to design, assess, communicate, and share digital public services across borders and sectors. The main stakeholders of TOOPRA are those directly involved in the TOOP project, the prospective users of the TOOP Reference Architecture that use it to build OOP services, and finally, the end users of the services that use the OOP services to retrieve their data.

In view of this, the main categories of TOOPRA users are: architects responsible for the design of cross-border solution architectures; business analysts responsible for assessing and studying the impact of changes in the IT systems; developers responsible for design, development and implementation of software solutions for interoperable digital public services (across borders and sectors); as well as portfolio managers responsible for maintaining the catalogue of assets related to the design and implementation of eGovernment solutions and for making investment decisions on these assets.

The architecture principles are the underlying general rules and guidelines for the use and deployment of IT resources and assets. The principles underlying TOOPRA include the following, among others:

- Give preference to open specifications and standards.
- Develop TOOP architecture as a reusable solution, reuse Building Blocks (BB) when possible.
- Integrate the requirements for and contribute through the TOOP Solution Architecture to the development of the High-level Reference Architecture for SDGR [8].
- Put in place processes to select relevant standards and specifications, evaluate them, monitor their implementation, check their compliance, and test their interoperability.
- Establish interoperability agreements in all layers.
- Clarify and formalize organizational relationships between the participants in the Once-Only processes.
- Decide on a common scheme for interconnecting loosely coupled service components and design the necessary infrastructure for establishing and maintaining European public services.
- Design a shared infrastructure of reusable services and information sources that can be used by all public administrations.
- The TOOP architecture should use trust services according to the eIDAS Regulation [9] that ensure secure and protected data exchange in public services.
- The information exchanged between the participants of the system should be limited to the data required to complete the process for which the information is requested.
- The information exchanged between the participants of the system should only be used for the explicitly agreed purpose.
- When the consent of the user is necessary for data protection purposes, it shall be obtained in accordance with Regulation (EU) 2016/679 [10] and Regulation (EU) 45/2001 [11].
- Develop interfaces with base registries and authoritative sources of information, publish the semantic and technical means and documentation needed for others to connect and reuse available information.

A typical information system has many requirements. Some of these - for example, those related to efficiency or reliability - influence the system architecture, but many requirements, for example, related to specific reports, do not. For TOOPRA, over forty ASRs that have an essential impact on the architecture were highlighted. The requirements were structured according to the standard Software/System Product Quality Model (ISO/IEC 25010) and Data Quality Model (ISO/IEC 25012). Some examples follow:

- DC must be informed about the conditions and terms of use of the retrieved information (Functional Suitability).
- DP should communicate the expected level of service associated with the processing of the request for data from the DC (Performance Efficiency).
- DP must be able to automatically process requests for evidence from DC (Interoperability).
- The transmission of an evidence from DP to DC must guarantee the confidentiality of the exchanged evidence (Security).
- The level of availability of the exchange process must comply with the legal requirements (Reliability).

- It must be possible to operate the evidence exchange process according to various deployment models: component on premise, service on premise, mutualized and centralized service (Usability).
- The legal value and meaning of data should not be altered crossing a national border (Data Accuracy).
- The User has the possibility to preview the evidence to be used by the DC and to check the validity of the retrieved information (Data Consistency).
- The User may be able to add information not provided by the DP(s) (Data Completeness).
- The authenticity of the data transmitted by DP must be trusted by DC (Data Credibility).

3 Development of the Architecture

The architecture follows the TOGAF Architecture Development Method (ADM) cycle in a continuous development process integrating new requirements emerging from pilots, stakeholders, and EU regulations. The first version of the architecture addressed mainly the initial pilot requirements and the regulations in force at that point in time. Along the development process, the architecture incorporated the requirements derived from SDGR [8] and the new pilot requirements resulting from the extension of business use cases.

The architecture requirements comprise requirements from several areas: pilot requirements, General Data Protection Regulation (GDPR) [10], EIF, legal requirements, as well as the SDGR and the Guidelines for the implementation of the SDGR [12]. The SDGR is the main driver for OOP implementation at the EU level as it provides the legal context to achieve the desired goals. This Regulation has the objective of reducing administrative burden on citizens and businesses, in compliance with national legislation and procedures while ensuring the functioning of the internal market. SDGR states that it is mandatory for Member States (MS) to provide 21 digitized administrative procedures in an interoperable and secure way.

The TOOP architecture requirements include Article 14 of SDGR which, among others, states that the technical system for the cross-border automated exchange of evidence and application of the OOP should enable the processing of requests for evidence at the explicit request of the user, the transmission of the evidence between competent authorities and the possibility for the user to preview the evidence to be used by the requesting competent authority. Also, it states that the evidence made available to the requesting competent authority shall be limited to what has been requested and shall only be used by that authority for the purpose of the procedure for which the evidence was exchanged.

The TOOP Architecture team cooperates and seeks to align its work with other relevant EC Initiatives, especially within the ISA^2 program [13].

4 The TOOPRA Views

The TOOP Architecture embodies in its components the principles and requirements guiding its design and evolution. The overall architecture description contains a collection of artifacts that document the TOOP architecture. The architecture views are the key artifacts in the architecture description.

As an Architecture Description Language (ADL), ArchiMate® [4], has been used starting from the very first version of the architecture. The goal was to describe the layers of an enterprise (business, information systems, technology). Also, the architecture was developed taking into consideration interoperability concerns and is compatible with EIRA [2].

4.1 Introduction

The architecture is described along the business, information system and technology dimensions.

The Business Architecture is a representation of business concerns through capabilities, end-to-end value delivery, information, and organizational structure, and the relationships among these business elements.

The Information System (IS) Architecture describes how the Business Architecture is realized by the Information Systems. The IS architecture includes the data and application architecture and describes (1) the structure of an organization's logical and physical data assets and data management resources, and (2) the individual application systems to be deployed, their interactions, and their relationships to the core business processes of the organization.

The Technology Architecture describes the logical components and services that are required to support the deployment of business capabilities and deployment components described in the IS Architecture. This includes IT infrastructure, middleware, networks, communications, processing, standards, etc.

Specific views addressing cross-cutting quality concerns, such as Security Architecture and Trust Architecture, and Management aspects complement the TOOPRA.

4.2 Business Architecture

The Business Architecture is a description of the structure and interaction between the business strategy, organization, functions, business processes, and information needs [7].

The TOOPRA Business Architecture is presented via the operational processes (process model, capabilities views (capability map), and business interactions.

The Process Model is useful to get a basic overview of the TOOP Business Architecture. It gives an overall upper-level view of the TOOPRA Business Architecture processes. There are two kinds of processes: operational and managerial. The operational processes specify end-to-end processes of executing Once Only Principle. The management processes are responsible for management of the resources required in the operational processes.

The Capability Map diagrams are useful to understand required capabilities and responsibilities of each actor participating in the cross-border Evidence exchange.

The Business Interaction diagrams enable identifying and understanding the major organisational interoperability issues connected with the TOOP Business Architecture. The diagrams in this group specify the collaboration between the actors involved in cross-border Evidence exchange.

The goal of the OOP activities is to retrieve already existing information which is needed for completion of the existing process. The exchanged information is therefore, in alignment with the definition used in the SDGR [8], labelled "evidence" as it is used to fulfill requirements of the current process.

The operational processes specify the end-to-end processes of executing the OOP as part of the delivery of a public eService. It must be noted that the once-only process of retrieving an evidence from another competent authority as shown in the diagram is only a small part of the complete business process that is executed to meet the requirements of the public service that is being provided to the user.

The main actors involved in the cross-border evidence exchange business process are the following:

- User: the entity, which can be either a natural or legal person, that initiates the execution of a procedure.
- Evidence Subject: the entity, whose data is needed to complete the procedure initiated by the User. The Evidence Subject may be a legal entity or a natural person. This is often the same entity as the User, but it can also be an entity related to the User, for example the legal representative of a company which needs to prove a clean criminal record in a procurement procedure. In case the Evidence Subject is a natural person, they may be referred to as a Data Subject and their consent may be necessary for data protection purposes in accordance with GDPR [10] and Regulation (EU) 45/2001 [11].
- Data Consumer (DC): the public organization that executes a procedure for a specific User and which needs to obtain data on one or more Evidence Subjects for the proper execution of the procedure. This data can be provided directly by the User or retrieved from another organization to which the required data has already been provided.
- Data Provider (DP): a public (e.g., Base Registry) or a private organization (e.g., Aggregator, Maritime Recognized Organization) able to provide data about an Evidence Subject, upon request from a DC.

Due to being a reference architecture, TOOPRA is generic in design and therefore does not describe an actual business process but shows what activities are required to integrate the once-only principle in a broader business process.

The process starts from a procedure, offered through a Public Service by a Competent Authority (DC) located in MS A, which has some requirements to be fulfilled by the User who triggers this procedure. The fulfillment of requirements needs to be supported by evidence, which are to be provided by a DP in MS B, to which the User has earlier provided the required information. Per request of the User, the Competent Authority can retrieve the evidence from the DP and as such acts in the role of DC.

As part of the normal business process of executing the procedure, the DC authenticates the user, identifies the required evidence (including identification of the Evidence Subject), asks for confirmation to retrieve the evidence, finds and retrieves evidence from the DP and continues the main process with the retrieved evidence. The DP checks legitimacy of the evidence request, extracts the data for the Evidence Subject, and issues the evidence.

Figure 2 presents an upper level view of the TOOPRA Business Architecture operational processes. For readability, the diagram omits administration processes like data set registration. At this highest level, the specifics of implementation are hidden.

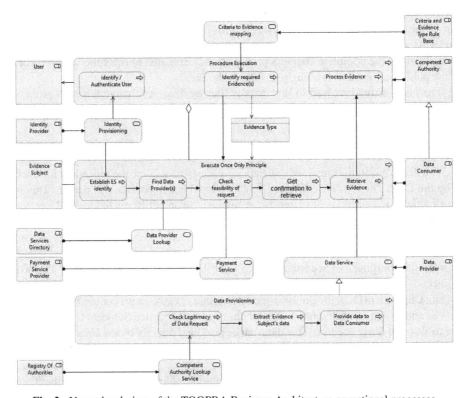

Fig. 2. Upper-level view of the TOOPRA Business Architecture operational processes.

Depending on the requirements of the actual business processes in a domain, several variations can exist in the way the individual process steps are executed.

For example, the DP that can supply the required evidence may be pre-defined in a domain. Also, the actual evidence exchange may vary and can be a two-step process where the DP first provides meta-data on the available Evidence and the actual Evidence is retrieved later in a second step. The retrieval of the actual Evidence data can even be done by another Competent Authority than the one making the original request.

As shown above, several shared services need to be available for the operational processes to function. It is evident that these shared services need to be managed as well, therefore in the model roles have been assigned to these services.

How these services are managed, and as such how these roles will be implemented, will however depend on the domain and the governance agreements made within that domain or even across domains. The definition of these processes is left to the domains. From an architectural point of view, the shared services in the TOOPRA require an underlying governance process, but the choice of the model for these processes is left to the domains and, consequently, they are not presented here.

In the second view component of the Business Architecture, TOOPRA uses the concept of capability – the ability to execute a specified course of action. The business capabilities are identified from the business processes and logically grouped by resources required in their deployment. They are mapped to the Information System level functions. This view of the business architecture is compliant with EIRA ArchiMate representation of the Organizational View Concepts in the Business Architecture.

A capability map identifies business capabilities from the business processes and groups them logically by resources required in their deployment. This architecture view specifies each business role's responsibilities when participating in a TOOP Network. It generically should be interpreted in the following way: to participate in a TOOP Network in a certain Business Role, the organization must have the capability to execute the assigned business functions. The Capability Map enables the participants in a TOOP Network to efficiently and easily identify the required business capabilities associated with the role they will play. It is also a valuable tool for architects and designers to support gap analysis when transitioning to a TOOP environment.

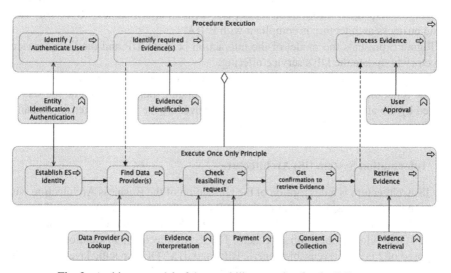

Fig. 3. Archimate model of the capability mapping for the DC process.

In the capabilities view of the Business Architecture, the processes are mapped to functions which the actors need to be able to perform to be capable of executing the processes. In TOOPRA development, only those capabilities are included that would be implemented as functions. In addition, the requirements from TOOPRA on an actor acting in a certain role are on a more detailed level than strategy. So to avoid duplication, capabilities are presented using the function notation.

Figure 3 shows this capability mapping for the processes executed by the DC, described at a generic level of abstraction, to support the goal of developing a generic reference architecture. The various business capabilities introduced are leveraged to support the deployment of the business processes.

The following Table 1 shows the DC capabilities and describes the purpose, outcomes, and required interaction.

Figure 4 shows how the DP capabilities are deployed in the evidence provisioning business process.

The following Table 2 shows the DC capabilities and describes the purpose, outcomes, and required interaction.

The third view component of the Business Architecture is focusing on the interactions between the actors involved in the OOP process. The models in this view show how the different functions of the actors work together, and which data is exchanged between them to enable the execution of the OOP process. It is in these interactions where the actors need to agree on common semantics and specifications to ensure interoperability.

A Business Interactions diagram enables architects and designers to identify efficiently and easily the major organisational interoperability points, as each Exchange of Business Information must be addressed from an interoperability perspective.

Figure 5 represents the most significant exchanges of business information between the main roles participating in an OOP system. It generically should be interpreted in the following way: as part of a Business Capability deployed by a Business Role, an Exchange of Business Information takes place with another Business Role. This view of the business architecture is compliant with EIRA.

Figure 6 presents the model of the interaction between DP and the Data Services Directory to update the DP's service offering.

The actor in charge of Data Services Directory role operates a business service to provide functionality to competent authorities to update their meta-data on the service offered by the authority. The business service is used by the service offering exchange so DPs can manage their dataset meta-data.

4.3   Information System (iS) Architecture

The IS Architecture is a description of the realization of the Business Architecture with IT components, taking into account the ASRs (top-down approach), reuse of Digital Service Infrastructure (DSI) BBs [14], and the TOOP Solution Architecture implemented for the TOOP pilots (bottom-up approach). The IS Architecture can therefore be seen as composed of 2 layers: i) reusable generic BBs, and ii) a TOOP specific layer, leveraging the generic building blocks to realize the TOOP functionalities.

The focal points in the IS architecture description are the following:

Table 1. DC capabilities, purpose, outcomes and required interaction.

Capability	Purpose	Outcomes	Required interaction
Entity identification/Authentication	Establishes the identity of the user and the evidence subject	The identity is known	Identity exchange
Evidence identification	Identifies the required evidence according to the criterion and the special context of the evidence subject	Evidence type corresponding to the criterion is identified	Evidence identification data exchange
Data provider lookup	Find a provider for an evidence related to a legal entity	Data providers identity is established	Data provider information exchange
Evidence interpretation	Links evidence to its business context	Information contained in the evidence is established	Evidence exchange
Payment	Payment for retrieving the evidence when required	Payment is negotiated, if needed	Evidence request exchange
Consent collection	Collects the consent of the user to retrieve the required Evidence	User consent is collected	Evidence request exchange
User approval	Manage the approval of the user to reuse the retrieved Evidence	User approval is collected	Evidence request exchange
Evidence retrieval	Request evidence from a (set of) data provider(s)	Evidence is retrieved	Evidence exchange

- Mapping of the business roles capabilities onto the operational capabilities utilised to operate the Once Only Evidence Processing and identifying the TOOP specific components, candidates for TOOP Building Blocks.
- Interoperability in the exchange of information.
- Reuse of Digital Service Infrastructure (DSI) Building Blocks (BB) to realize the application functions.

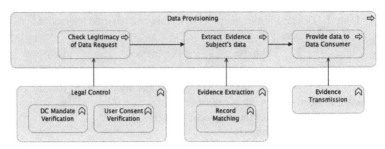

Fig. 4. Archimate model of the capability mapping for the DP process

Table 2. DP capabilities, purpose, outcomes and required interaction.

Capability	Purpose	Outcomes	Required interaction
Legal control	Checking the legitimacy of the evidence request	Evaluation of the legitimacy of the evidence request	Identity exchange, data provider information exchange, evidence request exchange
DC mandate verification	Data provider checks the mandate of the DC to request evidence	DC mandate is verified	Identity exchange, data provider information exchange, evidence request exchange
User consent verification	Checking that the requesting user authorized the access to the evidence	Evidence request is authorized	Identity exchange, data provider information exchange, evidence request exchange
Evidence extraction	Extracting the evidence from the providing competent authority	Evidence is retrieved	Evidence request exchange, evidence exchange
Record matching	Record matching is performed by the data provider based on identification attributes provided by the DC	The evidence subject record is found	Evidence request exchange, evidence exchange
Evidence transmission	Transmit the evidence to the requesting competent authority	Evidence is transmitted	Evidence request exchange, Evidence exchange

The TOOP IS Architecture description addresses these focal points by means of the following components:

- The *operational capabilities of the DC and DP* utilised to operate the Once Only Evidence Processing.

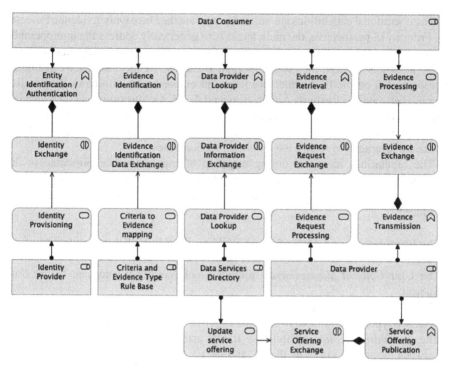

Fig. 5. Overview of the most significant exchanges of business information between the main roles participating in an OOP system interaction.

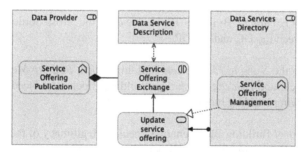

Fig. 6. Model of the interaction between DP and the Data Service Directory to update the DP's service offering.

- The *OOP Interoperability layer*, presenting the generic building blocks to realize the TOOP functionalities.
- The *IS Architecture Interfaces diagram*, depicting the main interactions among architecture building blocks, the way they communicate and the exchanged data.

The operational capabilities are utilised to operate the Once Only Evidence Processing. From an IS perspective, the main target is to generically address the interoperability concerns, i.e., the exchange of business information between participants of TOOP Network. In this section, the most important Business Architecture level capabilities are represented on the IS Architecture level and mapped to the Building Blocks. If a mapping between the Business Architecture and the IS Architecture level for a specific capability is not provided, then this capability is outside the scope of TOOPRA. Figure 7 specifies how the DC operational capabilities are realized and how the existing Building Blocks are leveraged to realize the required functionalities.

The capabilities identified during mapping of capabilities are presented in the OOP Interoperability layer as the generic building blocks that implement TOOP functionalities. For the DC, the following building blocks (shown in Fig. 7) are introduced:

- The *Identification and Authentication* Building Block establishes the identity of the User.
- The *User Consent Management* Building Block handles the consent of the Data Subject.
- The *Evidence Identification* Building Block enables the DC to determine which evidence types are available to the User to prove fulfillment of the requirement.
- The *Semantic Mediation* Building Block establishes semantic interoperability between the services used by the DC and DP.
- The *Data Provider Discovery* Building Block enables to determine the DP that can provide the information to be used as evidence in the procedure executed by the DC.
- The *Routing Metadata Discovery* Building Block provides the details for routing between the services of the participating authorities.
- The *Evidence Exchange* Building Block handles the cross-border exchange of Evidence between the DC and the DP.

In addition to the *Semantic Mediation* Building Block, *Routing Metadata Discovery* Building Block, and *Evidence Exchange* Building Block introduced above, the DP utilises the following building blocks.

- The *Legal Control* Building Block enables checking legitimacy of the data request.
- The *Evidence Extraction* Building Block makes possible to extract data of the Evidence Subject,
- The *Record Matching* Building Block allows to find the relevant record within a data set that applies to the Evidence Subject.

The IS Architecture Interfaces diagram shows the main interactions among architecture building blocks, the way they communicate, and which data is exchanged. The process diagram shows all the steps required in a cross-border Evidence exchange and depicts the entire process from user authentication to Evidence retrieval. There is only one Dynamic Service Location component and it is queried by both DC and DP. The DC discovers the routing metadata by accessing Capability Lookup of the DP and the DP by accessing Capability Lookup of the DC.

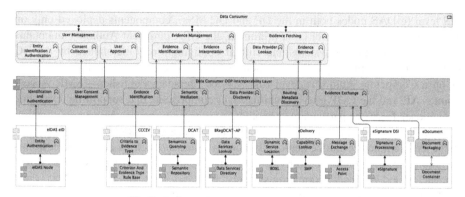

Fig. 7. Information system DC architecture.

Conceptually, the TOOPRA distinguishes between the OOP Core Semantic Model (CSM) (TOOP specific concepts), the core vocabularies (general application related concepts), and Domain Semantic Models (DSM), which are domain specific, e.g., health, public procurement. The OOP CSM describes entities relevant to the application of the OOP. These entities are generic and not affected by the domain where the architecture is applied. The core vocabularies are used in most or all services (e.g., CPSV [15] and CCCEV [16]). The methodology for creating Domain Semantic Models (DSM) is used in the context of OOP in specific domains.

4.4 Technology Architecture

The Technology Architecture provides logical components and services that are required to support the deployment of business capabilities and application components described in the IS Architecture. It comprises both the European infrastructure components and the components within the MS responsibility. The components within the MS responsibility include the components maintained by the MS and by its Competent Authorities. The current Technology Architecture model comprises two views: the *Deployment Topologies* view, and the *Network and Communication* view.

Due to a wide variety of information systems that can be developed using the Technology Architecture, there is no fixed way of how to deploy TOOP services. In the *Deployment Topologies* view we consider three different deployment topologies. Each deployment topology comprises the central European infrastructure components, components deployed on the MS level, and components deployed on a Competent Authority level.

The central European infrastructure components providing the TOOP Network Management are the same in every variation. They comprise the services provided by the Criterion and Evidence Type Rule Base (CERB), the Semantic Repository (SR), the Data Services Directory (DSD), as well as the Business Document Exchange Network Location (BDXL) Server and the DNS Server that are composed to realize the BDXL component.

Components provided on an MS and Competent Authority level can be of three types with respect to the level of their deployment: components deployed only on the

MS level (eIDAS nodes both in the DP and DC MSs), components deployed only on a Competent Authority level (as a minimum, the DP Competent Authority maintains its backend information systems and similar configuration is maintained by the DC Competent Authority), as well as components that can be deployed both on a national or on a Competent Authority level (the Service Metadata Publisher – SMP, Access Point – AP, and the OOP interoperability layer components that support the exchange of Evidence from one participant to another).

The diagram on Fig. 8 shows a variation of how the application components defined in the IS Architecture can be deployed to nodes in the technology architecture. In this variation, the Competent Authority acting as the DC operates its own SMP, AP, TOOP Connector, and backend information system.

Deployment topology depicted on this diagram enforces significant additional workload on the DC Competent Authority, who needs to adjust its business organization, deploy, and maintain all three components: TOOP Connector, SMP, and AP.

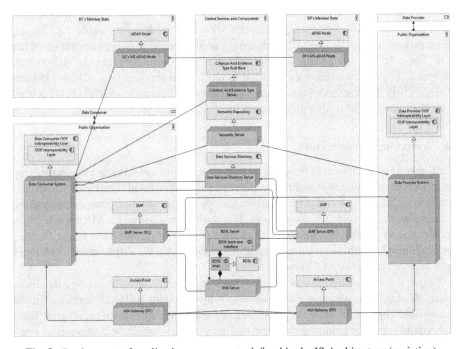

Fig. 8. Deployment of application components defined in the IS Architecture (variation).

On the MS level, the effort required seems minimized at first sight. Still in case of widespread usage of the TOOP architecture by various Competent Authorities, there is a very high probability that implementation of SMP and AP on MS level is needed anyway. So, this option may be not really advantageous form the MS view in the long-term perspective.

As a conclusion, this option may be preferred in the initial phase of introducing TOOP architecture on a MS level, when there is insufficient level of MS infrastructure

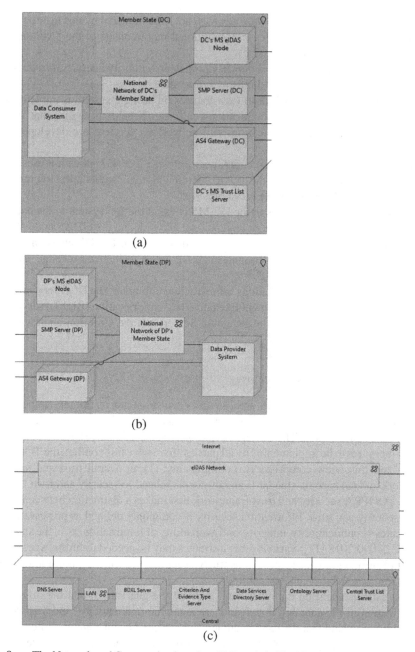

Fig. 9. a. The Network and Communication view (DC part). **b.** The Network and Communication view (DP part). **c.** The Network and Communication view (Internet part between DC on the left and DP on the right).

and some advanced Competent Authorities wish not to be hindered by this insufficiency. Additionally, it may be useful in case of additional requirements to the SMP and AP from some Competent Authorities.

Similar conclusions apply when the DP Competent Authority operates its own SMP, AP, TOOP Connector, and backend information system.

The *Network and Communication* view focuses on how the system is implemented from the perspective of the communications engineer. It helps to assure that within the system, appropriate communications and networking services are developed and deployed by relevant stakeholders.

From the network and communication perspective, a TOOP application uses communication networks in the MSs, the TOOP central communications infrastructure, the eIDAS network, and the Internet (Fig. 9a, 9b, 9c).

The communication networks in the DC MS connect the DC system to the national network of data consumers. Through this national network and the eIDAS node server, the DC connects to the eIDAS network for user identification. The DC also connects to the SMP server for the DP discovery and to an AP for the evidence exchange. Similar connections are used in the DP MS.

The TOOP central communications infrastructure comprises the DNS servers, local area networks, the Business Document Exchange Network Location (BDXL) server, the Data Services Directory server, the Semantic Server, and the Criterion and Evidence Type server.

4.5 Security and Trust Architecture

In view of recent trends in the IS area, security and trust are of primary importance for TOOPRA. At the same time, a project based on such architecture would involve many diverse stakeholders. Therefore, it would be too restrictive to propose just specific security measures to be implemented by all parties. To resolve this conflict, the TOOPRA security and trust view comprises two components: (1) an overall trust and security framework and (2) specific standards and protocols related to security and trust.

The TOOPRA security and trust framework first makes a distinction between information security and trust. Information security is commonly defined as preservation of its attributes - confidentiality, integrity, and availability of information, as in the standard ISO/IEC 27000:2018 [17]. Various other attributes may be needed to further specify the concept of information security, such as trustworthiness, authenticity, non-repudiation, accountability, reliability and traceability.

Trust establishment on the other hand is about the guarantees, that the origin and the destination of the data and documents are authentic (authenticity) and trustworthy (trustworthiness), and that data and documents are secured against any modification by untrusted parties (integrity) [18–20]. Additional trust management can include authorization, accountability, non-repudiation, traceability, and confidentiality. The main difference between information security and trust is the focus on specific concepts. As an example, information security usually does not involve trustworthiness of the data origin. From the other side, trust usually does not involve availability, reliability, and confidentiality.

Using the ISO/IEC 27000 series of standards, the TOOP security and trust architecture introduces the concept of Information Security Management System (ISMS) for all organizations involved in an OOP project. An ISMS comprises policies and procedures together with necessary activities and resources that are used and managed to protect information assets. To establish and maintain its ISMS, the organization needs to identify information assets and information security requirements associated with these assets. Security risks must be assessed and treated, including selection and implementation of controls to manage unacceptable risks. Effectiveness of ISMS must be maintained and improved.

The TOOP security and trust architecture uses the CEF eDelivery AS4 profile for message exchange, the CEF eDelivery profile of the BDXL specification, the OASIS Service Metadata Publishing 1.0 (BDXR SMP) specification, the OASIS RegRep v4.0, the CEF eID BB, and the CEF eIDAS Profile, among other building blocks, standards and interfaces.

5   Architecture Profiling

Based on the reference architecture, different profiles for application domains can be created. Application profiles are collections of variations of the basic TOOPRA model. These variations may be in the form of:

- explications, giving more detailed specifications of an existing TOOPRA component;
- extensions, providing additional functionalities or capabilities to TOOPRA; or
- modifications, introducing changes to TOOPRA structure or components.

To create a profile, it is recommended to i) understand the goals, legal foundations, stakeholders, and specific requirements leading to the profile development; ii) identify components that need to be detailed, extended, or modified; and iii) introduce, test, and document the variations.

The following profiles have been developed from TOOPRA after analysing the goals, legal framework, and specific requirements of the three piloting areas of the TOOP project:

- General Business Mobility
- eProcurement
- Online Ship and Crew Certificates

The goal of the General Business Mobility profile is to facilitate the mobility of companies in terms of doing business within the EU. It demonstrates how information can be automatically retrieved from a company's country of origin, avoiding duplicated effort, and eliminating paperwork and red tape for business management. The use cases covered by this profile are targeting European business needs and are aligned with the SDGR [8], which facilitates online access to information, administrative procedures and assistance services.

The goal of the eProcurement profile is to support businesses in public procurement. By implementing this profile, businesses will no longer have to provide all information they have already delivered in the past during public procurement. The eProcurement profile intends to use the TOOP infrastructure in order to demonstrate how the provision of evidence during an eTendering procedure can be faster and seamless. More specifically, it focuses on the automatic retrieval of the necessary information and qualification documents of tenderers at any phase of the process (pre-award, award or post-award) using the existing national European Single Procurement Document (ESPD) [21], eCertis and available eTendering Services. The main variation to TOOPRA introduced by the eProcurement profile is that the evidence exchanged in the reference OOP process is explicated as a national ESPD. Additionally, there are two different kinds of transactions with the DP: Get Evidence Metadata and Get Evidence. This is a variation mentioned in connection with the TOOPRA Business Architecture operational process model (the exchange of the Evidence information can also be a two-step process where the DP first provides meta-data on the available Evidence and the actual Evidence is retrieved later in a second step).

The Online Ship and Crew Certificates profile addresses problems in the maritime sector, related to accessing Ship and Crew Certificates which are currently issued and maintained in paper format and stored by national Maritime Administrations. The process of validating and checking ships and their crew can be streamlined by making the certificates accessible for Maritime Administrations directly from the issuer, not through the Master of the ship. This approach is fully in line with OOP principle, namely that instead of burdening citizens and businesses with proving compliance, administrations access and re-use information already existing in other administrative bodies. Models in this profile do not use the Criterion and Evidence Type Rule Base, because the Maritime Administrations already know which certificates they need, to perform the inspection. The Data Services Directory is still included to find the Maritime Administrations of other countries.

6   Sustainability of TOOPRA

To stay useful in the long run, components of TOOPRA need to be maintained and sustained. Different components need varying levels of sustainability effort by different stakeholders. First, the TOOPRA itself requires maintenance, including the following components:

- The wiki component of TOOPRA, currently maintained in the TOOP documentation space in Confluence.
- Views of TOOPRA specified by models expressed in ArchiMate, currently maintained in a git repository.
- The support history and open issues of TOOPRA, currently maintained in the JIRA platform.

The BBs and their components needed to implement TOOPRA are currently maintained by CEF. They comprise the CEF eDelivery building block, the CEF eID building block, and the CEF eSignature building block, among others.

The standards and other components needed to implement and maintain TOOPRA are maintained by the organisations driving the development, convergence, and adoption of these standards. It is assumed that the long-term maintenance of these artefacts is outside the TOOP scope. They comprise the AS4 Profile of ebMS 3.0 Version 1.0 OASIS Standard, the ebMS3 OASIS ebXML Messaging Services Version 3.0, the OASIS Business Document Metadata Service Location Version 1.0, the OASIS Service Metadata Publishing 1.0 (BDXR SMP) specification, standards from the ISO/IEC 27000 and ISO/IEC 25000 series of standards, ISO/IEC/IEEE 42010:2011, as well as the TOGAF® Standard, a standard of The Open Group.

7 Conclusions

The main goal of TOOP Reference Architecture is to overcome the main technical challenge in OOP application across the EU – the diversity of organisations, procedures, data, and services on all four main levels of interoperability.

This goal is achieved by using standard solution blocks, by designing the Reference Architecture and standard solution blocks in line with legal requirements, as well as by using tested, mature, inter-connected and interoperable standards and BBs.

TOOP Reference Architecture is developed in cooperation with the TOOP pilots and the TOOP Solution Architecture. It relies on proven Enterprise Architecture methodology, ensuring consistent standards, methods, and communication among Enterprise Architecture professionals.

To ensure sustainability of TOOPRA, its different components still need varying levels of maintenance effort by different stakeholders.

The results of the TOOP architecture represent the main technological innovation of TOOP: the generic federated OOP architecture that supports the interconnection and interoperability of national registries at the EU level – together with other investigations needed to generalize, extend, and sustain the TOOP results.

References

1. The New European Interoperability Framework. https://ec.europa.eu/isa2/eif_en, Accessed 26 Aug 2020
2. European Interoperability Reference Architecture. https://joinup.ec.europa.eu/collection/eur opean-interoperability-reference-architecture-eira/about, Accessed 26 Aug 2020
3. European Commission: European Interoperability Framework – Implementation Strategy. Communication from the Commission to the European Parliament, the Council, the European Economic and Social Committee and the Committee of the Regions, no. COM (2017) 134 final: 9 (2017)
4. ArchiMate® 3.1 Specification, a Standard of The Open Group. https://pubs.opengroup.org/architecture/archimate3-doc/chap01.html#_Toc10045268, Accessed 12 Oct 2020
5. Proper, H., Lankhorst, M.: Enterprise architecture – towards essential sensemaking. Enterp. Model. Inf. Syst. Arch. 9(1), 5–21 (2014). https://doi.org/10.1007/s40786-014-0002-7
6. Chen, L., Babar, M., Nuseibeh, B.: Characterizing architecturally significant requirements. IEEE Softw. 30(2), 38–45 (2013). https://doi.org/10.1109/MS.2012.174
7. The Open Group: TOGAF®, an Open Group Standard. Open Group Standard (2011)

8. European Union: Regulation (EU) 2018/1724 of the European Parliament and of the Council of 2 October 2018 establishing a single digital gateway to provide access to information, to procedures and to assistance and problem-solving services and amending Regulation (EU) No 1024/2012 (Single Digital Gateway Regulation). OJ L 295, 21.11.2018, pp. 1–38 (2018)

9. European Union: Regulation (EU) No 910/2014 of the European Parliament and of the Council of 23 July 2014 on electronic identification and trust services for electronic transactions in the internal market and repealing Directive 1999/93/EC (eIDAS Regulation). OJ L 257, 28.8.2014, pp. 73–114 (2014)

10. European Union: Regulation (EU) 2016/679 of the European Parliament and of the Council of 27 April 2016 on the protection of natural persons with regard to the processing of personal data and on the free movement of such data, and repealing Directive 95/46/EC (General Data Protection Regulation – GDPR). OJ L 119, 4.5.2016, pp. 1–88 (2016)

11. European Union: Regulation (EC) No 45/2001 of the European Parliament and of the Council of 18 December 2000 on the protection of individuals with regard to the processing of personal data by the Community institutions and bodies and on the free movement of such data. OJ L 8, 12.1.2001 (2001)

12. European Commission: Commission notice—Guidelines for the implementation of the Single Digital Gateway Regulation—2019–2020 work programme, C/2019/4881. https://op.europa.eu/en/publication-detail/-/publication/877b88c4-b356-11e9-9d01-01aa75ed71a1/language-en/format-HTML/source-105856679, Accessed 26 Aug 2020

13. ISA^2 - Interoperability solutions for public administrations, businesses and citizens Homepage. https://ec.europa.eu/isa2/home_en, Accessed 26 Aug 2020

14. European Union: Regulation (EU) No 283/2014 of the European Parliament and of the Council of 11 March 2014 on guidelines for trans-European networks in the area of telecommunications infrastructure and repealing Decision No 1336/97/EC, OJ L 86, 21.3.2014, pp. 14–26 (2014)

15. Core Public Service Vocabulary Application Profile (CPSV-AP). https://joinup.ec.europa.eu/solution/core-public-service-vocabulary-application-profile, Accessed 26 Aug 2020

16. Core Criterion and Core Evidence Vocabulary (CCCEV). https://joinup.ec.europa.eu/solution/core-criterion-and-core-evidence-vocabulary, Accessed 26 Aug 2020

17. ISO/IEC 27000:2018. Information technology—Security techniques—Information security management systems—Overview and vocabulary

18. Cofta, P.: Trust, Complexity and Control: Confidence in a Convergent World. Wiley, Hoboken (2007)

19. Gaurav, R., Sarfaraz, M., Singh, D.: Survey on Trust Establishment in Cloud Computing. In: 5th International Conference the Next Generation Information Technology Summit (Confluence). IEEE, Noida (2014)

20. Winslett, M.: An introduction to trust negotiation. In: Nixon, P., Terzis, S. (eds.) iTrust 2003. LNCS, vol. 2692, pp. 275–283. Springer, Heidelberg (2003). https://doi.org/10.1007/3-540-44875-6_20

21. European Union, Commission Implementing Regulation (EU) 2016/7 of 5 January 2016 establishing the standard form for the European Single Procurement Document, OJ L 3, 6.1.2016, pp. 16–34 (2016)

Testing Methodology for the TOOP Pilots

Andriana Prentza[1]([✉]), Marie-Laure Watrinet[2], and Lefteris Leontaridis[3]

[1] Department of Digital Systems, University of Piraeus Research Center, 18532 Piraeus, Greece
aprentza@unipi.gr
[2] Luxembourg Institute of Science and Technology (LIST), Esch-sur-Alzette, Luxembourg
[3] Unioncamere Europa, Brussels, Belgium

Abstract. The Once-Only Principle project (TOOP) is an initiative, financed by the EU Program Horizon 2020, with the aim to explore and demonstrate the Once-Only principle through multiple sustainable pilots, using a federated architecture on a cross-border collaborative pan-European scale, enabling the connection of different registries and architectures in different countries for better exchange of information across public administrations. The deployed systems in the different Member States for the different piloting domains are being monitored and tested following the TOOP testing methodology that was developed during the TOOP project and with the use of specifically developed TOOP tools in order to monitor, identify errors and improve the quality of the pilots. The specific piloting tests and milestones are customized per pilot domain and are followed by all Member States piloting in the specific domain. The methodology starts from a technical view at the own Member State level with the verification of a check list, continues with onboard testing and connectivity testing and as the last step a connectathon between different Member States takes place.

Keywords: eGovernment · Interoperability · Connectathon · Testing methodology · Pilot

1 Introduction

Testing is an important phase in the software lifecycle where the systems developed are tested to uncover errors and gaps in program function, behavior, and performance [1]. The software developed is tested to find out whether stakeholder requirements are matched and to ensure that it is bug-free. The testing process involves the execution of the software components using manual or automatic tools in order to evaluate one or more dimensions of interest.

Testing includes a set of activities that can be planned in advance and can be conducted systematically. For this reason, a testing methodology and testing tools need to be defined in the testing process.

The TOOP project ran pilots in three different domains: General Business Mobility (GBM), eProcurement and Maritime and in fifteen Member States (MS) [2].

R. Krimmer et al. (Eds.): The Once-Only Principle, LNCS 12621, pp. 164–190, 2021.
https://doi.org/10.1007/978-3-030-79851-2_9

For the purposes of the GBM pilot, it is considered that someone (Legal or Natural Person) requires data about their company to use in a service (to issue a certificate for their company for instance). Instead of them filling their information manually, the service that they are using (called Data Consumer – DC) can get their information for them through the TOOP service. To do this, a Concept Request is sent which contains information about who is participating in this data exchange and what data is required. This request is sent to a service which can provide this kind of data (Data Provider – DP). The DP then sends a Concept Response which contains the data that has been requested back to the DC through TOOP along with some information about it.

For the purposes of the Maritime pilot, it is considered that someone (Legal or Natural Person) requires a certificate for their or their company's ship and crew. Instead of them filling their information manually and submitting it, the service that they are using (DC) is able to get their information for them through the TOOP service. To do this, a Document Request is sent which contains information about who is participating in this data exchange and what certificates are required. This request is sent to a service which can provide this kind of data (DP). The DP then sends back to the DC a Dataset Response which contains either the certificates that have been requested or a list of all the available certificates that the user of the DC can choose from. This request for data is done in two steps. In the first step, the DC receives a list of certificate IDs and in the second step the DC uses those IDs to request the actual certificates from the DP as requested by the user of the service.

For the purpose of the eProcurement pilot, the objective is to get qualification evidences from DPs for Economic Operators (EOs) that are submitting a tender and need to satisfy specific criteria using the existing national European Single Procurement Document (ESPD) or eTendering Service. The retrieval may take place at any phase of the process (pre-award, award or post-award). An EO and a Contracting Authority (CA) send Concept Requests generated from the ESPD Response to a DP that sends back a Concept Response which contains in the final step the qualification evidences.

MS piloting in the same domain need to test against each other and this adds complexity to the testing process, hence the need of the well-defined and structured approach. Therefore, TOOP defined a testing methodology and developed a set of testing tools to facilitate the process of testing between the different MS in the three different domains piloting in TOOP. The testing methodology has first been generically defined, and adapted to the context of each pilot. It is also updated all along the project in association with the technical updates. The testing methodology starts at a low level that is more technical, to finish at a higher level by testing the connections between the different MS in a same piloting domain. This is done by organizing connectathons. Connectathons are being used in Integrating the Healthcare Enterprise (IHE), which is a world-wide initiative that enables healthcare IT system users and suppliers to work together to enable interoperability of Information Technology (IT) systems [3]. The Connectathon gives vendors an opportunity to test the interoperability of their products in a structured and rigorous environment with peer vendors. It also enables the IHE Technical Framework itself to be tested in the form of trial implementation/deployment settings. Participating companies test their implementation of IHE Integration Profile specifications against those of other vendors using real-world clinical scenarios [4]. The connectathons organized in TOOP have been adapted taking into account the TOOP environment, goals and requirements. The aim of using Connectathon in TOOP is to demonstrate that the deployed MS systems of the DPs and the DCs are interoperable and have fully implemented the TOOP technical specifications.

The next section describes the infrastructure and testing tools developed in TOOP to help MS developers to monitor their progress in terms of components deployment. An overview of the testing methodology from test preparations to connectathons is presented in the third section. The testing process along with the tools used in each step is analyzed in the fourth section, whereas test monitoring is presented in the fifth section. The results documentation is presented in detail in the sixth section. Finally, main conclusions are presented in the last section of the chapter.

2   Infrastructure and Testing Tools

2.1   Overview of TOOP Architecture

From the TOOP reference architecture described in previous chapter, the TOOP solution architecture was developed [5], as a set of fully implementable technical specifications, along with a suite of common software components (common components) that physically implements the solution architecture and can be used in the pilot environments by the participating MS, as well as a set of testing tools needed for the onboarding of pilots and the verification of end-to-end transaction capabilities achieved by each MS system connected to TOOP.

The TOOP solution architecture depicted in Fig. 1 below, includes MS systems that act as DC or DP and components that are either deployed nationally or centrally.

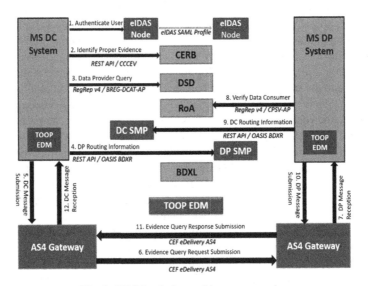

Fig. 1. TOOP solution architecture overview

The MS DC system is the system that is going to request and consume data from the DPs. The DC system authenticates the user via the eIDAS node [6]. It then consults the Criterion & Evidence Type Rule Base (CERB), which is a central authoritative system that maps specifics sets of data as evidence that prove specific requirements/criteria, to identify the proper evidence type that can be requested as an evidence for a specific Data Subject. The DC discovers the DPs that can provide the evidence they require by querying the Data Services Directory (DSD), which is a core service that acts as a catalogue of datasets that the DPs can provide upon request.

The Registry of Authorities (RoA), which is a core service that acts as a catalogue of procedures that the DCs can execute, is used in order to show whether a DC is authorized to request evidence for a specific procedure.

The Service Metadata Publisher (SMP) services provide the metadata about the eDelivery access point(s) (AS4 gateways) used by DCs and DPs in the evidence exchange. The SMP provides the access point metadata and BDXL is used to find the location of the SMP.

Both DC and DP model their messages according to the TOOP Exchange Data Model (EDM). The TOOP EDM uses the functional capabilities provided by the RegRep V4 Query Protocol to model the data request and response as queries.

The different infrastructure and testing tools that TOOP developed to facilitate the deployment of the TOOP artefacts in the MS are summarized in the following Table 1.

Table 1. TOOP infrastructure and testing tools

Tool	Infrastructure	Testing
TOOP connector	YES	
TOOP playground	YES	YES
TOOP simulator		YES
Reference DC/DP systems		YES
TOOP playground tracker		YES

The subsections below describe in detail the TOOP infrastructure and testing tools developed in order to monitor successful implementation of TOOP technical specifications and interoperable data exchange between the different Member States.

2.2 Connector

The TOOP connector is a software artefact developed by TOOP that includes different functionalities of the DC or the DP system and it was developed in order to facilitate the onboarding process of the MS systems in the TOOP infrastructure along the different releases. The TOOP connector is designed as a simplification for piloting countries to act as a glue between the national DC/DP software and the shared standard components (SMP, AS4, DSD). The connector needs to be installed by each of the MS when a new release is provided. The TOOP component offers different interfaces for different architectural use cases. The following Fig. 2 shows the TOOP connector in orange.

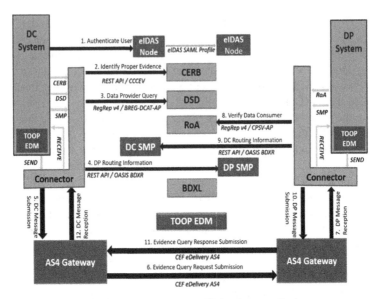

Fig. 2. TOOP connector (Color figure online)

More details are provided in the following Fig. 3. The specific interfaces with the DP or the DC system are depicted with the orange arrows.

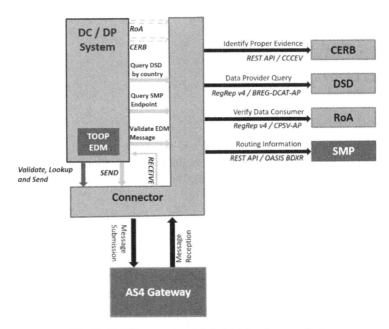

Fig. 3. TOOP connector detailed (Color figure online)

The different connector APIs with their name, relative URI and description are presented in the following Table 2.

Table 2. Connector APIs

Name	relative URL	Description
Query DSD by country	/dsd/dp/by-country	Query the DSD by doctype + country
Query DSD by DP type	/dsd/dp/by-dp-type	Query the DSD by doctype + data provider type
Query SMP Service-Group	/smp/doctypes	Query the SMP by participant ID for all supported document types
Query SMP Endpoints	/smp/endpoints	Query the SMP by participant ID and document type ID for all endpoints
Validate EDM Request	/validate/request	Validate a TOOP EDM Request against the XSD and the Schematron
Validate EDM Response	/validate/response	Validate a TOOP EDM Response against the XSD and the Schematron
Validate EDM Error Response	/validate/error	Validate a TOOP EDM Error Response against the XSD and the Schematron
Send AS4 message	/send	Send out an AS4 message to a specific receiver (metadata + payloads)
Simple Validate, Lookup and Send	/user/submit/request	Validate, SMP Lookup and AS4 sending of an EDM Request in a single call
Simple Validate, Lookup and Send	/user/submit/response	Validate, SMP Lookup and AS4 sending of an EDM Response in a single call
Simple Validate, Lookup and Send	/user/submit/error	Validate, SMP Lookup and AS4 sending of an EDM Error Response in a single call

2.3 Playground

The TOOP playground provides the infrastructure used for testing the pilot implementations. It simulates the behavior of a DC (fictitious MS Freedonia) and a DP (fictitious MS Elonia). Therefore, each MS can connect and test the data exchange with the fictitious MS. The aim of the TOOP playground is to emulate a virtual Europe for a more realistic deployment environment, for testing the developed TOOP artefacts and improving the reliability of each TOOP component.

The playground consists of:

- A reference Data Consumer (Freedonia),
- A reference Data Provider (Elonia),
- Core services (DSD, RoA, SMP, CERB),
- A distributed logging service (Tracker).

The following Fig. 4 presents an overview of the playground. In the left part of the figure, Freedonia includes the DP system, the eIDAS node of the fictitious MS and the AS4 gateway of the DP. In the middle part, there are the core services of the playground and in the right part, Elonia includes the DC system, the eIDAS node of the fictitious MS and the AS4 gateway of the DC.

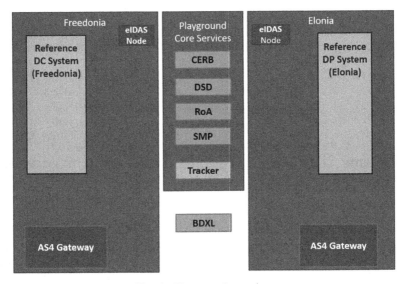

Fig. 4. Playground overview

2.4   Simulator

The TOOP simulator is the main local testing tool. It aims in facilitating the development of DC and DP services, by simulating the whole infrastructure. It also makes it possible for an MS to test its DC and DP only by using its own environment and mocking up the behavior of the respective DP or DC. Then, the MS can do transactions using only their infrastructure.

Three different simulation modes are possible:

- DC mode (simulating the infrastructure and the DP),
- DP mode (simulating the infrastructure and the DC), and
- Sole mode (simulating the infrastructure).

The following Fig. 5 on the left and Fig. 6 on the right show the TOOP simulator working in DC mode and in DP mode respectively. The TOOP simulator working in DC mode allows a MS to test its DC deployed system only by using its own environment and mocking up the behavior of the respective DP. Respectively, the TOOP simulator working in DP mode allows a MS to test its DP deployed system only by using its own environment and mocking up the behavior of the respective DC.

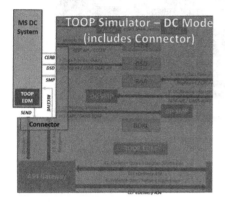 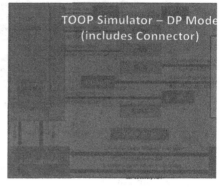

Fig. 5. TOOP simulator – DC mode   **Fig. 6.** TOOP simulator – DP mode

2.5 Reference DC and DP systems

The reference DC system is called Freedonia and the reference DP system is called Elonia.

Freedonia DC is a test DC implementation, which supports all types of queries and document types as defined by the pilots. It provides a UI for initiating TOOP data requests (https://dc-freedonia.acc.exchange.toop.eu/). It is used mainly for the connectivity testing step, as it will be discussed in the next section. It is also available as a war file, a standalone application and as a Docker Image, for facilitating local testing.

Elonia DP is a test DP implementation, which supports all types of queries and document types as defined by the pilots. It is discoverable through the discovery process of TOOP. It is also used mainly for the connectivity testing step. As for Freedonia DC, it is also available as a war file, a standalone application and as a Docker Image, for facilitating local testing.

2.6 Playground Tracker

The playground package tracker supports connectivity testing: when executing each step of the test scenario of a specific pilot, a MS uses it to check the transaction log on both DC and DP. It is a distributed logging service and it is used for testing purposes, providing the ability to see log messages from both ends of a test transaction. The tracker has been created to enable a user to see the actual message exchange of TOOP, that is not visible from the frontend.

The following Fig. 7 shows an example of the package tracker and the logs it displays. The primary objective of the tracker is to be used as a demonstration/presentation tool

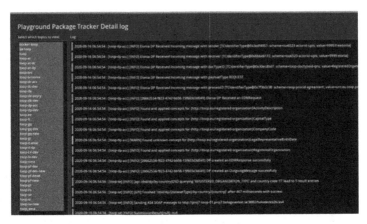

Fig. 7. Playground package tracker

and as a tool to examine the exchange of messages in TOOP during the development of the common components.

The principle, as presented in the diagram below (Fig. 8), is that the TOOP common components hosted in the TOOP playground will notify the package tracker at various

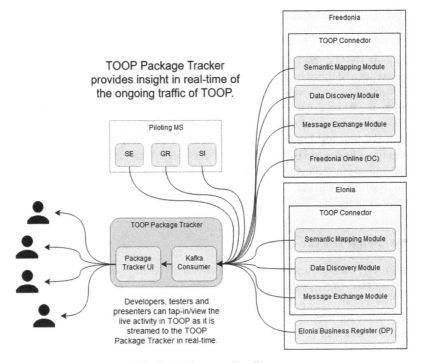

Fig. 8. Package tracker diagram

points during the TOOP data provisioning process. The package tracker collects and presents the received messages in a sequential manner to the user.

3 Testing Methodology: From Test Preparation to Connectathons

TOOP has defined a 4-step process to conduct tests, checking the readiness and maturity of the pilot MS implementations. Each testing step must be properly executed by every MS that implements a pilot, and the results are properly gathered and documented for completeness and monitoring. It includes the test preparation verifying a checklist, the technical tests to be done at MS level (onboard testing), the tests with fictional MS Elonia and Freedonia (connectivity testing), and the connectathon tests between the MS consisting in connectathons. More specifically, the TOOP testing methodology includes the following steps as these are presented in the following Fig. 9:

1. *Preparation for testing*, where a technical checklist verifies whether the national environment is ready for testing.
2. *Local testing*, where the MS use the TOOP simulator to verify their own TOOP environment by doing automatic testing.
3. *Connectivity testing*, where the DCs can use the datasets of the Elonia fictional MS and the DPs can use their datasets with the fictional MS.
4. *Connectathons*, where the DC MS connect with valid data using dataset of another DP.

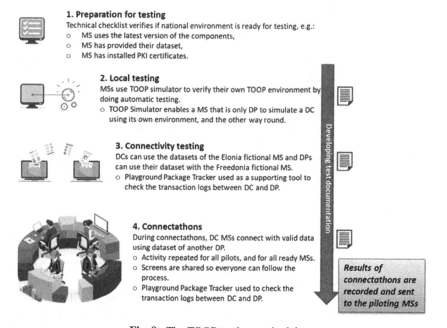

Fig. 9. The TOOP testing methodology

The methodology has been applied several times in the project lifetime. For the GBM pilot, a first session already took place from December 2018 to February 2019 with the participation of less MS, a second session took place from May 2019 to April 2020. Finally, the third session started in May 2020 until the end of the project. For the Maritime pilot, the methodology was applied as the MS were getting ready to pilot and for the eProcurement pilot, testing took place during the last period of the project from autumn 2020 until March 2021.

The four steps of the TOOP testing methodology are detailed in the following subsections.

3.1 Preparation for Testing: Checklist Before Testing

As part of the preparation for testing, the very first thing that the different MS have to do before starting to test is to verify that they have completed the checklist provided to them. The checklist consists of eight elements to verify at the MS technical level. The elements are presented in the following Table 3.

3.2 Local (Onboard) Testing

The second step of the end-to-end testing process includes automatic tests at the MS level using the TOOP simulator described in previous subsection (see Sect. 2.4). At this stage, the MS tests its own environment, a detailed user guide is provided on the wiki to help them using it.

3.3 Connectivity Testing

Before starting the connectathons, the different MS have the possibility to test their own DC and DP with fictional countries: Freedonia and Elonia. This is connectivity testing.

Connectivity testing enables to prove that the DC/DP system implemented by a MS is able to communicate properly under a sandbox environment which has been implemented by the TOOP team.

Elonia is a DP system that simulates a DP in the fictional country Elonia. A DC can do connectivity testing requesting data from the Elonia DP, using the Elonia's dataset.

Freedonia is a DC system simulating a DC in the fictional country of Freedonia. A DP can do connectivity testing triggering TOOP Requests from Freedonia DC towards his DP implementation. A screen shot of Freedonia can be seen above in Fig. 10.

3.4 Connectathon

Connectathon test sessions are organized via conference calls with shared screen. The environment where a TOOP connectathon takes place is a controlled and neutral environment where ready DC MS can test with ready DP MS (ready means the MS has passed successfully the three steps before connectathons). The connectathon is an opportunity for all the MS to identify errors in their implementations and to improve them. There is no negative effect in the case of an error in the implementation, on the contrary it serves as an incentive for improvement [7]. The improvement can be a refinement in the TOOP specifications or in the specific implementation at the MS deployed system.

Table 3. Testing preparation checklist

1. Use last version of TOOP Connector.
The MS must use the last version of TOOP Connector. A documentation is provided on the TOOP internal wiki to help the MS update their current release to the last one.
2. Use last version of TOOP SMP.
The MS must use the last version of TOOP SMP. The TOOP SMP is provided in two versions: either Docker container, or deployable war file. The MS must configure properly the TOOP SMP server for a good communication and for trust inside the TOOP infrastructure. Documentation for the SMP deployment and configuration is provided in the internal wiki.
3. Use last version of Document Type Identifier.
The MS must use the last version of Document Type Identifier. The Document Type Identifier lists the different capabilities of the DC to receive and process specific types of responses.
4. Use last version of a compatible AS4 gateway.
The MS must use the last version of a compatible AS4 gateway, e.g., HolodeckB2B.
5. Have provided their own DP dataset.
Each MS should provide their own DP dataset that is added in the dedicated TOOP wiki. They should provide their dataset according to the last concept namespaces used n the project.
6. Have ordered and installed received PKI certificates.
The MS need to have ordered and installed received PKI (Public Key Infrastructure) certificates to be used by keystore(s) TOOP services/components. Each deployment instance requires a certificate to join the TOOP infrastructure from a trusted Certificate Authority (CA): the TOOP connector, AS4 Gateway, SMP Server and backend systems (DCs and DPs) need to sign their messages using certificates trusted by the TOOP PKI.
7. Have registered the DC/DP supported document type capabilities and gateway endpoints to SMP
Each MS should have registered the DC/DP supported document type capabilities and gateway endpoints to SMP. Explanation is provided in the pilot wiki, depending on the MS pilot domain and role (DP or DC).
8. Have registered the SMP to SML.
The MS must register the SMP to SML (Service Metadata Locator).

Fig. 10. Screenshot of Freedonia

A typical connectathon session in the GBM pilot is described below, where Greece participates as DC, Slovakia participates as DP, and Sweden participates as both DC and DP. Greece that is only DC is ready to test as well as Slovakia (only DP) and Sweden (DC and DP). Greece, Slovakia and Sweden have realised successfully each of the three steps before the connectathon (checklist before testing, onboard testing and connectivity testing according to Elonia and Freedonia). The two DPs (Slovakia and Sweden) have provided their dataset.

The connectathon session can start:

1. Greece DC shares its screen and starts testing with Slovakia, using Slovakia DP dataset. The tests are done with a valid identifier and in a second step with an invalid identifier to be sure the correct global error message is displayed.
2. Greece continues testing with Sweden using Sweden DP dataset, with valid and false identifier.
3. Then Sweden shares its screen as DC and tests using Slovakia DP dataset with valid and false identifier.

The results of the connectathons are then reported on the TOOP pilot wiki, and a report is sent by mail to all the piloting MS.

An example with the respective screenshots and playground tracker details is shown below for the connection between Germany DC and Austria DP. First, Germany DC shares its screen, copies Austria's DP identifier and selects Austria in the list (see Fig. 11).

Fig. 11. Connectathon between Germany DC and Austria DP - selection of Austria DP

Then, Germany requests the corresponding DP information through TOOP (see Fig. 12).

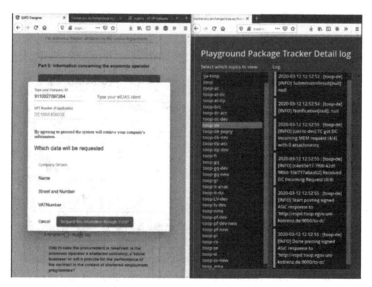

Fig. 12. Connectathon between Germany DC and Austria DP - request information

In the following Fig. 13, one can see that the data request is in progress between Germany and Austria.

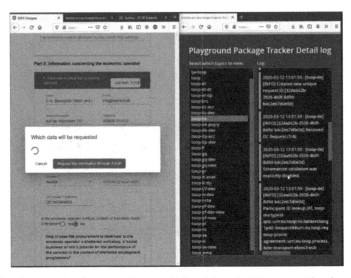

Fig. 13. Connectathon between Germany DC and Austria DP - request data in progress

The data requested is then received from Austria DP, and Germany needs to agree to receive it (see Fig. 14).

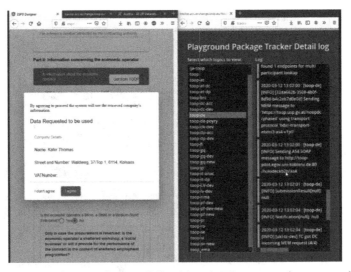

Fig. 14. Connectathon between Germany DC and Austria DP - agree on data requested to be used

Finally, the information is visible on Germany DC, and the test is successful (see Fig. 15).

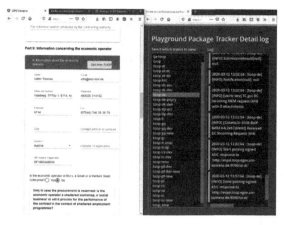

Fig. 15. Connectathon between Germany DC and Austria DP - successful result

When the connectathon is finished, a reporting is done with the current results as presented in Sect. 5.

4 Testing Process

This section presents an overview of the steps of the testing methodology along with the tools that are being used in each step. Local MS system testing (Subsect. 4.1) and local infrastructure testing (Subsect. 4.2) form part of the local testing step.

4.1 Local MS System Testing

In the following Fig. 16, the MS DC system checks whether it is able to create messages to be sent using the TOOP simulator and receive messages from the TOOP simulator.

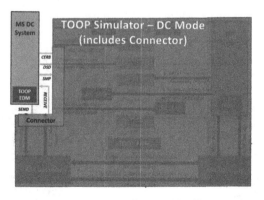

Fig. 16. Local MS system testing with the use of the TOOP simulator

4.2 Local Infrastructure Testing

In the following Fig. 17, the DC using a local DC instance checks whether it is able to send a request to the playground (Elonia), using its own deployed infrastructure (SMP, AS4 gateway).

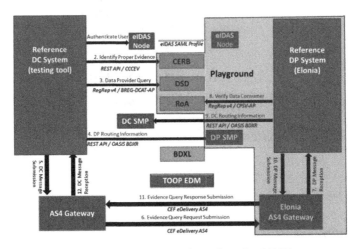

Fig. 17. Local infrastructure testing using a local DC instance

4.3 Connectivity Testing

In the following Fig. 18, the DC using its deployed system (and not a local DC instance) checks whether it is able to send a request to the playground (Elonia), using its own deployed infrastructure (connector, SMP, AS4 gateway).

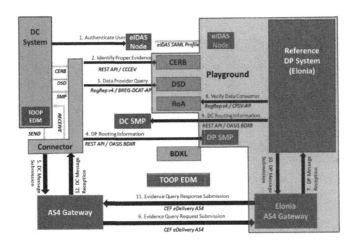

Fig. 18. Connectivity testing

4.4 MS to MS Connectathon

In the following Fig. 19, the DC using its MS deployed system checks whether it is able to send a request to all the other DPs using its own deployed infrastructure and accept back the response provided (both TOOP error and successful TOOP responses).

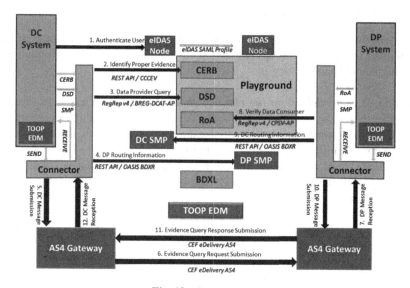

Fig. 19. Connectathon

5 Test Monitoring

As there are many MS deploying their systems either with the role of DC, or with the role of DP or with both roles (DC and DP) and getting ready for connecting using different releases that are available in the project, it is necessary to supervise the process, monitor the status of each MS participating in the testing process and organize the respective testing sessions in a structured way.

The testing manager is responsible for this role. She supervises the testing process, monitors the status of each MS participating in the testing process, and plans each connectathon. The testing manager interacts with each MS in order to keep track of the MS that are ready to participate in a connectathon, and plans the agenda of each connectathon. The agenda includes the connections along with the specific test cases that need to be tested. A DC ready MS will test with all the DP ready MS. This is repeated for all DC ready MS and the results are registered. Different reporting views of the results are adopted, as described in detail in the next section.

For the pilot test status tracking, a pilot test monitoring factsheet was initially developed, and is described in Subsect. 5.1. The test monitoring factsheet was applied in consecutive testing sessions, it was adapted and improved taking into account the feedback from the MS and the developers' teams and it was also aligned with the new releases of the TOOP components and the evolvement of the solution architecture and the adoption of the new EDM. This led to the identification of specific pilot milestones for each testing step and ways of verifying them. The pilot milestones are described in Subsect. 5.2.

5.1 Pilot Test Monitoring Factsheet

For this reason, monitoring information is asked to the MS, based on the four steps defined in the testing methodology subsection. Each MS has to indicate information for each pilot they are participating in:

1. ***Readiness to participate in the connectathon.*** Information is captured (updated) whether the MS is a DC and/or DP, if they are using eIDAS, and if they are ready to participate in a connectathon. The MS that are ready to participate in a connectathon proceed with filling the rest of the monitoring document.
2. ***Check list.*** The MS indicates information relevant to the check list part of the testing method. The following information is filled in:
- TOOP Connector installation: if it is done, current version and date it was installed, next version and date planned to install.
- TOOP SMP installation: if it is done, current version and date it was installed, next version and date planned to install.
- Document Type Identifier installation: if it is done, current version and date it was installed, next version and date planned to install.
- AS4 gateway installation: if it is done, which compatible AS4 gateway is installed (e.g. HolodeckB2B), which version and when it was installed.
- Provision of the MS own dataset: if it is done, and if yes, when.
- Ordering and installation of received PKI certificates used by keystore(s) TOOP services/components: if it is done and when.
- Registration of the DC/DP supported document type capabilities and gateway endpoints to SMP: if it is done and when.
- Registration of SMP to SML: if it is done and when.
3. ***Onboard testing.*** The MS indicates if they have performed successfully onboard testing as a DC and/or as a DP, what was the result (classified as (1) passed, (2) partly passed or (3) failed), and if it is not already done, when it is planned to be done. There is also space available for comments.
4. ***Connectivity testing.*** The MS indicates if they have performed connectivity testing. This means that if they act as a DC, they have to indicate the connectivity testing result of their DC system to the fictional Elonia MS, and if it is yet not done, they need to inform on the planned date. If they act as a DP, they have to indicate the connectivity testing result from the fictional MS Freedonia to their DP system, and if it is not yet done, they need to inform on the planned date. There is also space available for comments.
5. ***Connectathon.*** This part of the monitoring document includes information on the participation of the MS as a DC or as a DP or both as a DC and DP in the last connectathon and the respective results. There is also space available for comments.

5.2 Pilot Milestones Check

Five pilot milestones were identified along the four steps of testing for better monitoring the progress in the deployment of the TOOP components in each MS system. Milestone 1 aligns with testing step 1: preparation for testing, milestones 2 and 3 align with testing step 2: local testing, milestone 4 aligns with testing step 3: connectivity testing and milestone 5 aligns with testing step 4: connectathon. More specifically:

- *Milestone 1*: the MS must integrate the new EDM in their piloting system.
- *Milestone 2*: it concerns the transaction implementation; the MS system should be able to create messages to be sent using the TOOP simulator and to receive messages from the TOOP simulator.
- *Milestone 3*: the system's infrastructure (connector, SMP and AS4 gateway) must be properly deployed and correctly configured locally.
- *Milestone 4*: it is about the playground connectivity: DCs and DPs will test that their system deployed can connect to the playground (the fictive countries of Elonia and Freedonia).
- *Milestone 5*: it is about the connectathon where DCs and DPs will test with other MS. The MS system is able to communicate and execute correctly a transaction using each own system and infrastructure.

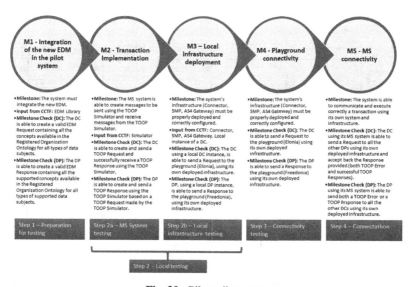

Fig. 20. Pilot milestones

The pilot milestones together with the way to verify them (as a DP, or as a DC) are presented in Fig. 20 above. The figure also presents what input is necessary to be provided by the team that develops the common components (Common Components Task Force – CCTF).

Milestones 1, 2 and 3 are checklist. The answers of the DCs and DPs can be one of the following:

1. Yes: the milestone is achieved.
2. Partly: the development to achieve the milestone is in progress but not yet finished.
3. No: the milestone is not achieved. It can be skipped, e.g. in the case of Austria that skipped milestone 2 and went directly to milestone 3.
4. Planned: the milestone is not started yet but is planned to be started.
5. Not decided: this is in case an MS has not taken a decision whether to proceed with the update of their system with the next release of the components. This can be due to resource reasons or change of policy.

For milestone 4, connectivity test with the playground needs to be completed. For milestone 5, testing during connectathon needs to be done. For both milestones 4 and 5, the results can be classified as:

1. Passed: the MS successfully passed the test.
2. Partly passed: the connection has been tested but partly passed and needs to be retested.
3. Failed: the MS did not pass the test.
4. Planned: the test not yet done.
5. Not decided: the MS has not taken the decision to proceed with the test.

Fig. 21. Pilot milestones MS status

For a direct interaction and support of the MS technical teams, recurrent technical and testing calls are put in place each week. The calls consist of two parts. During the first part of the call, the MS technical members are presented the latest technical updates of the TOOP components, and they can ask questions. The second part of these calls is dedicated to testing milestone 4 and milestone 5, with the MS that are ready. The participants really appreciate these calls that are dedicated to them and help them in completing their work.

During these calls, the status of the MS respective to the milestones is presented in a dashboard visualisation (see above Fig. 21). The three first columns show the MS and the pilot it is participating in (General Business Mobility and/or eProcurement). If the MS is green, it means that the MS participated in at least one connectathon, being ready for milestone 5. Orange means that the MS is about to be ready. No color indicates that the MS did not start any milestone for the moment. The other columns are grouped by milestone. For each milestone, the status of the MS achievement for the specific milestone according to the classification presented above is shown as a DC and as a DP. If a role (DC, or DP) is not applicable, then the cell is marked in grey.

6   Results Documentation

Results are reported in different views in a consistent way, easily traceable back in what was done in each connectathon, and easily comparable regarding the progress in each connectathon. Different reporting tables and graphs present the results, and a summary of the successful connections is presented in a map of results. The following subsections present the different reporting methods.

6.1   Reporting to MS

After each connectathon, an email is sent to all piloting MS with the results of the current connectathon. The email summarizes textually the results of the connectathon with the addition of a table presenting the results of connections done during the connectathon. A link is also provided to the pilot wiki where more information can be found. The results are classified as (1) passed, (2) partly passed, and (3) failed.

6.2   Global Results Table

After each connectathon, a global results table is updated. The columns of this table include the following information:

- The DC MS.
- The DP MS that are going to provide data to the specific DC MS.
- The status of each DC-DP connection. This is classified as (1) to be tested, (2) retested, and (3) already passed.
- The connectathon results of the current connectathon using two test cases: (1) valid identifier, (2) invalid identifier, and comments in case of failure.
- The connectathon results of the last connectathon (same information is provided as for the current connectathon).
- The general results updated with current connectathon results: results using test case (1) valid identifier, results using test case (2) invalid identifier and the date of the last connectathon.

The following Table 4 presents a snapshot of the global results table after a connectathon that took place on September 23rd, 2020.

Table 4. Connectathon global results table

DC	DP	Status	Connectathon results on 23.09.2020			Connectathon results on 16.09.2020			General result updated		
			Result valid Identifier	Result false identifier	Comment	Result valid Identifier	Result false Identifier	Comment	Result valid id	Result false id	Date last connectathon
Austria	Italy - IC	Already passed				Passed	Passed	Fix natural person id issue	Passed	Passed	16.09.2020
	Estonia	Already passed	Passed	Passed					Passed	Passed	23.09.2020
	Norway	Already passed	Passed	Passed					Passed	Passed	23.09.2020
	Poland	To be tested									
	Romania	Already passed				Passed	Passed		Passed	Passed	16.09.2020
	Slovakia	Already passed				Passed	Passed		Passed	Passed	16.09.2020
	Slovenia	Already passed				Passed	Passed		Passed	Passed	16.09.2020
	Sweden	Already passed				Passed	Passed		Passed	Passed	16.09.2020
Estonia	Austria	Already passed				Passed	Passed		Passed	Passed	16.09.2020
	Italy - IC	Already passed				Passed	Passed		Passed	Passed	16.09.2020
	Norway	Already passed	Passed	Passed					Passed	Passed	23.09.2020
	Poland	To be tested									
	Romania	Already passed				Passed	Passed		Passed	Passed	16.09.2020
	Slovakia	Already passed				Passed	Passed		Passed	Passed	16.09.2020
	Slovenia	Already passed				Passed	Passed		Passed	Passed	16.09.2020
	Sweden	Already passed				Passed	Passed	Need to add "SE/EE" to the legal id	Passed	Passed	16.09.2020
Germany (UKL)	Austria	Already passed				Passed	Passed		Passed	Passed	16.09.2020
	Estonia	Already passed	Passed	Passed					Passed	Passed	23.09.2020
	Italy - IC	To be retested				Partly passed	Partly passed		Partly passed	Partly passed	16.09.2020
	Norway	Already passed	Passed	Passed					Passed	Passed	23.09.2020
	Poland	To be tested									
	Romania	Already passed				Passed	Passed		Passed	Passed	16.09.2020
	Slovakia	Already passed							Passed	Passed	29.07.2020
	Slovenia	Already passed							Passed	Passed	29.07.2020
	Sweden	Already passed							Passed	Passed	05.08.2020

6.3 Reporting Tables

Two types of tables are updated after each connectathon summarising the status of the pilots: the MS implementation status and the connectathon status. These two tables are used to communicate results within the project but also to external stakeholders in a tabular way. The MS implementation status table presents the status of each milestone per MS and per pilot. The connectathon status table presents the status of the connectathon per MS and per pilot. The status in both tables can be (1) completed (coloured dark green), (2) in progress (coloured light green), (3) planned (coloured yellow), or (4) not started (coloured orange). Examples of these tables below reflect the results of a connectathon that took place on September 23rd, 2020 (see Table 5 and 6).

Table 5. MS implementation status

PILOT WG: General Business Mobility					
Member state	Milestone 1	Milestone 2	Milestone 3	Milestone 4	Milestone 5
Austria	Completed	Not started	Completed	Completed	Completed
Germany - UKL	Completed	Completed	Completed	Completed	Completed
Germany - Pöyry	Not started				
Greece	Completed	Completed	Completed	Completed	Completed
Estonia	Completed	Completed	Completed	Completed	Completed
Italy - ANAC	In progress	Completed			
Italy - Infocamere	Completed	Completed	Completed	Completed	Completed
Norway	Completed	Completed	Completed	Completed	Completed
Poland	In progress				
Romania	Completed	Completed	Completed	Completed	Completed
Slovakia	Completed	Completed	Completed	Completed	Completed
Slovenia	Completed	Completed	Completed	Completed	Completed
Sweden	Completed	Completed	Completed	Completed	Completed

Table 6. MS connectathon status

PILOT WG: General Business Mobility													
Member state		Germany -	Germany -				Italy -						
DC/DP	Austria	UKL	Pöyry	Greece	Estonia	Italy - ANAC	Infocamere	Norway	Poland	Romania	Slovakia	Slovenia	Sweden
Austria			Not started		Completed		Completed	Completed	In progress	Completed	Completed	Completed	Completed
Germany - UKL	In progress		Not started		Completed		In progress	Completed	In progress	Completed	Completed	Completed	Completed
Germany - Pöyry	Not started				Not started		Not started	Not started	Not started	Not started	Not started	Not started	Not started
Greece	Completed		Not started		Completed		Completed	Completed	In progress	Completed	Completed	Completed	Completed
Estonia	Completed		Not started				Completed	Completed	In progress	Completed	Completed	Completed	Completed
Italy - ANAC	In progress		Not started		In progress		In progress	In progress	In progress	In progress	In progress	In progress	In progress
Italy - Infocamere													
Norway	In progress		Not started		In progress	In progress			In progress	In progress	In progress	In progress	In progress
Poland	In progress		Not started		In progress	In progress	In progress			In progress	In progress	In progress	In progress
Romania													
Slovakia													
Slovenia	Completed		Not started		Completed		Completed	Completed	In progress	Completed	Completed		Completed
Sweden	Completed		Not started		In progress		Completed	In progress	In progress	Completed	Completed	Completed	

6.4 Reporting Graphs

The connectathon results are visible through different graphs presenting a different kind of information. The following graphs present a result summary for the current connectathon with a valid identifier (on the left, see Fig. 22) and with an invalid identifier (on the right, see Fig. 23). In both figures, the percentage of successful connections is shown in green, the percentage of partly passed connections is shown in orange, and the percentage of failed connections is shown in red.

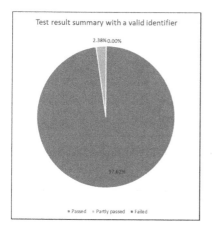

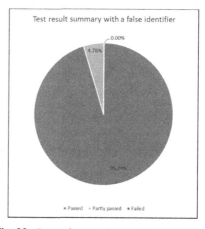

Fig. 22. Reporting graph - result summary with valid identifier (Color figure online)

Fig. 23. Reporting graph - result summary with invalid identifier (Color figure online)

The following graph (Fig. 24) presents the results for each MS (DC and/or DP) with a valid identifier. For each MS DC and each MS DP, the number of connections is shown (in green the number of connections that were successful, in orange the number of transactions that was partly passed, and in red the number of transactions that failed).

Other graphs are also updated after each connectathon, presenting the progress of results such as the one below presenting the total number of connections at each connectathon, including successful connections in green, partly passed connections in orange and failed connections in red. In Fig. 25, one can see that the number of connections increases from one connectathon to another, and the number of green connections also

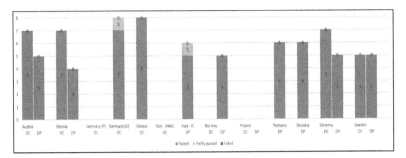

Fig. 24. Reporting graph - results by MS with valid identifier (Color figure online)

increases. The objective is ideally to have all connections successful which will be the end of a connectathon session. This might not be possible for instance if a MS pilot becomes inactive at one time. In Fig. 26, one can see the same kind of graph as above but per MS. Only a part of this last graph is presented.

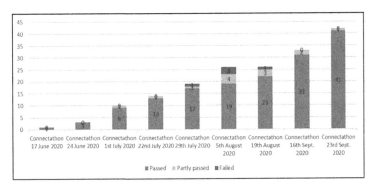

Fig. 25. Reporting graph - progression of results with valid id over time (Color figure online)

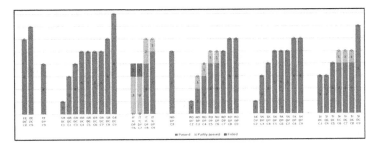

Fig. 26. Progression of results by MS: MS DC and MD SP with a valid identifier

6.5 Map of Results

A map of connections is visible on the TOOP website [8] and can be seen below (Fig. 27). This interactive map realized by the TOOP communication team enables to view the MS participating in the GBM pilot. A table on the right shows which MS are connected as DC and which MS are connected as DP. The table offers the possibility to select the countries for which the user wants to see the connections that are then visible as green arrow (successful connections) on the map.

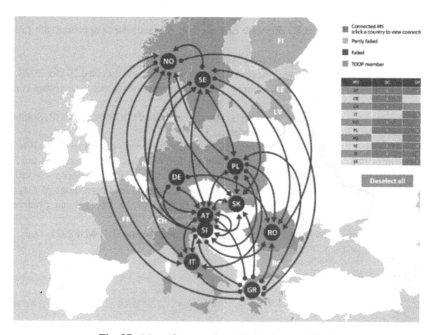

Fig. 27. Map of connections (Color figure online)

7 Conclusions

As presented in the current chapter, the TOOP testing methodology, process, monitoring, and reporting has been a structured effort to monitor the progress of different pilots, deploying different releases of TOOP components and participating in different domains and has been a very useful instrument to monitor and to support and to improve the quality of the pilots. It was first put in place for the General Business Mobility pilot starting with few participating MS, it was adapted to be used by the Maritime pilot participants and it was further adapted and used by the eProcurement pilot during the last session of testing during the project.

The methodology is also updated to respond to the needs of the common components development team, in parallel to the new releases of TOOP Components, and to respond to the needs of the MS.

Each two weeks, the piloting MS have been meeting via conference call to realize the well-known connectathons that also provide the possibility to keep good contact between the MS, and to identify possible issues that can be then corrected by the common components development team.

As a generic approach, this structured testing methodology can be applied in different context after a small adaptation.

References

1. Pressman, R.S., Maxim, B.R.: Software Engineering, A practitioner's approach, 8th Edition (2015)
2. TOOP pilots https://www.toop.eu/pilots. Accessed 31 Jan 2021
3. Integrating the Healthcare Enterprise (IHE) https://www.ihe.net/. Accessed 20 Dec 2020
4. What is the Connectathon, IHE Europe https://connectathon.ihe-europe.net/what-connec tathon. Accessed 31 Mar 2021
5. TOOP Solution Architecture http://wiki.ds.unipi.gr/display/TOOPSA20/TOOP+Solution+ Architecture+v2.0+-+2020+Edition. Accessed 31 Mar 2021
6. CEF eID offers digital services capable of electronically identifying users from all across Europe https://ec.europa.eu/cefdigital/wiki/display/CEFDIGITAL/eID. Accessed 31 Jan 2021
7. Lampoltshammer, T.J., John, K., Helger, P., Piswanger, C.-M.: Connectathons - a sustainable path towards development in european large-scale pilots. In: Proceedings of Ongoing Research, Practitioners, Posters, Workshops, and Projects of the International Conference EGOV-CeDEM-ePart 2019, pp. 207–214 (2019)
8. TOOP pilot connections https://toop.eu/pilot-connections. Accessed 31 Mar 2021

TOOP Pilot Experiences: Challenges and Achievements in Implementing Once-Only in Different Domains and Member States

Andriana Prentza[1(✉)], David Mitzman[2], Madis Ehastu[3], and Lefteris Leontaridis[4]

[1] Department of Digital Systems, University of Piraeus, 18532 Piraeus, Greece
aprentza@unipi.gr
[2] Infocamere, Padova, Italy
[3] Ministry of Economics and Communication (MKM), Talinn, Estonia
[4] Uniocamere Europa, Brussels, Belgium

Abstract. The Once-Only Principle (OOP) enables public administrations to support citizen and business life-cycle oriented issues as opposed to mere integration of administrative systems designed to serve bureaucratic ends. The Once-Only Principle project (TOOP) was funded by the EU Program Horizon 2020, with the aim to explore and demonstrate the OOP through multiple sustainable pilots in different domains, using a federated architecture on a cross-border collaborative pan-European scale, enabling the connection of different registries and architectures in different countries for better exchange of information across public administrations. The different pilot domains (eProcurement, Maritime and General Business Mobility) identified potential use cases suitable to show the OOP, defined the goals and expected benefits of TOOP based on motivational scenarios and process analyses and provided requirements to the TOOP Reference and Solution Architectures. Especially for the General Business Mobility domain requirements were provided also from the Single Digital Gateway Regulation. These requirements guided the development of the TOOP specifications and the TOOP components, the Member States deployed the TOOP specifications and components and participated in different connectathons demonstrating the OOP.

Keywords: eGovernment · Interoperability · Once-Only · Pilot

1 Introduction

At the start of the TOOP project [1], the state of the Once Only Principle (OOP) in the different Member States (MS) was very different from the points of view of policy, organization (of public administrations), technology and infrastructure. The participating piloting MS found themselves at various levels of "maturity" regarding general awareness of the Once Only Principle (OOP) and the implementation of procedures, organisations and infrastructures to support this principle at the national level. Concrete experiences and developments at the international level were almost exclusively limited to bilateral interoperability agreements between nations already closely tied politically,

© The Author(s) 2021
R. Krimmer et al. (Eds.): The Once-Only Principle, LNCS 12621, pp. 191–207, 2021.
https://doi.org/10.1007/978-3-030-79851-2_10

economically and culturally (e.g., Scandinavian countries, Benelux, etc.) as well as domain-specific interoperability initiatives not centrally aimed at implementing OOP (e.g., eProcurement, BR domains).

Countries which already had some degree of national standard – architecture and infrastructure in accordance with national legislation – included Estonia, Slovenia, Italy, Greece, Sweden and Norway. Except for the Scandinavian cases, these systems were neither interconnected nor even aware of each other. They served national purposes of data exchange between public administrations with varying degrees of emphasis on creating benefits for citizens, businesses and the administrations themselves. The European dimension was not yet contemplated.

Three pilot areas were chosen for the TOOP project. Two of these focused on cross-border exchanges of company data, one in the context of cross-border services (Pilot Area 1: Cross-border eServices for Business Mobility) and the other on exchange of registry data (Pilot Area 2: Updating Connected Company Data). The third pilot area is inherently cross-border in essence (Pilot Area 3: Online Ship and Crew Certificates). The main criteria for their selection were cross-border relevance, potential to reduce administrative burden, and feasibility of implementation.

The pilot of cross-border eServices for Business Mobility was based on the assumption that government administrations from different countries expose eServices directed at Economic Operators from various countries. During the respective service provision company-related information is needed. The aim was to show how such information can be automatically retrieved from the Economic Operators' country of origin without the business representative having to enter it again. Use cases include participation in public procurement procedures cross-border, extending business presence cross-border, administrations checking the mandates of business representatives.

The pilot of updating connected company data foresees a central role for the Business Registers. Company data are officially stored, at each MS level, in the Business Registers following the different European Company Law directives, regulations and national commercial codes. The data from the Business Registers are authoritative, up-to-date and have a recognized legal value. However, the same (or part of the same) data are also stored for other purposes by various public administrations in the same and other MS. Keeping these data up to date is a real challenge, especially when they are related to foreign companies.

The last pilot focused on online ship and crew certificates. The problem from OOP perspective with ship and crew certificates is that they are currently issued and maintained in paper format, resulting in delays in delivery to the vessel and extra costs.

The next section presents the TOOP pilot domains and the way the TOOP project worked towards piloting. Main achievements of the TOOP pilots are described in the third section. The fourth section presents the lessons learnt and the experiences of the different Members States. Main conclusions are presented in the last section of the chapter.

2   The TOOP Pilot Domains

TOOP followed an agile, iterative approach that starts from real user needs encapsulating the ambitions of pilot participants and proceeds by gradually building pilot prototypes that will ultimately result in production-level pilots capable of real transactions, which will be handed over to their owners in governmental organisations and businesses.

The starting point in the process was the compilation of use case descriptions in the form of motivational scenarios from the pilot coordinators together with the interested MSs, starting from the indicative usage scenarios identified during proposal phase when the selection of the piloting domains was done. MSs were closely involved in reviewing and validating the motivational scenarios. Each motivational scenario was subscribed to by several MSs. Taking into account the prioritizations of the MSs, six pilot use cases were identified in the three Pilot Areas (PAs):

- PA1: Cross-border eServices for Business Mobility

  - eProcurement
  - Licenses and Permissions
  - Company Data and Mandates

- PA2: Updating Connected Company Data

  - Business Register Data Provision
  - Business Register Interconnection

- PA3: Online Ship and Crew Certificates

  - Online Ship and Crew Certificates

The pilot coordinators together with the MSs took the motivational scenario descriptions and followed business process modeling in order to model certain aspects that are important for arriving at the extraction of requirements. PA virtual meetings and face-to-face plenary sessions were opportunities to discuss extensively and finalize the results.

As a next step, pilot coordinators and piloting MSs, looking at the entire range of the motivational scenarios and engaging in a process of abstraction and synthesis, a conceptual view of the once-only principle was created, the common patterns emerged and a more generic flow of events was described that depicts the generic data exchange that takes place along all the different motivational scenarios. These generic patterns were documented as Baseline Piloting Scenarios. Each motivational scenario can be projected to the generic flow of the baseline scenarios.

As a last step in the pilot design process a deployment architecture was created which was necessary for the development and rollout of TOOP-compliant common components, and a rollout and implementation plan was made available, featuring the main milestones expected for the project implementation.

Starting from the motivational scenario description and modelling, MSs committed to their national piloting scope and produced a pilot plan including all information necessary to understand who will pilot what, and what should be expected from each country in terms of functionality and infrastructure.

Each MS pilot plan included:

- the scope and ambition of the piloting MS including description of the national pilot scenario(s) by making reference to the Motivational Scenarios already described in the Pilot Areas but providing the national versions and possible variations and actual actors involved, and information on the data provider capability targets and data consumer functionality and system(s) to be connected as well as the data type(s) the MS intends to consume from TOOP,
- the motivation and goals providing a list of national goals to be used for post-pilot evaluation later in the project and why the pilot is important for the country, what are the national priorities and policy objectives to be met and what is the value expected for which stakeholders,
- the implementation strategy with details on organizations involved nationally and their role, and commitment of all relevant stakeholders, tentative planning of implementation anticipating also aspects of national readiness or dependencies on other European initiatives, and overall feasibility of the pilot including the main risks at national level but also at project level that may be factors that influence the execution of the pilot plan.

As the project was moving towards implementations that have specificities relevant to the business domains, domain ownership was needed and relevance to be manifested within the project and visible outside the project by domain stakeholders which include different MS organisations and different EC policy units. Therefore, the project decided to consider the approach of Working Groups (WGs) that complements the original approach referring to Pilot Areas (PAs) and does not contradict or substantially modify the original rationale of targeting pilots. It merely extends it, as a natural step in the evolution of pilots. PAs were use case-oriented, whereas WGs are business domain-oriented. The WG view relates to business domains where the legal basis is different, and this makes a difference in requirements, implementation, and future governance proposals when the pilot results are delivered to the MS but also the business domains.

The direct mapping from PA use cases to WGs can be seen in Fig. 1 below.

Therefore:

- The **eProcurement WG** includes the *eProcurement* from PA1.
- The **General Business mobility (GBM) WG,** which aligns well with the part of the proposed Single Digital Gateway Regulation (SDGR) that concerns company-related data includes two use cases from PA1: *Licenses and Permissions* and *Company Data and Mandates*; and two use cases from PA2: *Business Register Data Provision* and *Business Register Interconnection.*
- The **Maritime WG** includes the *Online Ship and Crew Certificates* from PA3.

Pilot implementation has the following dimensions which are specific to business domains, as reflected in the WG view:

a. Business stakeholders are different.
b. Data modelling is domain-specific and therefore WG-specific.

c. Transaction patterns are also domain-specific, hence WG-specific.
d. Connectathons (cross-border testing events) have WG-specific scenarios due to differences in data and transaction patterns. Testing happens among implementers within each WG even though some (e.g., Business Registers) may belong in more than one WG.

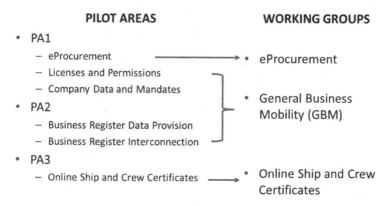

Fig. 1. Mapping from Pilot Areas use cases to Working Groups.

The TOOP pilot activities were therefore organised according to domains of interest defined by the business services they wished to enable: the eProcurement WG was a specific area created around eProcurement procedures (already an area of international interoperability development) and the Maritime WG was a specific area in the Maritime sector; the GBM WG was a more general area concerned government services promoting the European mobility of companies and their services.

Different MS piloted in the three workgroups. There were deviations from initial commitments, as changes in political and organizational priorities, changes in responsibilities, shortage of personnel, delays in tendering and choosing subcontractors had as a result some MS not to finally pilot in the workgroup they had initially committed. Subsections 2.1 to 2.3 present more details regarding the piloting workgroups and the MS that finally piloted.

2.1 eProcurement Pilot

The eProcurement Pilot intended to use the TOOP infrastructure in order to demonstrate how the provision of evidences during an eTendering procedure can be simplified. More specifically, the use case focuses on the automatic retrieval of the necessary evidences for a specific Economic Operator (EO) using the existing national European Single Procurement Document (ESPD) [2] or an eTendering Service implementing the ESPD. The pilot describes how an ESPD system can integrate the TOOP infrastructure to facilitate the discovery of designated data providers and evidence and send the relevant requests to retrieve the necessary information through the TOOP architecture. The retrieval may take place at any phase of the process (pre-award, award or post-award).

The provision of evidences to selection and exclusion criteria of a public procurement may be cumbersome for businesses and discourage them from participating. According to the Public Procurement Directive 2014/24/EU [3], when being awarded, an EO must provide all required evidences (declared in the ESPD at the phase of participation) in order to conclude contract with contracting authorities. Moreover, the contracting authorities can request at any time the provision of all supporting documents in order to proceed with the award and/or the contracting procedures.

Providing a pre-filled version of the ESPD may make this process more easy and less time consuming for both the EO and the contracting authorities. According to the use case, the required evidences will be automatically retrieved by the competent authority (business registry or aggregation/pre-qualification service) of the country in which the tenderer is registered. Thus, businesses will no longer have to upload information, already provided in the past, directly by their local IT infrastructure since data will be provided directly by the business registry. Moreover, the contracting authority can choose to be notified each time there is a change in the tenderer's situation. Finally, since data is provided by an authoritative source it will be reliable, trusted and have legal validity.

The Data Consumer Agencies that participated in the eProcurement pilot in TOOP consist of the Directorate for Management, Development and Support of the National eProcurement System in Greece, Italian National Anti-Corruption Authority (ANAC) from Italy and in Germany the University of Koblenz which developed an ESPD system that can be used by Economic Operators and Contracting Authorities to request, reference and validate evidences through evidence metadata.

The Data Providers that participated in the eProcurment pilot in TOOP included BR from Norway providing company information, the Register of Financial Statements from Slovakia and AFRY (pre-qualification company) from Germany as a prequalification body providing evidence information upon request.

The following Table 1 presents the MS that initially planned to pilot either as DC or DP or both DC and DP in the area of eProcurement. The MS that confirmed their intentions are marked as YES, and the ones that were not sure are marked as TBC (To Be Confirmed).

Table 1. Overview of MS planned to pilot as DC and DP in eProcurement.

TOOP PLANS – eProcurement Pilot																	
DATA CONSUMER Commitment of Member States																	
AT	BG	DE	DK	EE	FI	FR	GR	IT	LV	NL	NO	PL	PT	RO	SE	SI	SK	TR
		YES					YES	YES					TBC					
DATA PROVIDER Commitment of Member States																	
AT	BG	DE	DK	EE	FI	FR	GR	IT	LV	NL	NO	PL	PT	RO	SE	SI	SK	TR
		YES				TBC		YES			YES			YES			YES	

Table 2 presents the MS that finally piloted either as DC or DP or both DC and DP. The MS that reached technical readiness and participated in connectathon are marked as YES, the ones that did not pilot are marked as NO, and the ones that worked on their pilot but did not manage to participate in a connectathon for various reasons are marked as PARTLY.

All MS that planned to pilot as DC in eProcurement participated in the eProcurement pilot. The ones that were not initially confirmed, finally did not pilot. From the 5 MS initially planning to act as DP, Romania did not connect as DP due to lack of resources. Italy started the deployment but did not have enough time to participate in the connectathon.

Table 2. Overview of MS piloted as DC and DP in eProcurement.

TOOP RESULTS – eProcurement Pilot																		
DATA CONSUMER Commitment of Member States																		
AT	BG	DE	DK	EE	FI	FR	GR	IT	LV	NL	NO	PL	PT	RO	SE	SI	SK	TR
		YES					YES	YES					NO					
DATA PROVIDER Commitment of Member States																		
AT	BG	DE	DK	EE	FI	FR	GR	IT	LV	NL	NO	PL	PT	RO	SE	SI	SK	TR
		YES				NO		PART LY			YES			NO			YES	

2.2 GBM Pilot

The GBM WG had clear relations with the initiatives spawned by the European Services Directive [4]. Additionally, the TOOP services investigated in the GBM pilot were chosen with specific attention to those requiring data provision from cross-border Business Registers, in order to exploit the previously developed relations between EU BRs and the EU regulations on BR data exchange.

During the course of the TOOP Project, developments in the GBM pilot proceeded in strict symbiosis with the evolving Single Digital Gateway (SDG) initiative – the regulation, itself [5], as well as the conception and specification of the national and European organisations and infrastructures supporting it.

The main roles that TOOP Partners play in the GBM scenario are:

- Data Consumers: Public agencies offering services to companies – both domestic and foreign – in compliance with regulations governing the promotion and exercise of business activities, or the establishment of businesses and services, in their territories.
- Data Providers: Business Registers, or equivalent government-mandated authorities, that are "officially responsible" for maintaining and distributing company information required to identify and authorize the Economic Operators which are subjects of the DC services.
- Technical agencies serving DCs and DPs: Agencies organized to serve specific administrations or agencies already charged with a transversal role in managing or interfacing National OO-Layers.

The most frequent Data Consumer Agencies represented in TOOP consist of Points of Single Contact (PSCs) for example from Slovenia and Poland. Other Data Consumers are the Tax Agency in Sweden, the Directorate for Management, Development and Support of the National eProcurement System in Greece, business Portals from Austria, Estonia and Norway. Some of the services which they offer are business registration, licenses, and other different services regarding business mobility.

The Data Providers are primarily BRs providing company information included BRs from Sweden, Norway, Italy, Estonia, and other government portals from Austria, Poland, Romania, Slovenia, and Slovakia, dealing with business promotion and regulation.

Some other actors involved in the provision of TOOP-enabled services are legal persons, the subject of the TOOP-enabled service; the authorized representative of the Legal Person; eID providers and other EU and National infrastructures for security, payments, translation, etc.

The goals of all these actors, almost independent of their roles in OO processes were established early in the project and confirmed at several checkpoints along the way as:

- Reducing administrative burden for companies and citizens (Legal Entities) required to use cross-border DC services;
- Increasing the efficiency of these services – saving time and costs for both subjects and administrations (Front-office and Back-office operations);
- Automating data retrieval and procedural interoperability between administrations resulting in improved data quality and better, swifter processing;
- Increasing trust in administrative procedures – the right data furnished at the right place at the right time; reduced complaints or even lawsuits for damages caused by administrative errors;
- Compliance with EU regulations and a more harmonized business marketplace.

The European dimension of the project made partners acutely aware of the need to use standard technical solutions and open specifications of architectures, procedures and interfaces. Strong preference was given to CEF building blocks and interoperability standards emerging from other EC initiatives. Such standards are being continuously re-evaluated and updated at all levels of interoperability: technical, semantic, procedural, legal.

The following Table 3 presents the MS that initially planned to pilot either as DC or DP or both DC and DP in the area of GBM. The MS that confirmed their intentions are marked as YES, and the ones that were not sure are marked as TBC (To Be Confirmed).

Table 4 presents the MS that finally piloted either as DC or DP or both DC and DP. The MS that reached technical readiness and participated in connectathon are marked as YES, the ones that did not pilot are marked as NO, and the ones that worked on their pilot but did not manage to participate in a connectathon for various reasons are marked as PARTLY.

From the 9 MS initially planning to act as DC, finally Italy and Romania did not connect as DC. Germany which was to be confirmed, finally acted as DC with an ESPD application consuming business data. Estonia (not initially considered in the planning) also connected its business registry as DC. Turkey due to legal restrictions did not continue piloting after the 1st year. The Netherlands are marked with partly* as they did

Table 3. Overview of MS planned to pilot as DC and DP in GBM.

TOOP PLANS – GBM Pilot																		
DATA CONSUMER Commitment of Member States																		
AT	BG	DE	DK	EE	FI	FR	GR	IT	LV	NL	NO	PL	PT	RO	SE	SI	SK	TR
YES	TBC						YES	YES		YES	YES	YES		YES	YES	YES		TBC
DATA PROVIDER Commitment of Member States																		
AT	BG	DE	DK	EE	FI	FR	GR	IT	LV	NL	NO	PL	PT	RO	SE	SI	SK	TR
YES	TBC	YES					YES	YES		YES	YES	YES		YES	YES	YES	YES	TBC

not piloted with eDelivery but with direct API connection to Sweden and Norway and with an earlier model of the TOOP Exchange Data Model and did not continue to next releases.

Table 4. Overview of MS piloted as DC and DP in GBM.

TOOP RESULTS – GBM Pilot																		
DATA CONSUMER Commitment of Member States																		
AT	BG	DE	DK	EE	FI	FR	GR	IT	LV	NL	NO	PL	PT	RO	SE	SI	SK	TR
YES	TBC	YES					YES	NO		PARTLY*	YES	YES		NO	YES	YES		NO
DATA PROVIDER Commitment of Member States																		
AT	BG	DE	DK	EE	FI	FR	GR	IT	LV	NL	NO	PL	PT	RO	SE	SI	SK	TR
YES	NO	YES					NO	YES		NO	YES	YES		YES	YES	YES	YES	NO

From the 11 MS initially planning or considering to act as DP, business registries from Greece, the Netherlands and Germany finally did not connect to the TOOP architecture.

2.3 Maritime Pilot

The aim of the maritime pilot was to fulfill the needs of a Port State Control Officer (PSCO) in the context of a ship inspection. Ship and crew certificates are today issued and maintained in paper format, resulting in delays on delivery to the vessel and extra costs. Certificate data exists in Maritime Administrations' (MA). There are different associated problems:

- The ship has to submit same certificate data for every port of call, e.g. ship submits the copy of the Tonnage Certificate, which is used for calculating port dues, pilot dues etc.

- The Port State Control (PoSC) may not have enough time to check the certificates thoroughly during ship's port stay or crew's rest time is used for inspection, both resulting in increased risk of marine accident.
- Withdrawn certificates are not removed from circulation, increasing the risk that "more favourable" certificates are being presented to the PoSC.
- Falsification of paper certificates is rather easy.
- Paper certificates are sent on board via courier service, which is costly (in most extreme cases, a ship may need to wait for paper documents to arrive via post up to several weeks) and an administrative burden. A ship may leave the port before the certificates arrives, thereby increasing the risk of the detention.
- In case the vessel changes flag, the losing Flag State's registry has to submit all relevant data to the receiving Flag State's register. Such data is mainly concentrated onto ship certificates (Regulation (EC) 789/2004 [6] and IMO res. A. 1053(27) [7]).

The aim of the pilot was to provide a proof-of-concept that these problems can be solved.

The main roles that TOOP Partners play in the Maritime scenario are:

- Data Consumers: The DC is the PSCO. The PSCO needs to get access to information about existence and validity of certificates and information within certificates. The required certificates are at least all the conventional certificates. In order to achieve this status, the Data Providers need to commit to providing all the required data services.
- Data Providers: The DP (MA ship registry, MA seafarer registry, RO ship registry ...) needs to provide all the information that is agreed that the PSCO requires.

The following Table 5 presents the MS that initially planned to pilot either as DC or DP or both DC and DP in the area of Maritime. The MS that confirmed their intentions are marked as YES, and the ones that were not sure are marked as TBC (To Be Confirmed). Table 6 presents the MS that finally piloted either as DC or DP or both DC and DP. The MS that reached technical readiness and participated in connectathon are marked as YES, the ones that did not pilot are marked as NO, and the ones that worked on their pilot but did not manage to participate in a connectathon for various reasons are marked as PARTLY.

Table 5. Overview of MS planned to pilot as DC and DP in maritime.

TOOP PLANS – Maritime Pilot																	
DATA CONSUMER Commitment of Member States																	
AT	BG	DE	DK	EE	FI	FR	GR	IT	LV	NL	NO	PL	PT	RO	SE	SI	SK	TR
	YES		YES	YES	YES		YES	TBC	YES		YES						
DATA PROVIDER Commitment of Member States																	
AT	BG	DE	DK	EE	FI	FR	GR	IT	LV	NL	NO	PL	PT	RO	SE	SI	SK	TR
	YES		YES	YES	YES		YES	TBC	YES		YES						

Table 6. Overview of MS piloted as DC and DP in maritime.

TOOP PLANS – Maritime Pilot																		
DATA CONSUMER Commitment of Member States																		
AT	BG	DE	DK	EE	FI	FR	GR	IT	LV	NL	NO	PL	PT	RO	SE	SI	SK	TR
	PAR TLY		YES	YES	YES		PART LY	NO	PART LY		YES							
DATA PROVIDER Commitment of Member States																		
AT	BG	DE	DK	EE	FI	FR	GR	IT	LV	NL	NO	PL	PT	RO	SE	SI	SK	TR
	PART LY		YES	YES	YES		PART LY	NO	PAR TLY		YES							

Out of the seven MS that planned to pilot as DC and DP in the Maritime pilot, the four made it to the successful connectathons. Bulgaria, due to delays in subcontracting, deployed both DC and DP capabilities as initially planned, but did not have the time to participate in Connectathon, therefore is marked as partly piloted. Greece also only partially implemented the pilot, as it encountered several difficulties, mostly related to the limited availability of online data for ship and crew certificates from the competent authorities holding such information in Greece, in paper from (a typical "network externalities" effect at the DP level). In addition, the ambivalence of the position of the government authorities has not favored the investment of specific resources in this pilot.

Latvia, due to unexpected technical and personnel problems, did not succeed to fully implement the pilot and take part in the Connectathons.

In the maritime domain, there was a good common understanding regarding once-only and semantic, organisational, legal and technical agreements on some elements and on some there was not. However, a more important question was whether sufficient business need was recognised by the participating organisations. The process the maritime domain focused on involved enough of sensed "pain" that it was quite easy to gather support for the initiative. This was also analytically confirmed in the process mapping exercise. As for all the interoperability elements, it was felt that these are not major hurdles. Since shipping is a global and historical domain there has been time to achieve a good common understanding on semantics. The organisation is there, EMSA and DG MOVE at EU level and IMO globally. Legally, the PSCO process is quite well defined both at EU level and at IMO. As regards technical aspects, there are systems existing at EU level, most notably the Thetis system. There was enough interoperability to deem the pilots' quality goals achievable. During the project, this was confirmed. Once there was a platform to use, setting up the data exchange and testing whether it works was quite straightforward, without major issues.

3   Advances Attained in TOOP Pilot Domains

As mentioned above, the state of implementation and awareness of OO procedures was quite varied in the different Pilot Partner MS. Thus, different configurations of TOOP components/CEF building blocks were implemented according to the architectural needs of the Partners. Some partners were able to exploit existing local or national infrastructures to maximize benefits and reduce costs of implementation. The following diagram illustrates the different approaches to TOOP integration for the connection of DCs and DPs to the TOOP Federated network. Data Aggregators represent intermediate levels of implementation of OOP, for example in regional or domain-specific contexts (Fig. 2).

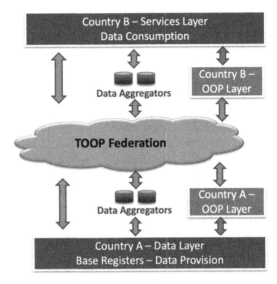

Fig. 2. Connection of DCs and DPs via the TOOP federation network

In any scenario of cross-border business mobility, country A (origin) could be considered the MS where a company or a professional is registered and as country B (destination) the country where the company or professional wants to do business. If the DC and the DP are in different countries, then a variety of infrastructures may sit between them, each of the two countries will have a combination of national once-only layer, aggregators or ad-hoc pairings.

If we extrapolate to an EU-27 environment that is entirely heterogeneous, it becomes clear that in order to ensure DC-DP data exchanges and implement the OOP cross-border, either a lot of ad hoc connections must be made (not a scalable option) or a federated architecture must be put in place.

TOOP was established with one core objective: to define, implement and pilot a federated architecture that enables the discovery and interconnection of data providers and consumers, so that its instantiation into a cross-border infrastructure can be used to implement the OOP cross-border.

Having adopted a basic model to describe once-only data exchanges and established the need for a federated architecture, it is necessary to project these views onto the real situation in Europe, where:

• Architectures are heterogeneous and infrastructures rarely interoperate even inside certain countries, let alone internationally.

- There are already certain data exchange networks deployed or emerging at European level (e.g., BRIS, Tax Authorities, EESSI [8], PEPPOL [9] etc.)

The following figure paints the landscape within which TOOP came to design a federated architecture and deploy an interoperability infrastructure to facilitate DC-DP data exchange (Fig. 3).

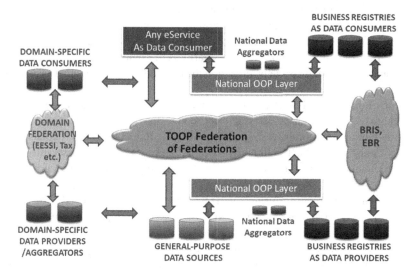

Fig. 3. The TOOP piloting landscape

The DP side is important, since it is important that data is accessible. In business mobility processes, where mostly company-related data are involved, there are three categories of data providers:

- The Business Registers (BRs), which are a special category since they operate under their own legal basis nationally and at EU level.
- Domain-specific providers or aggregators (e.g., in the eProcurement domain).
- General-purpose data sources which are not Business Registers (other base registers).

Some of these systems may already be connected to cross-border exchange networks – the BRs are connected to BRIS. The eProcurement platforms are starting to be connected to PEPPOL, the tax agencies are also interconnected, etc. These networks are not interoperable among them – even networks such as BRIS and PEPPOL, which both use eDelivery, use it in different "flavours". At the same time, each country has its own infrastructure (combination of national OOP layers, aggregators and ad-hoc pairings).

In such a complex field, it is generally not possible to exchange data between an eService sitting in a country wishing to act as a data consumer and the sources of data which are needed in a cross-border mobility scenario. Unless a system is already connected to one of the few existing international networks, it cannot communicate outside its country. Even the ones connected to the existing networks can only communicate within their silos.

In this wider landscape, the need for the federated TOOP architecture and infrastructure becomes even more apparent. In fact, it is important that it becomes a federation of federations, being able to pull data from the existing silos if it is more difficult to connect to the original data sources. In a world of national OOP layers that extend over the vast array of data provided and consumed in each country, it would suffice to connect these layers; but this is not enough at the moment as these layers are not as widespread as it could be wished for. For some data types it might be more efficient to link TOOP to an existing network (e.g., BRIS), thereby making TOOP a cross-federation infrastructure.

TOOP pilots came to explore these scenarios and come up with solutions on the technical and the governance levels, involving the MS participants and other institutional stakeholders.

The flexibility of the TOOP architecture permits all combinations of configurations simultaneously. The Swedish Tax Authority, connected to TOOP via a national OO Layer is able to request company information from the Italian Business Register, which is directly connected to the TOOP network, in the same way as it requests information from the Slovenian Business Portal, an aggregator which connects different government authorities.

In the maritime domain, during the TOOP project, EMSA and DG MOVE had developed an alternative data exchange system, where all ship certificates would be sent to a central repository that would serve the central Thetis system. Implementing TOOP in this situation would mean that there is no central repository and all data is exchanged directly between the participating countries. A central repository allows for more control and stability in the system as well as follow the existing model where EMSA is a central service provider to the maritime authorities. Implementing TOOP would have changed that organizational/ cultural setting. Though the EMSA approach only tackles ship certificates where the exchanged data is not sensitive. If at some point it is decided to start to exchange crew certificates, which may include sensitive personal information, a decentralized TOOP approach should fit better as it takes out a central mediator and leaves control and responsibility with the DP and DC.

4 Lessons Learnt

The existence of OO infrastructures in the different MS was usually an advantage for implementation of TOOP components and services, but there were still several factors involved. Although experience in integration and interoperability at the international level helped make MS aware of the different issues involved the state of the PA procedures and information networks still heavily condition the way that OOP could be implemented. In particular, traditional PAs and their information systems are designed for vertical, bureaucratic info handling with different info silos adopting completely different approaches to information handling and service provision. The "products" of these information silos – reports, certificates, profiles, etc. - are usually specific to the administration involved, using techniques language and even concepts not widely known and used in other administrations. This is why technical integration is so very different from true interoperability which requires seamless compatibility of procedural, legal, organizational and semantic entities.

Public Administrations in Member States which had promoted National OO Layers had already faced this issue of providing information, which was useful in other administrative contexts, but working at the national level means that there is still a common legal framework and a common bureaucratic culture of certificates, procedures and the basic language and concepts being regulated. The main source of interoperability difficulties arise from the "culture shock" that occurs when cross-border procedures meet.

To create useful, fully OO-enabled applications government agencies must not only abandon their own particular "mindsets" and adapt to the needs of other administrations, but they must embrace the concept of life-cycle processes for citizens and businesses and prepare their information products to support the critical life-cycle events they entail. This will involve deconstructing existing reports and certificates, but it is not just a question of providing direct access to elementary data items. Too much semantic information would be lost in such a case.

For the maritime pilot, some lessons learnt are presented below:

- They partners should have "gone out of the building" before they started designing and building. While they talked to maritime authorities and business partners, they didn't sufficiently talk to the European Commission to confirm that whether their MVP met the basic requirements of the customer.
- The good thing is that the quality goals will most probably be achieved, even though through another solution. But, a centralized approach misses out on the possibility to implement other business cases, with other types of organisations (e.g. business registers, tax authorities, toll, police etc.) and is much riskier when dealing with sensitive information.
- When developing a data exchange layer, the close collaboration between the platform team (Technical team in TOOP's case) and the product teams (the pilots) is vital while the platform team needs to be the more active part.

5   Conclusions

Cross-border piloting in a large-scale pilot project is definitely challenging, especially, when there is a moving target. TOOP started as a far more exploratory project, aiming to define its perimeter, its architecture and its pilots and then disseminate and exploit its results and find whether there is impact. However, when SDGR was introduced, this meant taking into account the legal requirements of a new Regulation and building a solution for its implementation. The project and particularly the pilots in PA1 and PA2 had to shift focus. The project shifted to a project implementing specifications for regulation, and therefore the impact was assured, if the specifications piloted were close to the Implementing Act.

TOOP raised to the occasion and met its objectives as well as the expectations around its pilots. For this to be done, it was necessary to have a careful and meticulous project execution. The pilots were closely monitored and supported in order to ensure that they meet their goals. The tools and support that were provided by the technical team were highly appreciated by all piloting partners. Taking into account all the different updates and incremental releases, especially in the GBM WG, this would not have happened otherwise. A structured environment for onboarding and roll out was necessary.

It is also important to mention that TOOP piloting had a big impact on OOP solutions nationally and contributed to a faster development of national OOP-functionality.

It should be mentioned that in the maritime domain, although the pilots did not go further that the proof-of-concept, the pilot was a good catalyst for dialogs with the (primarily EU) maritime legal and business domain, but met constraints and did not find the required external policy and strategy support.

Concluding, cross-border piloting is a wonderful way to show the key problems and issues and how the real issues emerge then, and it allows to provide a concrete picture/solution of a before abstract legal text and give it a realistic future. This is the most important thing that through piloting, real complex change is possible!

References

1. Krimmer, R., Kalvet, T., Toots, M., Cepilovs, A., Tambouris, E.: Exploring and demonstrating the once-only principle: a European perspective. In: Proceedings of the 18th Annual International Conference on Digital Government Research, pp. 546–551 (2017)
2. European Commission, (2016). Commission Implementing Regulation (EU) 2016/7 of 5 January 2016 establishing the standard form for the European Single Procurement Document, OJ L 3, 6.1.2016, pp. 16–34 (2016)
3. European Commission: Directive 2014/24/EU of the European Parliament and of the Council of 26 February 2014 on public procurement and repealing Directive 2004/18/EC Text with EEA relevance, OJ L 94, 28.3.2014, pp. 65–242 (2014)
4. European Commission: Directive 2006/123/EC of the European Parliament and of the Council of 12 December 2006 on services in the internal market, OJ L 376, 27.12.2006, pp. 36–68 (2006)
5. European Union: Regulation (EU) 2018/1724 of the European Parliament and of the Council of 2 October 2018 establishing a single digital gateway to provide access to information, to procedures and to assistance and problem-solving services and amending Regulation (EU) No 1024/2012 (Single Digital Gateway Regulation). OJ L 295, 21.11.2018, pp. 1–38 (2018)
6. European Commission: Regulation (EC) No 789/2004 of the European Parliament and of the Council of 21 April 2004 on the transfer of cargo and passenger ships between registers within the Community and repealing Council Regulation (EEC) No 613/91, OJ L 138, 30.4.2004, pp. 19–23 (2004)
7. International Maritime Organization: Resolution A.1053(27) Survey Guidelines under the Harmonized System of Survey and Certification (HSSC), 2011, Adopted on 30 November 2011, Agenda item 9, 20.12.2011, pp. 1–169 (2011)
8. EESSI. https://ec.europa.eu/social/main.jsp?catId=869&langId=en
9. PEPPOL. https://peppol.eu

Measuring the Impact of the Once Only Principle for Businesses Across Borders

Tjerk Timan[✉], Anne Fleur van Veenstra, and Kristina Karanikolova

Strategy and Policy, Netherlands Institute for Applied Scientific Research TNO,
Anna van Buerenplein 1, 2595 DA The Hague, The Netherlands
{tjerk.timan,annefleur.vanveenstra,kristina.karanikolova}@tno.nl

Abstract. The Once-Only Principle (OOP) holds that public administrations ideally collect data from citizens and businesses *only once* to share this information, within regulatory limits, with other administrative bodies and across Member States. The aim of the OOP is to simplify interaction with public services and contribute to administrative burden reduction. To demonstrate the cross-border application of the OOP for businesses, the Large Scale Pilot European project 'The Once Only Principle Project (TOOP)' develops pilots and identifies benefits and challenges as well as (potential) impacts of the adoption of this principle. In this chapter, we explore an Impact Assessment framework for measuring the impact of the OOP on cross-border services for businesses and subsequently validate this framework with members from the TOOP project. During stakeholder sessions organized for this purpose, we find that the OOP potentially has a high impact on government, e.g. by enabling fraud reduction, yet little is known about the impact of the OOP on businesses, and in particular on its cross-border impact. The expected benefits of the OOP likely emerge on the longer term, making identification of short-term impacts challenging. Nonetheless, based on our findings, we recommend to develop and implement methods and tools to measure the impact on the long-term to increase sustainability of the OOP.

Keywords: Once only principle · Impact assessment · Data sharing · Impact frameworks · Impact assessment

1 Introduction

The Once Only Principle Project (TOOP) is a Large Scale Pilot (LSP) European project that was carried out between 2017 and 2021 with the objective "to explore and demonstrate the once-only principle through multiple sustainable pilots" [21] to provide a basis for future implementation and wider use of the Once Only Principle (OOP). The pilots developed within the TOOP project focus on cross-border electronic services (e-services) for businesses. They explore use cases that demonstrate the impact of the OOP on doing business across borders, including expected benefits such as decreasing the administrative burden of businesses or making governmental processes more efficient. Impact Assessments aid organizations and governments to better understand the consequences

R. Krimmer et al. (Eds.): The Once-Only Principle, LNCS 12621, pp. 208–224, 2021.
https://doi.org/10.1007/978-3-030-79851-2_11

of adopting technologies into daily processes and workflows [4]. An important outcome of the project is, thus, to develop and validate an Impact Assessment (IA) framework that contributes to implementation and wider use of the OOP; it provides a basis for IA indicators and formulates recommendations for assessing OOP impacts. Since the TOOP project focuses on the cross-border aspect of the OOP for business, the IA framework also focuses on the *cross-border* aspect of the OOP for *businesses.* The development of the IA framework for the OOP across borders was carried out using an action research approach [52]. This means that the development of the IA framework was conducted in parallel to the technical work of the TOOP project and that an approach of diagnosis and intervention was taken, feeding back the policy objectives into the technical goals and vice versa. The OOP is a high-level policy objective and is mentioned as one of the principles stemming from the eGovernment Action Plan [9]. Such overarching principles need technical building blocks to put high-level principles in practice, but also, in turn, influence the effectiveness of policies: *"Pilot socio-technical systems are used to prove the viability and the feasibility of some policy objective that requires the usage of Information and Communication Technologies (ICT) platforms in order to be attained"* [34]. As part of our action research approach, we set up a series of focus group sessions throughout the project in which we invited project partners to jointly discuss impacts assessment and indicators. The added value of such sessions was to regularly capture key developments within the different pilot projects and to connect these developments with developments in the policy field in order to fine-tune and adjust views on the main impacts of the OOP and their measurability.

The IA framework and its discussion, thus, serves multiple purposes. The first is to guide the adoption of the OOP in cross-border services for businesses based on lessons learnt in the project and its pilots. Secondly, the IA framework contributes to the development of recommendations for the long-term sustainability of project results and its connection to other e-Government initiatives and regulations such as the Single Digital Gateway Regulation (SDGR) [12].[1] To this end, this chapter is structured as follows. In the next section, we explore benefits and challenges of the OOP, followed by a section on the how we went about developing an IA framework based on related impact indicators. After presenting the suggested framework, in section four we show how this framework was validated in a series of stakeholder focus groups aimed at discussing the framework and its indicators and connecting them to the TOOP pilots. Section five presents the discussion of the findings. Finally, in the conclusion section, we reflect on the IA methodology and describe impact areas to focus on when implementing the OOP.

2 The Once-Only Principle: Benefits and Challenges

The OOP holds that public administrations should aim to collect information from citizens and businesses *only once* and after that, when needed, share this data with other

---

[1] The SDGR envisions that by the end of 2023, more administrative procedures will be available online, national online procedures will be accessible cross-border and the OOP is applicable to a variety of procedures [12]. In this framework, the TOOP project can be seen as providing inputs and working towards the objectives of the SDGR.

administrative bodies or reuse it, while respecting privacy regulations and other requirements [20]. Within the EU, cross-border implementation of the OOP implies that all other EU Member States should be able to access and reuse certain data once this data has been collected in one Member State. This data can vary in terms of types of entries or mandatory basic information recorded by Member States due to different historical developments of bureaucratic processes. At minimum, this principle should allow governments to re-use basic registries across Europe. On a Member State level, there have been several initiatives that explore and demonstrate the uptake of the OOP. However, cross-border implementation of this principle has until now been limited [21, 22].

The implementation of the OOP is associated with significant benefits [23]. For businesses, the OOP may result in cost and time savings, thereby reduce their administrative burden [23]. For public organizations, the benefits are efficiency gains as a result of less paper mailing, faster processing, time savings due to decreased need for data collection, improved re-use of data, reduced number of unnecessary data submission demands, process optimization and the removal of duplication of tasks [55]. Such efficiency gains can lead to an increased quality of services, reduction of fraud and/or errors and less discrimination [23]. The TOOP website shows some recent success stories in which Member States in the European Union are using building blocks developed by the project [36], or where countries connected to Europe through the European Economic Area [13], for example, are taking up similar principles to make it easier to process EU applications and vice versa [37].

However, the implementation of the OOP across borders is also associated with several challenges. Especially, technical and interoperability issues are recognized among the most challenging problems for cross-organizational information systems due to their reliance on heterogeneous information and process models [25]. The challenges for the uptake of the OOP in a cross-border context not only stem from the type and the quality of data and underlying processes of data collection and retention, but also from non-compatible ICT infrastructures or differences between concepts and meanings of data (semantic interoperability) and interoperability on both national and international level [6, 34]. Interoperability is a key element for the success of implementing the OOP within a Member State as well as implementing it across borders. It can be defined as the "ability of different organizations to interact towards mutually beneficial and common goals, which involves the sharing of information and knowledge by means of the exchange of data between their respective ICT systems" [6, 34]. Besides applicable to technical aspects, interoperability can also apply to semantics, legal issues and organizational aspects [11].

Concerning *technical* interoperability, heterogeneity of ICT systems and the lack of national interoperability and national systems not meeting the OOP requirements are obstacles that affect EU-wide implementation of the OOP [6, 34]. Regarding *semantic* interoperability, the main challenge is to enable semantic interoperability between the IT systems of different governments on both a data-structure and data-label level (how are categories filled, what data formats are used etc.) as on a linguistic level [20]. *Legal* interoperability refers to organizations operating under different legal frameworks, policies and strategies, meaning public services may fall under different governmental departments and/or legal frames in the Member States. *Organizational* interoperability refers to the way in which public administrations align their business processes, responsibilities and expectations to achieve common goals [19]. In general, public sector organizations vary significantly in their requirements due to factors such as organizational and legal structure, size, legacy systems, topic/sector addressed, to name a few. This means that the solutions to enable cross-border OOP have to be highly compatible with, and adaptable to national and local existing ICT solutions and infrastructures [21]. Next to interoperability, there are other challenges, ranging from user acceptance and expectations to public administration progress in adopting certain processes and common semantics, and the uptake and implementation of digital innovation for government. In order to anticipate on potential impacts of novel technologies or principles such as the OOP, a go-to approach is to conduct an Impact Assessment (IA). To do this, an IA framework was developed by identifying impact indicators for TOOP.

3   Assessing Impact: Developing a Framework for the OOP

3.1   The Use of Impact Assessments (IA) for Technology and Policy

Impact Assessments (IA's) are often used in the process of policy making to evaluate policy options, such as deployed by the OECD [27] and the European Commission (EC) [10], as well as to assess the impact of (new) technologies [4, 40]. Typically, the EC performs IA's on initiatives that are "expected to have significant economic, social or environmental impact" [10]. The OECD uses them to "describe the cascade of cause and effect leading from an intervention to its desired effects" [27]. While an IA mainly focuses on whether an initiative achieves its expected *benefits*, other aspects also need to be taken into account, since impacts can be *positive* or *negative*, and *intended* or *accidental* [33]. This means that the scope of an IA can go beyond benefits only, while often being used to investigate the impact of a *specific* intervention to realize change [27, 33]. For TOOP, this would mean that an IA helps in a better understanding and anticipation of potential changes in day-to-day government processes once the OOP is implemented. The development of an IA for the OOP as an information system means that it is a *technical* impact assessment [3] as well as a *policy* impact assessment, which means that policy goals are inherently tied to, and shaped by, the information systems they are channeled through.

Often IA's are performed in relation to *specific* issues, e.g. to investigate the impact of a policy on the environment, or to determine socio-economic effects of introducing a new technology [2, 16]. Since we are assessing a policy action as well as a technological implementation that is framed as a principle, potentially connecting to many other public services, the framing of the OOP is rather challenging. One starting point could be to draw on existing IA frameworks used in fields related to the OOP, such as digital government [31], social innovation and integrated service delivery. In such frameworks [31] however, the approach for gathering and evaluation of indicators for impact can vary widely, from highly structural quantitative methods to highly qualitative ones. Moreover, where the end-user is taken up in many indicators in these frameworks, their presence in evaluation methods is often lacking [1]. Looking at the variety of scoring mechanisms used, it becomes clear that there is no one preferred methodology when it comes to IA's in relation to analysing digitisation in and of public services. The available frameworks do offer useful suggestions on how to connect various high-level goals and expected impacts to measurement indicators. In earlier work [35, 38], we described how IA's are often concerned with addressing specific issues rather than performing a generic assessment.

In case of this IA, the focus is on assessing whether the objectives of the OOP will be achieved, yet, we also acknowledge that over the course of the development of the OOP, such values may change. Existing IA frameworks offer some important points for consideration. Firstly, an IA may consist of an approach that investigates multiple criteria or requirements (such as fairness or efficiency) across multiple aspects or fields (such as environmental, economic, or organizational), leading to a two-dimensional set of indices. This allows for specific recommendations that concern a combination of criteria or requirements. Secondly, IA's that aim to assess a specific topic can yield rich, in-depth findings as opposed to IA's that evaluate several options. In other words, small- and in-depth assessment approaches might turn out more valuable than trying to capture impacts broadly and for the long term.

3.2 A Impact Assessment Framework for the OOP

For the development of an IA framework for the OOP, we started by discerning different levels of government processes, such as institutional and environmental, legal and regulatory, organizational and managerial, or technological, or end-user satisfaction [15]. With the first two levels taken together (befitting the topic under study), this division of impacts can be capture in the following four categories:

1) Legal and institutional;
2) Organizational and business process;
3) Technical (data, data governance, and architecture); and
4) End-user (businesses or Economic Operators, EOs).

The first category deals with legal, institutional and/or political benefits. An elaborate overview of legal boundaries and connected frameworks regarding the OOP has been developed for different application areas [17], yet how these play out in an implementation phase remains unknown. Besides 'hard' legal boundaries, institutional rules and regulations as well as political climate play a major role in shaping the preconditions for the OOP implementation. Secondly, local organizational structures and habits can differ greatly within governmental administrative bodies and institutions. Day-to-day practices are often augmented when it comes to information and data exchange between Member States and herein lie great challenges and potential impacts. The OOP, thus, does not only need to 'pass' legal and political tests, it also needs to be adopted within day-to-day administrative organizational practices. Thirdly, ICT infrastructures need to be ready for OOP implementation. Technology or technological aspects include both aspects of data (sharing and harmonization) and data architecture. Finally, businesses and other end-users represent an important stakeholder group to assess the impacts of the OOP and should be of key importance in assessment [24].

These four categories are consequently mapped against the main impact (benefit) categories of the TOOP project (administrative burden reduction, quality of service, government efficiency, secondary impacts) to create a matrix. In each of the cross-sections of the matrix, potential impact indicators can be discerned. We have derived these indicators both based on eGovernment literature and they have been validated and extended during the project meetings with experts from the TOOP project. The indicators that are based on literature were derived from an explorative literature search. Since only few studies of the OOP specifically were found (notable exceptions being Cave [6] and Gallo et al. [14]), we explored adjacent terms and areas to widen our search. Furthermore, Gallo et al. [14] stress that the OOP is currently not, and should also not be, implemented in isolation, but rather within the wider context of eGovernment programs, being on a cross-border or a national level. Therefore, we also looked at topics related to the OOP, stemming from the wider field of eGovernment.[2]

Table 1 presents an overview of the indicators from each of the four categories described earlier and maps them onto the four impact categories. It should be noted that some of the impacts can be combined or shifted (e.g. simplification of the process and time/cost savings are related to user satisfaction and government efficiency as well as to administrative burden reduction). Below, the expected benefits of the OOP, based on the literature search, are summarized per TOOP objective.

3.3 Administrative Burden Reduction

A first expected benefit of the OOP is administrative burden reduction for end-users. This, in general, can be seen as reducing the amount of steps or simplification of a process that need to be taken for a business to comply with a specific procedure [6]. By having company data available digitally across borders, filling out forms, and walking through administrative procedures should become simplified for the end-users. This will ideally lead to a significant decrease in both time and costs of administrative procedures. Time saving is mentioned by Cave et al. [6], being savings on: process time (time spent locating, collecting and submitting information, completing administrative procedures and specifying services to the appropriate level of detail), and elapsed time (time needed to complete procedures from start to finish).

Besides operationalizing administrative burden reduction as time and cost savings, other aspects should be taken into account from the wider context of eGovernment. Bekkers et al. [43] mention the changing relations between stakeholders and the law, or in regulation in general as a major expected benefit contributing to administrative burden reduction. This is closely related to the notion of transformational e-government,

---

[2] The following search engines were used: Scopus, ResearchGate, Springer, the European Commission Database, and Google Scholar. Furthermore, sources used in the TOOP Grant Agreement were analyzed. Key search terms included 'OOP benefits', 'OOP KPI', 'OOP impact', 'eGovernment benefits', 'eGovernment KPI', 'eGovernment impact', 'eGov benefits', 'eGov KPI', 'eGov Impact', 'Impact Assessment Criteria', 'Impact Criteria', 'Integrated Service Delivery KPI', 'Integrated Service Delivery benefits', 'Integrated Service Delivery impact', and 'Integrated Service Delivery criteria'. Papers based on this search that are included in the literature review were selected on several criteria: number of expected benefits mentioned, applicability of the expected benefits as an indicator of the OOP, year of publication not older than ten years (> 2006), covering at least two different aspects, perspectives, or dimensions of impact, and maturity of the framework.

Table 1. Categorisation of expected benefits, secondary benefits and negative effects, per impact level – adapted from TOOP Deliverable D2.10 [35]

Expected benefit	Where (on which level) does the expected benefit occur?			
	Legal and institutional	Organizational and business process	Technical (data, data governance, architecture)	End-user (businesses or EOs)
Administrative burden reduction	• Transformation of stakeholders' relations and legislation	• Harmonisation of data	• Improved data quality, reliability and validity	• Simplification of processes • Time savings • Cost savings
Quality of service	• Non-discrimination • Reliability and trust	• Transparency and accountability	• Ubiquity, access and availability	• User acceptance • Responsiveness to the needs of society and legitimation
Government efficiency	• Fraud reduction and prevention	• Avoid duplication of tasks • Re-use and interconnectivity of building blocks	• Interoperability of data	• User satisfaction
Secondary benefits and negative consequences	• Improved collaboration between government organisations	• Improved organisation and ICT architecture • Performance and effectiveness • Start-up effects	• Security breaches • Platform dependency	• Improved mobility • Risk of identity theft • Digital dependency

or public sector transformation, referring to the radically changing ways in in which stakeholders interact with each other [41]. Due to novel – digital – ways of working, also relations among stakeholders alter, which in the end influences existing regulation as well. To ensure simplification of administrative processes, uniformity and consistency of data, such as adhering to standard formats with the same definitions, become essential: i.e. harmonization of data [44]. One way of achieving this is by setting up base registries [14].

This streamlining of public sector processes can take place organizationally by streamlining administrative processes, but also technologically by enabling automated data sharing and to replace redundant data collection with information requests, thereby flipping the process form dragnet-data collection to on-point information collection and sharing [22, 23]. Furthermore, to allow for harmonization, an important expected benefit is improving the quality, reliability and validity of data [44]. Reliability of data will likely increase, as data will be stored and therefore also updated in its original source. These elements are, thus, expected to be benefits that can be attributed to the OOP as well and that are likely to lead to administrative burden reduction.

3.4 Improved Quality of Service

A second category of expected benefits of the cross-border OOP is improving the quality of service of public services. A main expected benefit of the OOP is non-discrimination, by removing asymmetries in the treatment of domestic and cross-border individuals and businesses seeking services that require them to submit information to public authorities [43]. This is considered an important benefit of the OOP in the context of establishing the Digital Single Market. Besides non-discrimination, also other public values are important to achieve in the context of public services delivery. One important expected benefit in this context increased transparency and accountability [43]. When administrative processes change and data is harmonized and standardized, this allows for greater openness of processes and data repositories, which is increasingly common within the context of open data [44].

Furthermore, an expected benefit of the OOP is ubiquity, which refers to access to a service from any platform, at any time, from any physical location, which also means that ubiquity is not limited to public services but can also be provided by private service providers [42]. More generally, accessibility is an expected benefit of the OOP, meaning the level of ease and extent of access service users have to the services to which they are eligible [54]. For public services, user acceptance is an important expected benefit [6]. The acceptance of a public service by users and the responsiveness to the needs of society [43] is especially important, since their acceptance and relevance are strong determinants for the use – and thus the benefits for end-users. Therefore, improved quality of services is expected to increase trust and reliability of government services, as more citizens will be inclined to use public services [6].

3.5 Government Efficiency

Regarding efficiency of government processes, a main expected benefit of the OOP is the avoidance of duplication of tasks [53]. If tasks within public administrations can be performed more efficient, this is likely to result in a decrease of time spent on these tasks as well. As such, it is a mirrored benefit from administrative burden reduction for businesses. A second important expected benefit contributing to government efficiency is fraud reduction and prevention, which can be explained as the aim to minimize the extent, and improve the detection of attempts to obtain services by means of inaccurate or contradictory information [6]. Generally, these are the two main expected benefits for government organizations.

Furthermore, to allow for re-use of data and existing architectural building blocks, re-use and interconnectivity of building blocks is an expected benefit of realizing the OOP [6], as well as achieving interoperability of data [44]. The former refers to an administration-wide simplification of information management, while the latter refers to the development and use of standards for data exchange, allowing also for a machine readable format. These benefits, too, mirror the benefits for businesses since data harmonization was already mentioned as a main expected benefit for businesses. Generally, the impact of improved data quality and data harmonization can be seen to benefit organizations beyond those within the public sector, while interconnectivity of administrative building blocks and interoperability are expected to benefit public administrations most. Still, there is expected to be a clear link between the benefits of businesses and those of government.

Another expected benefit of the OOP is user satisfaction [24]. While this benefits businesses as well, it is considered especially important for public services, since it is a strong determinant of the use of a service as well as for trust in public administration [3].

More efficient government is expected to lead to more satisfaction among users, which, in turn, is expected to increase not only actual use and uptake of the services, but also of trust in public administration. Here too, it can be observed that it is hard to identify expected benefits for the OOP in isolation from eGovernment benefits in general.

3.6 Secondary Benefits and Unforeseen (Negative) Consequences

Besides expected benefits, an IA can also include unexpected and unforeseen benefits as well as negative consequences. Therefore, in addition to the expected direct benefits, an IA should offer a framework that captures secondary and negative effects as well. This allows an impact assessment along a broader spectrum, adhering also to realistic scenarios of risks and potential bottlenecks (be they on technical, organizational, legal, or economic aspects), and it helps to differentiate an IA from a more direct project evaluation. By allowing secondary benefits to enter the assessment, it is possible to touch upon larger scale impacts of implementation of the OOP. For some benefits it is hard to distinguish whether they are direct, primary benefits or second, larger scale impacts. Examples could be fraud reduction, transparency and accountability, and improved data quality. These can either be achieved by implementing the OOP directly or as a result of having implemented the OOP. For practical reasons, since we expect that in the case of the TOOP project pilots we may be able to observe these benefits directly, we took up the these benefits under the main categories of expected benefits. Regarding the benefits that we do not expect to occur within the project (for example, because we are only able to assess pilot settings rather than actual use in practice), but that may be expected to occur after implementation in a real-life setting, we consider secondary benefits.

Secondary benefits that we have identified include increased mobility of end-users as a result of non-discrimination and general improved services across borders[3]. Furthermore, a secondary effect of the OOP that is likely to occur is increased or improved collaboration between governmental bodies and institutions, also the ones who are not directly linked to the first OOP projects or practices. When interconnectivity of building blocks within administrative processes, interconnectivity of data, and data harmonization occur, it is likely that public administrations are able to find new and more efficient ways to collaborate also for other purposes. Besides efficiency gains from a financial and organizational viewpoint, better organization and IT architectures were found as expected secondary benefits from the wider context of eGovernment [45]. Generally, these types of secondary effects are expected to result in increased performance and effectiveness of government or 'performing with less', referring to the combined effects of improved user satisfaction, effectiveness and efficiency [43], or as a combination of resource utilization, accuracy, efficiency, and effectiveness [46].

A possible negative consequence on the short term could be start up effects[4]. This means that during the initial start-up phase, investments in both time and money are needed to allow for this re-adjustment of processes and ways of working, adaptation

---

[3] This was mentioned in one of the workshops that were held with the participants in the pilots, during the kick-off meeting Tallinn, 26 January, 2017.

[4] This was mentioned in one of the workshops that were held with the participants in the pilots, during a TOOP workshop Rome 22–24 May, 2017.

and mutual learning process between user and provider of a government service to the OOP. This likely influences the benefits identified in the assessment. A number of related aspects can be mentioned, such as the above mentioned developing organizational and IT architecture – aligning and orchestrating within and in between governmental bodies, which will likely demand a huge technical effort. This aspect can, thus, both be framed as a potential expected – secondary – benefit, but since the development may be cumbersome, this may also become a negative consequence. For end-users, start-up effects may result in (temporarily) maintaining parallel systems of digital and paper, which means that they – for a period of time - may have to maintain parallel links to government, including challenges related to archiving and data retention (think of maintaining duplicates of own or governmental digital archives, copies, user names and logins, identity verification, alteration of input, timeliness and 'freshness' of data).

Final potentially negative aspects include factors related to data security and 'lock-in effects' – on both the side of government and that of end-users. If data cannot be stored safely and if data is not treated in a proper and trustworthy manner, this could result in the risks of security breaches [47] with the possible risk of identity theft [48] and as a result, the OOP has little chance of success in terms of scaling and uptake [50]. Although this in part is an organizational aspect, the technical side of responsible data processing within government organizations lies in matters such as compatibility, firmware updates, the use of open or closed platforms, inter-software dependencies etc. Furthermore, potential negative aspects include 'lock-in effects' [50] on the side of governments (platform dependency), when they become dependent on the vendor platforms used for services delivery, or on the side of end-users when they become digitally dependent on governmental systems for service delivery and data provisioning [51].

4   Validating and Discussing the Framework with Stakeholders

In order to further assess our framework and criteria, we asked the TOOP project members for feedback. Following our action research approach, this was done via a series of seven stakeholder sessions that took place throughout the project.[5] In these sessions, project partners - (around ten to fifteen per session) developers of technical building blocks for the OOP and public administrators from different Member States - were invited to discuss the (expected) impacts of the OOP, the type of indicators proposed and how these connect to current ways of assessment of innovations in government as well as the benefits and challenges that they foresee once the OOP is implemented. In every session we refined the (expected) impacts based on the discussion and we updated the framework accordingly. In this way, through these stakeholder sessions we were not only able to validate the impact indicators identified from literature, but we could also explore to what extend the impacts that were set out at the start of the project changed due to experience gained during the development of proof-of-principles in the several pilot projects. Regarding the IA, we addressed the following questions:

---

[5] Meetings were held in Tallinn (25–27 January 2017), The Hague (18–19 April 2017), Rome (22–24 May and 2–3 October 2017).

- Are the impacts you expected at the start of the pilot the same as you see them now?
- Do you think these impacts will materialize once the pilot is actually implemented and how far in the horizon do you see this happening?
- What would be the strongest felt impacts, in your opinion, and what is further needed to achieve them?
- Which issues/problems of this public service will be resolved or minimized out through TOOP architecture?
- Some of the expectations are that the OOP will increase the data quality and reliability. On what is this outcome dependent and how has the pilot/use case approached this objective?

Several points were raised during the discussions. In general impacts were expected to materialize after OOP is adopted but provided that it is adopted widely enough. Regarding changing of impacts, the participants recognized some of these impacts but noted that not all will be immediately felt and some can be seen as more important than others. As an illustration, administrative burden reduction might be reached in the long-term but it can be expected that in the short- and medium-term the administrative burden might increase until the OOP is fully implemented. Government efficiency on the other hand might be much more important while yet difficult to measure as it might also involve re-organization of some procedures. Participants also noted that some legal/regulatory impacts may need to be emphasized more. It was also pointed out that TOOP needs key business cases to communicate how it can help in achieving higher-level goals. It was also noted that the categories of impacts as presented in the framework were not necessarily recognized by practitioners: the more specific they can be made, the better. Both member state representatives and technical experts from the pilots recommended to provide clear roadmaps for implementation after the project is finished. In summary, for the sustainability of the OOP its impacts need to be clear and convincing in order to stimulate uptake.

For each of the four categories of the framework, findings were captured from the stakeholder sessions. First of all, when we look at *legal and institutional* impacts, some the of the scenarios for OOP implementation might be challenging, mainly because some parts of business-or citizen registration data would need to be checked on authenticity and correctness by an authorised representative each time data is manipulated. Yet, if implemented, the OOP would allow authorities to directly share data with each other (provided that an agreement from the user is given), and this would ensure authenticity of the data and leading to increased reliability. If implemented following the right procedures, also beyond the business-to-business scenario, the OOP might help in fraud reduction, as several focus group participants stated that this is a highly important goal and marker (or driver).

Secondly, on the level of *organizational and business processes*, the participants stress that lessons learnt from TOOP should travel to other sectors and fields (e.g. private individuals data exchange). As the possibilities for cross-border exchange of information are quite wide and the SDGR priorities do not always match with the pilot area focus, the results from the TOOP pilots should be seen as examples that can be extrapolated to other sectors. Moreover, for the sustainability of TOOP, and to get a better grip on the demand side of OOP, statistics and monitoring mechanisms can also help estimate the potential demand for OOP solutions in the different sectors, thus helping countries prioritise their efforts. Realizing the benefits of the OOP could, however, be influenced by a variety of organizational factors - from internal (re)organization and digitization to international coordination of efforts. In the maritime sector for instance, introducing the OOP on an international level (rather than just European) has the potential to not only reduce the time and costs of ship inspections but also help authorities with examining foreign certifications.

Thirdly, on a *technical* level (data, data governance, and architecture), besides the semantic mapping, for full implementation of the OOP principle and its expansion beyond the tested scenarios, the work should also continue on the interoperability of the different systems and also in exploring a 'push scenario' where foreign registries receive notifications and accept as authoritative any changes of the data they already hold, thereby reducing the administrative burden for citizens and businesses who need to only introduce changes to their situation once.

Finally, regarding *end-users* (businesses), there is a need to establish a clear vision on the next steps in order to provide stakeholders with a roadmap and sustain the current momentum. As the cross-border OOP is not implemented, at this time, it can only be expected that the OOP will bring convenience, time and costs savings as the biggest impacts [5].

5   Discussion: Challenges of Measuring Impacts

Regarding the measurement of these impacts, a first key point of debate is that of quantitative versus qualitative forms of measuring the indicators as provided above. Due to the varying levels between member states of digital readiness for the OOP, and due to the exploratory nature of the TOOP pilots, measuring quantitively for instance, the administrative burden reduction at this point in time would be based mainly on speculation. What became clear during the stakeholder sessions, is that many see the IA framework more as a preparation for sustainability: to gather what should be monitored in the future in order to actually properly measure the impact of the OOP, but that for now, it was considered too early to assess impacts, especially quantitatively. Where previous studies predicted that applying the OOP across the EU could lead to "annual net savings of as much as €5 billion per year" [14], analysis of the overall impact of the OOP is difficult to estimate. This is due to, among others, differences among Member States in the use of OOP [14], the overall strategy of the OOP, the types of data that can be shared, and the number of digitized transactions [14].

Similarly, a study on different policy options and impacts for EU-wide adoption of the OOP concluded in 2017 that the impacts of the OOP as well as the associated costs are very difficult to quantify. The study further concluded that "[t]here are significant evidence gaps on costs and benefits, especially beyond Member State level. What can be measured does not cover the most socially important impacts, is not directly attributable to OOP and is not quantitatively significant. Moreover, available measurements do not capture business or citizen impacts" [6]. Instead of assessing the impact of OOP, looking at expectations and refining indicators to measure potential impact seems within scope. It should however be noted that these impacts are, thus, only expectations. These are based on the experience of the TOOP participants in the field of public administration and their experience with similar previous initiatives. Plotting lessons from the stakeholder sessions among the main four levels of impact, leads to a set of reflections, including possible impacts, benefits and challenges, that we have captured.

In general, the expected benefits were not so much questioned, yet priorities in discussion within multiple focus groups tentatively indicate that burden-reduction and fraud-detection, with main concerns around personal data protection and current procedures around inter-governmental data sharing were highlighted. The SDGR is generally seen a driver for OOP as well as the TOOP project which can provide lessons learned based on the pilots. Yet with so many currently existing systems still in the process of full adoption (an ENISA study from December 2017 on the adoption of eIDAS for example, concluded that there is a difference in the penetration of classical trust services - such as insurance of certificates - and defined services by eIDAS and that for 'certain services there are only a few providers in specific Member States' [7]), it remains challenging to predict the impact of TOOP in the landscape of digital government.

6 Conclusion

In this chapter we have shown how an Impact Assessment framework for the Once-Only Principle was developed and subsequently validated. Based on desk research and regular qualitative interaction with the pilots and Member State representatives, we set out to create different moments and methods of tacking stock of impacts during the development of the TOOP project. The Impact Assessment framework, developed based on these interactions and former similar Impact Assessment approaches, can help Member States to put in place processes and instruments to measure if and how the OOP is contributing to goals set by the different Member States. The main contribution of the framework is a starting point for actual measurement of impacts once first OOP-based services are put into place.

Concerning the measurement of impact, one of the main challenges is to find the right level of granularity for the impact indicators. On the one hand these indicators need to remain connected to the larger impact goals (or benefits) that the OOP is set out to bring, on the other hand, they need to be concrete to such an extent that they can connect to existing indicators. We found out that some impact indicators can be measured quantitatively, but that painting a complete picture of the impact will need qualitative work in the form of interpreting and synthesizing quantitative measurements.

Whereas the framework in itself seems to cover the main potential impacts of the OOP, the validation sessions revealed two key lessons. The first being that out of the many potential impacts, there are some that turn out be of key relevance and thus can be seen as key drivers – or potential barriers. Moreover, the way in which the impacts will be measured (quantitively or qualitatively) remains challenging especially since little is known about the size of the problem it aims to solve. This means that it is unclear if the OOP fills a latent need and/or if the lack of an OOP is currently withholding companies to engage in cross-border business. Another point of attention is the connection to current legislation and existing building blocks: these connections need to become more explicit in the pursuit of a sustainability roadmap for Member States or sectors implementing the

OOP. The OOP has a number of potential positive impacts, recognised by the pilots and their members. It is generally agreed among the research participants that most of the impacts will materialize shortly after the OOP is implemented. This however assumes that the OOP is successfully implemented among all business registries and in a critical mass of countries. Given that many Member States are currently arranging their regional and national data sharing processes and that this might imply some re-organization of registries and rights to share, the entire process will take a longer than initially foreseen. On the other hand, regulatory reforms such as the SDGR act as an accelerator for uptake by the Member States. The pace of implementation will differ per country and sector and also the readiness of some countries differs with regard to the implementation of some of the building blocks such as eIDAS, the European digital identity framework. The impacts of implementation of OOP will differ per Member State and are dependent on factors such as digital maturity of the administration, social attitudes toward governmental data sharing, the local legal framework and perceived need for the service both within and outside the public administrations.

References

1. Akkaya, C., Krcmar, H.: Towards the Implementation of the EU-Wide "Once-Only Principle": perceptions of citizens in the DACH-region. In: Parycek, P., et al. (eds.) EGOV 2018. LNCS, vol. 11020, pp. 155–166. Springer, Cham (2018). https://doi.org/10.1007/978-3-319-98690-6_14
2. Alene, A, Manyong, V., Coulibaly, O., Abele, S.: IMPACT: A Framework for conceptualizing Impact Assessment and promoting impact culture in Agricultural Research. IITA, Ibadan, Nigeria (2006)
3. Alarabiat, A., Soares, D., Fereirra, L., de Sa-Soares, F.: Analyzing e-governance assessment initiatives: an exploratory study. In: Proceedings of the 19th Annual International Conference on Digital Government Research: Governance in the Data Age, pp. 1–10, May 2018
4. Banta, D.: What is technology assessment? Int. J. Technol. Assess. Health Care 25(Supplement 1), 7–9 (2009)
5. Camilleri, M.A: Exploring the behavioral intention to use e-government services: validating the unified theory of acceptance and use of technology. In: Kommers, P. (Ed) 9th International Conference on Internet Technologies & Society, Lingnan University, Hong Kong. IADIS (2019). https://ssrn.com/abstract=3320327.
6. Cave, J., Botterman, M., Cavallini, S., Volpe, M.: EU-wide digital Once-Only principle for citizens and businesses. policy options and their impacts. Final Report for the European Commission, DG CONNECT (2017). https://doi.org/10.2759/393169
7. ENISA: eIDAS: Overview on the implementation and uptake of Trust Services: One year after the switch over. European Union Agency for Network and Information Security (ENISA), December 2017
8. European Commission, European eGovernment Action Plan 2016–2020. https://ec.europa.eu/digital-single-market/en/european-egovernment-action-plan-2016-2020. Accessed 29 Sept 2020
9. European Commission, eGovernment Action Plan. https://ec.europa.eu/digital-single-market/en/egovernment-action-plan-digitising-european-industry. Accessed 29 Sept 2020
10. European Commission, Impact assessments – the need for impact assessment. https://ec.europa.eu/info/law-making-process/planning-and-proposing-law/impact-assessments_en;

11. European Commission: European Interoperability Framework – Implementation Strategy. Communication COM(2017) 134 final (2017)
12. European Commission, The single digital gateway. https://ec.europa.eu/growth/single-mar ket/single-digital-gateway_en
13. Eurostat – Statistics Explained. https://ec.europa.eu/eurostat/statistics-explained/index.php/ Glossary:European_Economic_Area_(EEA)
14. Gallo, C., Giove, M., Millard, J., Thaarup, R.K.V.: Study on eGovernment and the Reduction of Administrative Burden: final report (2014). https://doi.org/10.2759/42896.
15. Gil-Garcia, J.R., Pardo, T.: E-government success factors: mapping practical tools to theoretical foundations. Gov. Inf. Q. **22**, 187–216 (2005)
16. Glasson, J., Therivel, R., Chadwick, A.: Introduction to Environmental Impact Assessment. Fourth Edition, Routledge (2012)
17. Graux, H.: Overview of legal landscape and regulations. Deliverable 2.5, TOOP project (2017)
18. Henman, P.: Of algorithms, apps and advice: digital social policy and service delivery. J. Asian Public Policy **12**(1), 71–89 (2019)
19. Henning, F.: A theoretical framework on the determinants of organisational adoption of interoperability standards government information networks. Gov. Inf. Q. **35**(4), S61–S67 (2018)
20. Kalvet, T., Toots, M., Krimmer, R.: D2.7 Drivers and Barriers for OOP (1st version). Deliverable D2.7 for the TOOP project (2017). http://toop.eu/sites/default/files/D27_Drivers_and_ Barriers.pdf.
21. Kalvet, T., Toots, M., Van Veenstra A.F., Krimmer, R.: Cross-border e-Government services in Europe: expected benefits, barriers and drivers of the once-only principle. In: Proceedings of the 11th International Conference on Theory and Practice of Electronic Governance, pp. 69–72, April 2018
22. Krimmer, R., Kalvet, T., Toots, M., Cepilovs, A.: Position Paper on Definition of the "Once-Only" Principle and Situation in Europe. Deliverable D2.6 of the TOOP project (2017). http:// toop.eu/assets/custom/docs/TOOP_Position_Paper.pdf
23. Krimmer, R., Kalvet, T., Toots, M.: Position paper on definition of OOP and situation in Europe (version V1.0). Deliverable D2.14 for the TOOP project (2017). http://www.toop.eu/ sites/default/files/D2.14_Position_paper_OOP_update.pdf
24. Mitseva, A., Peterson, C.B., Dafoulas, G., Efthymiou, A., Abildgaard, A., Bellini, S.: ISISEMD evaluation framework: for impact assessment of ICT pilot services for elderly with mild dementia, living in the community and their relatives. In: Proceedings of the Networking and Electronic Commerce Research Conference 2010, pp. 1–23. American Telecommunications Systems Management Association (2010)
25. Mocan, A., Facca, F.M., Loutas, N., Peristeras, V., Goudos, S.K., Tarabanis, K.: Solving semantic interoperability conflicts in cross-border e-government services, Semantic Services, Interoperability and Web Applications: Emerging Concepts. IGI Global, pp. 1–47 (2011)
26. Nielsen, M.M., Carvalho, N.R., Veiga., L.G., Barbosa, L.S.: Administrative burden reduction over time: literature review, trends and gap analysis. In: Proceedings of the 10th International Conference on Theory and Practice of Electronic Governance, pp. 140–148, March 2017
27. OECD Directorate For Science, Technology And Innovation: What is Impact Assessment. OECD, pp. 1–7 (2014). https://www.oecd.org/sti/inno/What-is-impact-assessment-OECDIm pact.pdf.
28. Passani, A.: Impact Assessment of Collective awareness Platform for Social innovation and Sustainability (CAPS) - the IA4SI framework. IA4SI project (2014)
29. Podhora, A., et al.: The policy relevancy of impact assessment tools: evaluating nine years of European research funding. Environ. Sci. Policy **31**, 85–95 (2013)
30. Sanderson, I.: Evaluation, policy learning and evidence-based policy making. Public Adm. **80**(1), 1–22 (2002)

31. Savoldelli, A., Misuraca, G., Codagnone, C.: Measuring the Public value of e-Government: The eGEP2. 0 model. Electron. J. e-Government, **11**(1), 373–388 (2013)
32. Sivarajah, U., Irani, Z., Weerakkody, V.: Evaluating the use and impact of Web 2.0 technologies in local government. Gov. Inf. Q. **32**, 473–487 (2015)
33. Streatfield, D., Markless, S.: What is impact assessment and why is it important? Perform. Meas. Metrics **10**(2), 134–141 (2009)
34. Tepandi, J., et al.: Towards a cross-border reference architecture for the once-only principle in europe: an enterprise modelling approach. In: Gordijn, J., Guédria, W., Proper, H.A. (eds.) PoEM 2019. LNBIP, vol. 369, pp. 103–117. Springer, Cham (2019). https://doi.org/10.1007/978-3-030-35151-9_7
35. Timan, T., Karanikolova, K., Van Veenstra, A.F.: The Once-Only Principle Project 2nd Evaluation Report; Impact Assessment Framework – update. Deliverable D2.10 for the TOOP project, confidential (2019)
36. TOOP: Implementation of TOOP Solution: Italian Success Story. TOOP project. https://toop. eu/sites/default/files/italian-v2.pdf
37. TOOP: Implementation of TOOP Solution: Norwegian Success Story. TOOP project. https:// toop.eu/sites/default/files/norway-v6_03.pdf
38. Van Veenstra, A.G., Timan, t., Vermeulen, P., Congleton, H.: D2.9 OOP Impact Assessment framework (final version). Deliverable D2.9 for the TOOP project (2018)
39. Yannacopoulos, D., et al.: E-Government: a comparative study of the G2C online services progress using multi-criteria analysis. Int. J. Dec. Support Syst. Technol. **2**(4), 1–12 (2010)
40. Zamboni, A., et al.: ICT Impact Assessment Guidelines: Practical tools and guidelines for assessing ICT implications. European Commission (2018)
41. van Veenstra, A.F., Klievink, B., Janssen, M.: Barriers and impediments to transformational government: insights from literature and practice. Electron. Gov. Int. J. **8**(2/3), 226–241 (2011)
42. van Veenstra, A.F., et al.: Ubiquitous Developments of the Digital Single Market. European Parliament's Committee on Internal Market and Consumer Protec-tion, Brussels (2013). http://www.europarl.europa.eu/RegData/etudes/etudes/join/2013/507481/IPOL-IMCO_ET(2013)507481_EN.pdf.
43. Bekkers, V., Tummers, L, Stuijfzand, B.G., Voorberg, W.: FP7 LIPSE - Social Innovation in the Public Sector: An Integrative Framework. Working Paper Erasmus University Rotterdam, Version 0.5 (2013). http://lipse.org/userfiles/uploads/Working%20paper%201%20Bekkers%20et%20al.pdf.
44. Zuiderwijk, A., Janssen, M.: Open data policies, their implementation and impact: a framework for comparison. Gov. Inf. Q. **31**(1), 17–29 (2013)
45. Codagnone, C., Boccardelli, P.: eGovernment Economics Project (eGEP) – Measurement Framework Final Version, 2006. European Commission (2006). http://www.umic.pt/images/stories/publicacoes200709/D.2.4_Measurement_Framework_final_version.pdf.
46. Fotrousi, F., Fricker, S.A., Fiedler, M., Le-Gall, F.: KPIs for software ecosystems: a systematic mapping study. In: Lassenius, C., Smolander, K. (eds.) ICSOB 2014. LNBIP, vol. 182, pp. 194–211. Springer, Cham (2014). https://doi.org/10.1007/978-3-319-08738-2_14
47. Alsmadi, I., Abu-Shanab, E.: E-government website security concerns and citizens' adoption. Electron. Gov. Int. J. **12**(3), 243–255 (2016)
48. Whitson, J.R., Haggerty, K.D.: Identity theft and the care of the virtual self. Econ. Soc. **37**(4), 572–594 (2008)
49. Veugelers, R.: New ICT sectors: Platforms for European growth? Bruegel Policy Contribution, issue 2012/14, August 2012. https://lirias.kuleuven.be/bitstream/123456789/376464/2/New.
50. Farrell, J., Klemperer, P.: Coordination and lock-in: competition with switching costs and network effects. Handb. Ind. Organ. **3**, 1967–2072 (2007)
51. Reddick, C.G.: Citizen interaction with e-government: from the streets to servers? Gov. Inf. Q. **22**(1), 38–57 (2005)

52. Eden, C., Ackermann, F.: Theory into practice, practice to theory: action research in method development. Eur. J. Oper. Res. **271**(3), 1145–1155 (2018)
53. European Social Network (ESN): Policy Areas: Integrated Services. ESN website. http://www.esn-eu.org/integrated-services/index.html.
54. Richardson, D., Patana, P.: Integrating Service Delivery: why, for who, and how? OECD, Social Policy Division Discussion paper (2012). https://www.oecd.org/els/soc/Richardson_Patana%20INTEGRATING%20SERVICE%20DELIVERY%20WHY%20FOR%20WHO%20AND%20HOW.pdf
55. Carvalho, J., Soares, D.: Who is measuring What and How in EGOV Domain? In: Parycek, P., et al. (eds.) EGOV 2018. LNCS, vol. 11020, pp. 120–131. Springer, Cham (2018). https://doi.org/10.1007/978-3-319-98690-6_11

The Future of the Once-Only Principle in Europe

Robert Krimmer[1,2] ⓘ, Andriana Prentza[3](✉) ⓘ, Szymon Mamrot[4](✉) ⓘ,
Carsten Schmidt[1,2](✉) ⓘ, and Aleksandrs Cepilovs[1](✉) ⓘ

[1] Ragnar Nurkse Department of Innovation and Governance, Tallinn University of Technology
(TalTech), Akadeemia tee 3, 12618 Tallinn, Estonia
{robert.krimmer,carsten.schmidt}@ut.ee, {robert.krimmer,
carsten.schmidt,aleksandrs.cepilovs}@taltech.ee
[2] Center for IT Impact Studies, Johan Skytte Institute for Political Studies, University of Tartu,
Lossi 36, 51003 Tartu, Estonia
[3] Department of Digital Systems, University of Piraeus Research Center, 18532 Piraeus, Greece
aprentza@unipi.gr
[4] Łukasiewicz Research Network – Institute of Logistics and Warehousing, ul. Estkowskiego 6,
61-755 Poznań, Poland
szymon.mamrot@ilim.lukasiewicz.gov.pl

Abstract. The Single Digital Gateway Regulation (SDGR) and the underlying Once-Only Principle (OOP) outline that businesses and citizens in contact with public administrations have to provide data only once. The chapter gives an overview based on the findings of the EU-funded "The Once-Only Principle Project (TOOP)". The authors summarise the developments related to the once-only principle and the SDGR in Europe. They also outline a vision for the future of the OOP in Europe. The vision is based on the analysis and the key take-aways from the previous chapters of this book. It also highlights the next steps to further improve the technical and legal basis and the chances given by the update of the eIDAS regulation. Furthermore, an opportunity for the sustainability of the OOP and the TOOP is described.

Keywords: Once-Only Principle · Single Digital Gateway · SDGR · Digital Single Market · TOOP · Building blocks · e-Delivery · eID · eIDAS

1 Introduction

Even if the Once-Only Principle (OOP) itself is not an entirely new approach the implantation of the OOP on a supra national level opens a new dimension. The OOP is among the seven underlying principles of the eGovernment Action Plan 2016–2020, as well as the Tallinn and the Berlin Declaration, to make government more effective and simpler and to reduce administrative burdens by asking citizens and companies to provide certain (standard) information to the public authorities only once. The implementation is based on the common need that was identified by most of the Member States and European Commission. The legal framework for this is the Single Digital Gateway Regulation (SDGR).

R. Krimmer et al. (Eds.): The Once-Only Principle, LNCS 12621, pp. 225–236, 2021.
https://doi.org/10.1007/978-3-030-79851-2_12

2 The Dimensions of the Once-Only-Principle

The previous chapters summarise the key aspects of the OOP in Europe. In general, the political, theoretical, legal, and technical foundations were analysed. Within this chapter, the main outcomes of this analysis will be highlighted. These are especially the major drivers and barriers, impacts and take-aways of good practices in Europe.

2.1 The Implementation of the Once-Only Principle on a National Level

This chapter focused on the analysis of the deployment of OOP at national level, as the EU-wide implementation of the OOP to a large extent depends on national administrations that serve as data providers and data consumers. Here the diversity of EU Member States in terms of national implementations of the OOP comes into play: different administrative structures, legal frameworks, IT systems, database models, as well as other elements, affect the deployment of the EU-wide OOP. This is further exacerbated by the different maturity levels of the implementation of the OOP at national level.

Analysis of the implementation of the OOP at national level revealed a number of benefits. Firstly, OOP puts user at the centre of the service, reducing the red tape, improving the efficiency and quality of public service provision. Secondly, OOP leads to the significant improvements in data quality, as no data is duplicated across different registries and therefore is easier to maintain. All this also leads to significant cost reductions for citizens, businesses and public administrations. Bringing the OOP to the European level will help magnify these benefits, advancing the creation of the Digital Single Market.

To bring this a step further, TOOP project explored and developed a generic OOP IT architecture, and tested and demonstrated it in three pilots focusing on general business mobility, eProcurement, and maritime transport, with the support of over the lifetime of the project more than 20 Member States and EEA countries[1]. The high-level architecture and the technical specifications that were developed by TOOP were taken up as a basis in the implementation of the Single Digital Gateway – the next milestone in the development of seamless cross-border digital services.

2.2 Drivers, Barriers and Opportunities

The drivers and barriers for OOP were analysed within different Member States and associated countries based on the experiences and findings within the TOOP project. Though there are some influencing factors that are more prevalent in one piloting area than another, mostly the drivers and barriers are similar across the TOOP use cases and would therefore suggest the same for wider implementation. Institutional factors were found to be the most influential – OOP implementation was perceived to be easier in Member States where the existing legal landscape was in favour of the principle and the political priorities of the member state aligned with the priorities of the TOOP project and vice versa in Member States where the regulatory landscape was less favourable of the OOP. The involvement of international regulatory bodies was also considered an

---

[1] The number of participating countries and partners has changed over the duration of the project.

important factor for successful implementation as the enforcement of wider adoption of the principle was considered crucial for reaching the full potential. Organisational factors such as the inherent structure and pre-existing procedures in the various organisations involved were found to be much less of a barrier than initially perceived at the beginning of the project.

2.3 Good Practices of Once-Only Principle Across Europe

To sum up the findings from the OOP good practice analysis, the investigation has evidenced existing good practice cases and enablers in different Member States. However, the diffusion of OOP solutions is still scarce, especially at cross-border levels of the OOP solutions. Further research and efforts from the side of government actors are needed to successfully implement the OOP across borders. The TOOP project provides a federated reference architecture for enabling the provision of OOP solutions across borders. However, as the analysis of good practices has shown, the success of the OOP implementation depends on many different enablers. Putting such enablers in place demands further considerable effort along a holistic perspective on public service design and implementation with the OOP.

Some further general insights from the good practice research:

- While strategic policies in Europe extensively promote digitalization, networked systems and interoperability, digital transformation in practice and with the OOP as underlying paradigm is considerably lagging behind these visions.
- While OOP visions are promoted to create awareness of the potentials and benefits, these activities are not necessarily reaching out to those that in the end have to implement the OOP solutions.
- In particular, top-down implementation of digitalization needs to urgently be complemented with bottom-up engagement of relevant stakeholders by employing e.g., co-creation concepts, stakeholder engagement and similar to involve the relevant stakeholders in such digital transformations.
- Attempts of bottom-up stakeholder engagement to realize interoperable cross-border public services need to be complemented with qualitative research to systematically and rigorously understand barriers and challenges of actors in digital public service provisioning and to design OOP solutions that meet the users' expectations.

2.4 Impact of the Once-Only Principle for Businesses Across Borders

The analysis of the impact has shown that it is unclear if the OOP fills a latent need and/or if the lack of an OOP is currently withholding companies to engage in cross-border business. Another point of attention is the connection to current legislation and existing building blocks: these connections need to become more explicit in the pursuit of a sustainability roadmap for Member States or sectors implementing the OOP. The OOP has a number of potential positive impacts, recognised by the pilots and their members. It is generally agreed among the research participants that most of the impacts will materialize shortly after the OOP is implemented. This however assumes that the OOP is successfully implemented among all business registries and in a critical mass of countries. Given that many Member States are currently arranging their regional and national data sharing processes and that this might imply some re-organization of registries and rights to share, the entire process will take a longer than initially foreseen. On the other hand, regulatory reforms such as the SDGR act as an accelerator for uptake by the Member States. The pace of implementation will differ per country and sector and also the readiness of some countries with regard to the implementation of some of the building blocks such as eIDAS, the European digital identity framework. The impacts of implementation of the OOP will differ per Member State and are dependent on factors such as digital maturity of the administration, social attitudes toward governmental data sharing, the local legal framework and perceived need for the service both within and outside the public administrations.

3 Experiences from Running TOOP

3.1 Managing a Large-Scale Pilot

Management of large-scale pilots is challenging for a number of reasons. First, large-scale pilots are not typical research and innovation projects that are normally funded by the EU Framework Programme for Research and Innovation, and TOOP is also not a typical example of a large-scale pilot. The main reason for this is a very strong policy push and an expectation from the funding authority, and the community involved in the project, to deliver results. In classical research and innovation projects a certain probability of failure is tolerated, given the significant amount of uncertainty endemic to any research and innovation project. Hence, failure to reach some of the objectives set in the proposal is not necessarily interpreted as a failure of the project. Large-scale pilots operate at the boundary between innovation and deployment (TRL 8–9), and therefore bear a different level of expectations in terms of the certainty of project results.

Most large-scale pilots operate in an environment with certain policy expectations and the results of such pilots often feed into the legislative process, in particular in defining secondary (technical) legislation, such as delegated or implementing acts. TOOP was designed and initiated in a similar environment in terms of the overall policy landscape, and with the expectation to eventually feed into the legislative process; however, with the push of the Estonian Presidency of the Council of the EU for the adoption of the Single Digital Gateway Regulation (SDGR), the expectations towards the project changed in the middle of the project's life cycle. With the adoption of the SDGR, the project was expected to not only feed into the development of the secondary legislation defining the technical requirements for the implementation of the SDGR, but also to develop the core technical components that would eventually support the implementation. This shift in perspective and expectations created additional pressure on the consortium and therefore also on the management of the project.

Second, large-scale pilots often involve a significantly larger number of participants than classical research projects. In addition to the number of participants, large-scale pilots also involve diverse groups of participants, spanning academia, public sector organisations, and industry. It is therefore essential to strategically build the consortium already at the stage of designing the pilot to make sure the structure of the consortium will be balanced in terms of the overall objectives of the project, interests and capabilities of the participants, as well as expectations from the policy makers if the project is expected to support them. As mentioned elsewhere in this book, TOOP carried out three pilots with 19 Member States and associated country authorities. This allowed to develop and pilot solutions with a wide variety of use-cases and with a diverse set of national environments, ensuring that these solutions serve the ultimate goal of cross-domain information exchange.

Third, management of large-scale pilots requires a certain level of agility within a relatively complex environment. Considering that large-scale pilots involve a significant innovation component, agility is necessary in order to be able to respond to both changes in external environment as well as changes within the consortium, adapting the work of the project on the go, in order to make sure that the project achieves the set objectives on schedule, and on budget. The ability of the project to react, however, depends on one key factor – the funding programme and the specific requirements set for it.

As mentioned earlier, TOOP was supported by the Horizon 2020 Framework Programme. H2020 funding is mostly used for research and innovation projects, most of which fall below TRL7 (including), with the exception of pre-commercial and innovation procurement. In most cases, consortia involved in carrying out projects are relatively small and homogenous. As a result, the overall complexity of projects is rather limited. TOOP project, as a large-scale pilot, was very different in that sense. From the outset it had a two-tier structure of the consortium, with a number of sub-consortia at national level responsible for the implementation of the national pilots and other tasks. This two-tier structure was necessary to make the large consortium, consisting of around 50 partners, manageable, in particular when it comes to project governance and decision making.

Agility in the management of the TOOP project was achieved through a number of means, from the management of the development of the software components, to the management of the consortium, to the financial management of the project. Agility in the management of the consortium was necessary in order to allow for entry and exit of partners during the project. This allowed to maintain the consortium actively engaged in the work, in particular with the focus on piloting, and to introduce Member States and associated country authorities who couldn't join in the beginning of the project but were interested in piloting the TOOP solution. This also allowed to introduce the necessary competences that could not be identified at the beginning of the project.

With regard to financial management, to ensure tight control over partners' spending and maintain agility with regard to resource allocation, the project implemented an internal system of quarterly cost reporting. Reimbursements of costs for partners were based on their quarterly reports, which included also reporting on the work performed in the respective quarter. This allowed to ensure control of the project's resources, which is especially relevant in large consortia tasked with developing and piloting IT solutions. This approach diverges from the approach within classical Horizon 2020 research and innovation projects, where financial reporting is linked to periodic reporting defined by the funding authority (usually between 12–18 months). The more frequent financial reporting adds to administrative burden within the consortium and therefore puts additional pressure on the coordinator of the project.

First, the coordinator must ensure that a project management team is in place to oversee the overall governance of the project, internal financial reporting, as well as reporting towards the funding authority. Second, the coordinator must ensure that appropriate tools are in place to manage quarterly financial reporting in a way that is most convenient and efficient for all parties, and in particular to those who need to do the reporting. Last, but not least, the coordinator must ensure that the consortium agreement to regulate the operation of the consortium is fit for purpose.

Although the coordinator's project management team is essential for project's success in the long term, it is not sufficient, as many variables in the equation remain under control of the funding authority. First and foremost, the overall complexity of the Horizon 2020 grant agreement regulations requires a significant experience of the project management team within the specific funding framework to ensure that all rules and requirements are complied with, while at the same time ensuring fast action. Second, although the overall Horizon 2020 grant agreement framework is relatively flexible, the overall complexity makes it difficult to benefit from this flexibility. Third, it requires extensive coordination with the project officer from the funding authority to ensure efficient and effective project management.

To explain how this complexity plays out in practice, we provide an example. In TOOP project, consortium agreement foresaw the possibility to re-allocate funds on the basis of partner's contribution to the project in a dynamic way, using quarterly reporting as a reference point. For example, if one partner initially assigned to the task cannot perform the task, resources can be re-allocated to another partner who is willing and able to perform the task. While H2020 allows for such re-allocations in principle, when those are major and require re-allocation of responsibilities for tasks or work packages, these changes need to be implemented via an amendment to the grant agreement. If the consortium consists of ca. 50 partners, and in order to balance the project's budget, resource allocations for more than 50% of the partners involved may need to be changed. When these changes are combined with changes in the description of work, and some changes in the consortium structure (e.g., new or existing partner), and are implemented with one amendment request, the amendment request becomes very complex and therefore requires a significant time from the contracting authority to process and confirm. Often this requires corrections in the amendment request, which delays processing even further. In some cases, in particular in public administrations and publicly-funded universities, resources cannot be committed unless there is legal certainty regarding resource allocations. Hence, unless the amendment request is approved by the funding authority, some parties halt their involvement in certain tasks, thus affecting parts of or the entire project.

In the implementation of large-scale pilots, it is therefore essential to be aware of the limitations imposed by the specific funding instrument, and either choose a more flexible funding instrument (possibly with lower reimbursement rates), or plan ahead and incorporate long timelines for administrative procedures in the overall project plan.

3.2 Developing a Technical Architecture for a Large-Scale Pilot

As described above the number of partners and the technical involved are manifold. This causes one of the challenges for the development of a technical infrastructure for the

OOP at a large scale. The chapter on TOOP Trust Architecture provided an overview of the Trust Architecture as an indispensable component for the implementation of the OOP in context of cross-border services spanning different policy domains. The Trust Architecture as devised in the TOOP Reference Architecture (TOOPRA) focuses on the trust establishment between the actors involved in an OOP System to provide guarantees on the origin, destination, authenticity (property that the entity providing the data is what it claims to be), trustworthiness (property that the entity providing the data can be relied on as honest or truthful), and integrity of information that is exchanged between the actors.

To overcome the main technical challenges in OOP application across the EU and associated countries - the diversity of organisations, procedures, data, and services on all four main levels of interoperability - the TOOPRA were developed. In the respective chapter about the TOOP OOP architecture it is explained, how this goal is achieved by using standard solution blocks, by designing the Reference Architecture and standard solution blocks in line with legal requirements, as well as by using tested, mature, interconnected and interoperable standards and building blocks. It relies on proven Enterprise Architecture methodology, ensuring consistent standards, methods, and communication among Enterprise Architecture professionals. The TOOPRA is a common outcome of the partners involved of TOOP pilots and the TOOP Solution Architecture.

The scenarios addressed by TOOPRA can involve organisations that could have no previous interaction; therefore, the preferred choice is trust by liability, possibly in conjunction with trust by reputation. The trust by liability is, in turn, supported by some existing general-purpose trust-enabling tools, such as: electronic identity, electronic delivery, and electronic signature or seal. These services are provided by Trust Service Providers and provide legal value. This particular architecture enables a community-based approach to digital trust, based on the existence of a network of trusted nodes (Access Points), which provide the capability to establish a secure and trusted channel between different public and private organizations. The Technology layer is complemented by the Organizational layer and the Legal layer, which provide a basis for collaboration between different entities, and ensure that the exchanged information maintains its meaning.

In order to facilitate the cross-border provision of digital services, in particular those based in the OOP, diffusion of mutually recognised electronic identification is key; however, history of successful use of different OOP systems is as essential for building trust of governments, organisations and users. In that sense, TOOPRA provides a solid set of tools for efficient deployment of OOP services and for the design of trust as an integral part of their architecture.

3.3 Piloting at Large-Scale

From the first ideas to change organisational structures within the European Union until the implementation into reality it was a long and partly stony way. Based on several experiences in the past, starting in the 90th of the last century, the EC has developed the approach of the so called "Large Scale Pilot" Projects (LSP). The LSPs became the instrument of the EC and the Member States to support the transition into a digital society. LSPs can be defined as goal driven initiatives that propose approaches to specific real-life societal, industrial challenges. Based on the point of view of the EC, pilots are autonomous entities that involve different kind of stakeholders from supply side to demand side, and contain all the technological and innovation elements, the tasks related to the use, application and deployment as well as the development, testing and integration activities. In 2001 the EC has declared it a priority for Europe to set up cross-border digital public services, allowing citizens and businesses from a Member State to interact with a public service in another Member State electronically.

First, Member States and the EC identified a few key domains where it would be very beneficial to develop common solutions at European level. Three topics were identified in 2005, eID, eProcurement and eHealth. As a next step, the areas of business set up and justice got a special focus. Within five dedicated LSPs technical solutions were developed. Besides that, also suggestions for organisational improvements were made. The outcomes of the LSPs were focussed on the specific sectors and not foreseen to be re-used or extended to other areas. Therefore, the EC and the Member States decided to design specific LPSs with a focus on a technical and organisational cross-sectoral interoperability. First, as part of the e-SENS project, based on generic and extensible technical building blocks cross-sectoral solutions were developed. As a second step, cross-border and cross-sectoral services were designed within the TOOP project.

The results of the LSPs are picked up by the EC and MS in manyfold ways. To support the sustainability of the technical building blocks that were developed especially by the LSPs, the Connecting Europe Facility (CEF) was set up. The goal of the CEF is to fund and support the development of the common infrastructure components. As continuation with the CEF2 program the EC and MS will support and catalyse investments in digital connectivity infrastructures of common interest. This will be complemented by further programs like e.g. the Digital Europe Program (DEP). The support is not limited to financial contributions, it is also possible to amend the legal framework.

4 Sustainability of the Once-Only Principle

4.1 Implementation of the Once-Only Principle

Many European countries have started implementing the once-only principle at a national level, while its cross-border implementation is still fragmented and limited to a few services. In view of its contribution to the realisation of the Digital Single Market in Europe, the European Commission is strongly promoting the implementation of the OOP across borders. Therefore, once-only is one of the underlying principles stated in the European Union's "eGovernment Action Plan 2016–2020" and is part of several initiatives related to the European Digital Single Market.

TOOP is concerned with the demonstration of this principle in the context of cross-border services for business and to support the transition towards the SDGR. It is the first large-scale pilot (LSP) project under the Horizon 2020 Framework Programme of the EU.

The TOOP project was launched on 1st of January 2017 and during its lifetime more than 50 organisations from more than 20 EU Member States and associated countries were involved. The main objective of TOOP was to explore and demonstrate the once-only principle across borders, focusing on data from businesses via three distinct pilots. Via these pilots, TOOP wanted to enable better exchange of business-related data or documents with and between public administrations and reduce administrative burden for both businesses and public administrations.

4.2 ONCE-ONLY.ORG

Several initiatives around the OOP have started during the last years. These initiatives and projects are established in a national and supra-national context. Within these projects (e.g., TOOP), certain findings and results of a technical nature, including technical specifications and software components, have been developed. One of the main goals of the projects is to ensure that these important and potentially valuable outcomes are sustained, updated according to stakeholder requirements and available for use and exploitation, after the project's termination. They must also be maintained, i.e., to remain current e.g. in alignment with the specifications and architecture reflected into the SDG Implementing Act(s) and other relevant initiatives at EU level.

Therefore, the members of the TOOP project have endorsed ONCE-ONLY.ORG as organisation to sustain its results. ONCE-ONLY.ORG is an international not for profit association (AISBL – Association Internationale Sans But Lucratif) established under Belgian law, within the framework of the TOOP project, and as a part of its sustainability strategy. The purpose of the organisation is "to facilitate and promote international cooperation of public and private stakeholders aiming to advance and enhance the once-only principle and other underlying principles for e-Governance and the interoperability solutions and practices that support them". Furthermore, its activities under the statutes may include actions that aim to "ensure the sustainability of state-of-the-art solutions, specifications, technological building blocks, and services, as well as related governance schemes and frameworks".

An AISBL is a member-driven organisation, it is an Association of Members. It is therefore open to all interested parties who want to continue being involved in the support of once-only solutions and more specifically to the sustainability of TOOP results. The membership of ONCE-ONLY.ORG is an excellent way to influencing their future, even if they are not among the current IPR owners. As members, all organisations will determine the future of the Association.

As such, ONCE-ONLY.ORG will be a viable sustainability organisation to accept the stewardship of the IPR pertaining to the OOP technical artefacts, to maintain and further develop them, and to make them available for the purposes of supporting European public policy, on the implementation of the OOP.

4.3 Update of eIDAS

The OOP and electronic identification of natural and legal entities are strongly inter-connected. The setup of the regulation was a big step forward on the way to create a common legal basis for eIDs in the EU. But since the full entry into force of the eIDAS Regulation in September 2018, the implementation of digital identity even within the eIDAS framework is recognised as fragmented and not harmonized across the Member States. This leads into an interoperability issue.

Identity Matching

The databases used by the different administrations in the MS are mostly designed for specific cases or services. The underlying structure of the register quite often are set up before generic rules to exchange eIDs like in the eIDAS regulation were established. The data schemes are strongly related to the provided services. This causes a gap of attributes that allows an automated exchange of information and mapping of identities. Different information is collected about citizens and businesses and may identify people and organisation differently. To make it even more difficult, some Member States (e.g., Germany) do not have persistent identifiers or provide such persistent identifiers only as optional attributes. This causes a range of problems to match the identity of a legal or natural person already on a national but especially supranational level.

Record Matching

Identification in Europe happens via eIDs notified under eIDAS. In this case, there is a record matching issue depending on MS infrastructure. While using notified eIDs under the eIDAS Regulation, for the most part will allow data providers to match an identity with a record (evidence requested) using the attributes of the natural person provided by the eIDAS minimum data set, in some cases additional attributes are needed to ensure a match. This is based on a lack of interoperability and the credentials defined in the eID schemes of the MS.

The lack of a match with the regulated electronic identity circuits falls under the national sovereignty, and the consequent lack of a sound legal basis. The revision of the eIDAS regulation is the opportunity to put a stronger emphasis on the capacity to reliably link notified eIDs to any corresponding identities issued for the same person in another Member State on the basis of that notified eID. The Commission currently appears to be contemplating the creation and management of unique European electronic identities (a secure European e-identity, as proposed by President von der Leyen), which would be available to European citizens upon their request and based on their notified eIDs. This approach may be suitable, especially if that unique European identity (or the accompanying infrastructure) can also be used as a tool to interlink national electronic identities that would be derived from a notified eID (or from the European unique identity that would also be derived from the original notified eID) (Schmidt et al. 2021).

5   Future for Large-Scale Piloting Such as TOOP and the Once-Only Principle as Such

The main goal related to the future of the Large-Scale Pilots is, to find a sound way to generalize, extend, and sustain the results of the project(s) and to deliver a proposal for the way forward for the LSPs itself. Besides that, it is of utmost importance to provide a proposal for the future of the Once-Only principle, as the OOP can be seen as the basis for any kind of cross-border and cross-sector data exchange. The means that it contains and can therefore highlight all pros and cons of the e-Government sector.

As highlighted within the chapters of this book, TOOP is part of a family of Large-Scale Pilots. One of the perceptions of the research is that TOOP is the end of the cycle of LSPs. Now, it is important to outline the way forward. Besides that, during the TOOP project and the previous LPSs several technical, organisational and even legal gaps were identified. The COVID-19 pandemic has speedup the related process of identification and has - like through a burning glass - put a strong focus on the outcomes. Various political and administrative barriers (such as data protection and data-sharing requirements, implementation costs, public sector silo issues, and especially legal barriers and/or gaps) that could hinder the actual implementation of cross-border initiatives were recognised.

The next steps have to contain a proposal for the sustainability of the outcomes of the TOOP project and to cover the gaps identified. One of the conclusions of the research and development within the project were that the goals set for the LSPs are reached. It can be assumed that piloting at a large scale is a proper instrument to bring together stakeholders, develop technical solutions and identify open issues. Based on this outcome, it worthwhile to propose a new cycle of LSPs that focus on and have a new thematic context.

Furthermore, on the organisational side, it is important to continue the development related to the vertical networks. These networks like EUCARIS, BRIS etc. have to be sustained and extended into a wider context.

A logical next step would be to integrate the previously named vertical networks in the existing horizontal network set up by TOOP and to institutionalise its structures. This would be a step forward to use and strengthen the network. Thematically the network and future LSPs could focus on data ownership, data reorganisation and data responsibilities.

6 Conclusions and Future Research

TOOP has mastered an important challenge on the road to an integrated digitally transformed Europe by exploring, developing, demonstrating and piloting a pan-european data exchange layer that works. While it might have been just a first step where many are to follow: the paradigm that digital data should cross the border rather than physical paper evidence has shifted! But there still much to do, explore, learn and research, such as.

– How is trust established in digital for a cross-border Once-Only setting?
– How to develop semantics for cross-border exchange further?
– What is the actual impact of the cross-border data exchange applying the Once-Only Principle in real systems?
– How could the TOOP data exchange layer be extended?

  • How could a push scenario be realized?
  • How could the infrastructure be expanded using SSI, blockchain tech-nologies and architecture?

– How could a push scenario be realized?
– How could the infrastructure be expanded using SSI, blockchain technologies and architecture?
– How would the TOOP architecture look like if applied to other business sectors?

- How can existing networks like BRIS, ESSIE, EUCARIS etc. be connected or even integrated into a TOOP style horizontal data exchange layer?
- How can artificial intelligence help avoid fraud (e.g. amongst others through pattern detection)?
- Etc.

These interesting research questions and challenges will drive our future research around OOP. Our next checkpoint will be the 2023 digital government research (dg.o) conference, which is due to take place in Tartu, Estonia. The conference topic will be "Cross-Border Digital Public Services". We should be able to see, how TOOP helped shape the this new kind of public service provisioning and European lifestyle – despite or even because of a Covid-19 induced contactless service delivery!

Reference

Schmidt, C., Krimmer, R., Lampoltshammer, T.J.: "When need becomes necessity" - The Single Digital Gateway Regulation and the Once-Only Principle from a European Point of View – forthcoming (2021)

Annex

List of Beneficiaries and Linked Third Parties 2017–2021

Acronym	Official name	Start date	End date
Estonia (EE) Coordinator			
TalTech	Tallinn University of Technology	01/01/2017	31/03/2021
Austria (AT)			
BRZ	Bundesrechenzentrum GmbH	01/01/2017	31/03/2021
BMDW	Bundesministerium für Digitalisierung und Wirtschaftsstandort	01/01/2018	31/03/2021
DUK	Universität für Weiterbildung Krems	01/01/2017	31/03/2021
A-SIT	Zentrum für Sichere Informationstechnologie-Austria	01/01/2018	31/03/2021
BMF	Bundesministerium für Finanzen	01/01/2017	31/12/2017
BKA	Bundeskanzleramt der Republik Österreich	01/01/2017	31/12/2017
Belgium (BE)			
Time.Lex	Time.Lex	01/01/2017	31/03/2021
Bulgaria (BG)			
EAMA	Executive Agency Maritime Administration	01/01/2017	31/03/2021
Switzerland (CH)			
BFH	Berner Fachhochschule	01/03/2018	31/03/2021
Germany (DE)			
StraVV.DE	Strategische Verwaltungsvernetzung Deutschland	01/01/2017	31/03/2021
BMI	Bundesministerium des Innern	01/01/2017	31/03/2021
BVA	Bundesverwaltungsamt	01/01/2017	31/03/2021
MRN	Metropolregion Rhein-Neckar Gmbh	01/01/2017	31/03/2021
UKL	Universität Koblenz-Landau	01/01/2017	31/03/2021
Denmark (DK)			
DTI	Teknologisk Institut	01/01/2017	31/03/2021
DMA	Sofartsstyrelsen	01/01/2017	31/03/2021
DBA	Ministry of Business and Growth	01/01/2017	30/06/2018
Estonia (EE)			
MKM	Majandus ja Kommunikatsiooni Ministeerium	01/01/2017	31/03/2021
EMA	Veeteede Amet	01/01/2017	31/03/2021
RIA	Riigi Infosüsteemi Amet	01/01/2017	31/03/2021
RIK	Registrite ja Infosüsteemide Keskus	01/01/2017	31/03/2021

(*Continued*)

(Continued)

Acronym	Official name	Start date	End date
Finland (FI)			
TRAFI	Liikenne- Ja Viestintavirasto	01/01/2017	31/03/2021
France (FR)			
DINSIC	Direction interministerielle du numerique et du systeme d'information et de communication de l'etat	01/07/2018	31/03/2021
Greece (GR)			
UPRC	University of Piraeus Research Center	01/01/2017	31/03/2021
CERTH	Ethniko Kentro Erevnas Kai Technologikis Anaptyxis	01/01/2017	31/03/2021
UA	Panepistimio Aigaiou	01/10/2017	31/03/2021
GSCCP	Ministry of Economy and Development	01/01/2017	31/03/2021
MAR	Ministry of Administrative Reconstruction	01/01/2017	31/03/2021
MDG	Ministry of Digital Governance	01/09/2019	31/03/2021
Italy (IT)			
UC	Unione Italiana Delle Camere Di Commercio Industria Artigianato E Agricoltura Unioncamere	01/01/2017	31/03/2021
ANAC	Autorita' Nazionale Anticorruzione	01/01/2017	31/03/2021
IC	Infocamere Societa Consortile Diinformatica Delle Camere Di Commercio Italiane Per Azioni	01/01/2017	31/03/2021
UCE	Unioncamere Europa	01/01/2017	31/03/2021
Infocert	Infocert SPA	01/01/2020	31/03/2021
Latvia (LV)			
MAL	Valsts Akciju Sabiedriba Latvijas Juras Administracija* Maritime Administration of Latvia	01/01/2017	31/03/2021
Lithuania (LT)			
LMSA	Lietuvos Saugios Laivybos Administracija	01/01/2017	31/03/2021
Luxembourg (LU)			
LIST	Luxembourg Institute of Science and Technology	01/01/2017	31/03/2021
CAM	Commissariat Aux Affaires Maritimes	01/01/2017	01/01/2017
Netherlands (NL)			
MinBZK	Ministerie Van Binnenlandse Zaken En Koninkrijksrelaties	01/01/2018	31/03/2021
MinEA	Ministerie Van Economische Zaken En Klimaat	01/01/2017	27/07/2019
TNO	Nederlandse Organisatie Voor Toegepast Natuurwetenschappelijk Onderzoek Tno	01/01/2017	31/03/2021
KvK	Kamer Van Koophandel	01/01/2017	31/12/2017

(Continued)

(Continued)

Acronym	Official name	Start date	End date
RvO	Ministerie Van Economische Zaken En Klimaat	28/07/2019	31/03/2021
Logius	Logius	01/01/2017	31/12/2017
Chasquis	Chasquis	01/04/2019	31/03/2021
Norway (NO)			
BRC	Registerenheten I Bronnoysund	01/01/2017	31/03/2021
NMA	Norwegian Maritime Authority	01/01/2017	31/03/2021
Poland (PL)			
ILiM	Łukasiewicz Research Network – Institute of Logistics and Warehousing	01/01/2017	31/03/2021
Portugal (PT)			
E-Sens.Com	E-SENS COM GBR		
Vortal	Vortal-comercio Electronico Consultadoria E Multimedia Sa	01/01/2017	20/05/2019
Romania (RO)			
ICI	Institutul National De Cercetare-dezvoltare In Informatica Ici Bucuresti Ra	01/01/2017	31/03/2021
ONRC	Oficiul National Al Registrului Comertului	01/01/2017	31/03/2021
Sweden (SE)			
SU	Stockholms Universitet	01/01/2017	31/03/2021
Bolagsverket	Bolagsverket	01/01/2017	31/03/2021
Slovenia (SI)			
SI-MPA	Ministrstvo Za Javno Upravo	01/01/2017	31/03/2021
Slovakia (SK)			
PosAm	Posam, Spol Sro	01/01/2017	31/03/2021
SOSR	Statisticky Urad Sr	01/01/2017	31/03/2021
MFSR	Ministerstvo Financii Slovenskej Republiky	01/01/2017	31/03/2021
Turkey (TR)			
MEBI	Mebitech Bilisim Anonim Sirketi	01/01/2017	27/07/2019

Author Index

Printed in the United States
by Baker & Taylor Publisher Services